FALLING FOR TRUTH

FALLING FOR TRUTH

A SPIRITUAL DEATH AND AWAKENING

HOWDIE MICKOSKI

TAT Foundation Press

Published by TAT Foundation Press
Thomas Green Road
Roxboro, North Carolina 27574

Text font: Garamond

Main entry under title: Falling For Truth: A Spiritual Death and Awakening

1. Body-Mind-Spirit 2. Spirituality

ISBN: 978-0-9864457-4-3

Table of Contents

Acknowledgements

To:

Shawn Nevins at the TAT Foundation, who spent four years constantly showing me why my manuscript was not yet ready for publication, and what would be needed to do to improve it. I think he finally just gave up, and accepted the book you are now reading, so he could back to making his documentaries and writing poetry.

David Scoma took lots of his free time to clean up the poor grammar and sentence structure some three versions ago. When I asked him how good the writing actually was he said, "It's not *20,000 Leagues Under the Sea.*"

My wife, Gro Anita Skilbrei, who encouraged me to complete the book so it might get her invited to attend a TAT Foundation meeting.

My mother, who when still alive, would ask me in each of her weekly phone calls if I was finished with the book yet.

Elin Snaprud, who read the first version of this manuscript and responded, "well, it's an alright first attempt."

All of the people who came to my lectures in the first few years during the writing process as I was learning how I wanted to present this material. In a few years all of them would no longer come to talks or accept my phone calls.

Ken Kazemi who shared death with me, then dropped Richard Rose and Jed Mckenna on my lap and changed my spiritual direction. You have him to blame.

Vera Duman who kept me going in the worst of stomach troubles, questioning me if Castaneda would like what I was writing.

And finally to my beautiful cat who...well she never had anything critical to say about me or my book. She just would stay curled up or stretched out beside me, no matter what I was writing. I looked at her and asked her why she wasn't critical of my book. She stared at me, and I heard her voice in my mind, "I don't need to be critical, you have had all these other good people to do that for you. So I can just sit with you, and wish you well. Meow."

AWAKE

So you want to wake up?
And go somewhere to do it.
But there is nowhere to go,
No place to walk to,
No path will get you there.
Realization is where you are right now,
It is here, not there.
No paths, no walking, no goals, no guides.
Why?
When you truly know that answer,
You will be awake

2006

Coming Attractions

"The books we need are the kind that act upon us like a misfortune, that make us suffer like the death of someone we love more than ourselves, that make us feel as though we are on the verge of suicide, or lost in a forest remote from all human habitation—a book should serve as an axe for the frozen sea within us." (Franz Kafka)

Chapter 1

CONFESSION

Loose Footing

"Know myself? If I knew myself, I would run away."
(Goethe)

I am dead. No longer a normal human. I guess that in some way makes me abnormal, but in this new way of seeing...

"Wait," my editor interjects looking up from reading this manuscript. "You can't start a book by claiming to be dead."

"Why not?"

"Well, you're obviously not dead. You are writing the book. And besides, you are sitting right there across the table in front of me."

I purse my lip. "I don't mean dead from the standpoint of the body. The body is still very much here. I meant dead from the standpoint of what I have always thought of as me, or my personality. Maybe not dead. But those things that I always had total faith in, I can no longer believe in their totality."

"You have to explain that at the start of your book," he replies.

"I just did."

☙

May 28, 2005

"Oh no, now we're in trouble." I whispered those words after understanding the situation confronting us. Stupidly I got too close to the dangerous river within Johnston Canyon, just 20 yards from one of the largest natural waterfalls in Canada. Even more stupidly, I fell in. Ripped by the current I sensed the great danger and pulled my best Johnny Weissmuller imitation to swim back to my friend Kris on the shore. This Tarzan was in desperate need of help. Upon reaching him, I did stupid thing number two. I pulled my on-land saviour into the water with me, hence uttering the words, "oh no, now we're in trouble," as the current of water ripped me down the canyon. Time was stilled, moving millisecond by millisecond. Thought ceased, and all that arose were what I would call clusters of information, bubbles of something that were complete understanding, but not thought itself. They came up complete and full, held still as if a painting before my eyes, then would fade or vanish—and the next cluster would arise. What I would normally think of as "my mind" was not there to be found, yet something else much deeper seemed to be working.

In that microsecond came the realization, "So this is how I am supposed to die. Who would have guessed it would be like this?" It seemed so laughable that of all possible ways one could die, this was the way that it was going to happen to me. And it was fine. There was no great wish to continue living. I was going to die in a few seconds, and all it would be was the end of my story, and I was going to have front row seats to witness it. Pure acceptance came over me, and something that I had always known as me, died. In that moment came what best I can describe as a sort of computer download. For one of the seconds, it was like a mass of data was placed inside me. It has been a long process to work through these "files" and find out what was in the download.

The next microsecond, as the water ripped me towards the canyon wall, my head turned to gaze at Kris, dog-paddling to stay still in the slower part of the current. A new thought cluster arose, "well if I don't get out, how the hell is Kris going to get out?" It was like some new force animated and took over the body, determined not to go over the falls. My right leg slammed hard into an underwater boulder, deflecting the body off course a bit towards the bank. A lucky break. My feet grazed the bottom and I began to crawl out, all the while yelling at Kris "over here, it's shallow." Reaching the shore, I saw Kris already crawling out as well. He hadn't needed me.

After sitting mostly quietly for an hour, we began to discuss and reconstruct the experience we both had. We were amazed with a few things. First was how perfect the experience was. Nothing could have been added to it, or been taken away from it, to make it any better. Even the falling in was perfect. Second was how different time was in the experience. We could explain an hour of perception experience in what in relative time lasted perhaps a few seconds. Third, we had, each in our own way, accepted our death in the moment, with no struggling to try to extend it. And we both realized that what crawled out of that canyon was not the thing that fell in. We were new things, and we had no idea what that meant. We still don't.

For eight years previously, I was on a search for Ancient Egypt's "secret," studied most every tradition of spirituality and mysticism— and I thought I had found answers. Yet falling into the canyon turned everything on its head. It put my years of searching under the microscope and showed that I had spent most of it in a veiled search of trying to get my hopes validated. Falling caused me to re-look at everything. I have not been on solid footing since.

In the short term, for as much as a year, a deep clarity appeared, and many delusions of the world and spiritual community were recognized. Fear did not exist. However, there was a problem. As always, that problem is ego. A very deep realization damages ego, thus following any Awakening much false can be detached from, as calmness and clarity come in. But while egoic layers were damaged, they were not removed. It is amazing to see how fast the ego reorganizes itself into something different, then comes back in control with even more fear and self-importance than before. Sadly, this was the case here.

The problem was I got lazy. Any realization is so strong, shattering, and overpowering—that it is easy to think that there was nothing left to do but be like a retired old man who just sits on his porch and watches the world go by. As Richard Rose might say, you can't just HAVE a realization, you have to BECOME the realization. The work has to continue, or as the Zen teachers say, *"When you get to the top of the mountain, keep climbing."* To have a realization, on any level—without continued work to integrate it, is likely going to lead to egoic distortions. Much of spiritual work is on the physical and psychological levels; the areas most spiritual seekers use their spirituality to avoid. Part of the work is indeed to lift to the clouds for new perspectives and understandings, but to keep one's head in the clouds permanently is not to develop any grounding.

℘

My editor, Anders, again looks up from his reading and sort of stares at me.

"What?" I ask him.

"That's it?"

"That's what?"

"Your authority to write a book on spirituality comes from falling into a canyon?"

I think about the irony of that for a moment. "Ya I guess it does," I laugh.

"Come on."

"Well I mean there was like a decade of seeking and researching and contemplating before that—exercises, sacrifices, tests, beautiful moments, expanding awareness—but in the end, a few microseconds of time in the canyon revealed more than all of the 10 previous years of hard work combined."

He shakes his head. "You know this is not what most spiritual seekers expect, or really want to hear. It is not what they read in the major books."

"Exactly. In a sense, it was many years later when I began to realize that my experience and revelation in that canyon was genuine. I doubted it for a long while. It wasn't like anyone else's experience, nor was it the wished for beautiful occurrence that would make me somehow more special than others. It came to me from being a careless fool, after many years of basically fooling myself that I had been "a very spiritual person." Then those two fools combined, and for a split second between them, my death came, and so did a realization that I could have never expected. I mean if someone has an experience that is exactly what they read or what they hope for, you can never be sure it is genuine and not just a wishful projection, or a fantasy you made manifest to feel better. Really, until someone has an experience that, even though perhaps having some similarities to someone else's but still in some way unique and unexpected, they can never know for sure if it is genuine revelation or egoic projection. Actually, books like this are more valuable after an experience has happened, for it can help someone to understand much of the confusion that comes afterwards. But what is realized in the experience itself is all beyond words, and I am trying to spend 200 pages, and over 100,000 words to help shed light on those two seconds after being a fool. That is why it has taken me so many years to put this manuscript together."

"100,000 words about being a dead fool," Anders laughs.

"You know, there is a reason the Tarot Fool has been given the number zero."

☙

I must confess. I rarely read introductions. I don't know why. The author spent just as much time working on the introduction, but for some reason when I start a new book I jump right into the first chapter. It makes no sense. I'm not sure what that says about me, but it did influence my reasoning to start with chapter one. However, and with great irony I know, I thought that I should introduce myself and this book.

It looks like you have a spiritual book in your hands. Just like any of the other thousands that are found overflowing on bookstore shelves. Spiritual writing and lecturing today is big business. Generally, they are written by people who believe they are special. Authors writing to show how you can be more happy, successful, important, loving, unique, or the case of religion—destined for a wonderful future once you are dead. You know special, like the author. Some even believe they have been chosen to be a divine spokesperson or wonder healer. The spiritual book marketplace brimming with expert after expert claiming to have "all the answers." How then, can we trust that any of the information out there is genuine, and not just another game of delusion? Is there a way to test what someone really knows? And what reason is there for you to continue to read my book?

Modern spiritual books tend to come in two specific formats. The first is presented from the point of view of "I am the expert," and is written similar to books on how to fix a transmission or grow your own vegetables. These books tend to promise that if you follow the formula being presented (usually something simple—meditate, be quiet, be in the now, think happy things) then you can reach a level of perfection where you can make all of your wishes come true. How they have gained such authority to write such a book is generally vague or not convincing.

The second type of spiritual writing tends to run in a semi-novel form (either fictional or autobiographical). In this model, the story follows the standard format set up by Carlos Castaneda in 1960's. The book *Beauty of the Primitive* explained it as,

"Many fictional and semi-fictional tales of power follow a certain pattern. First the narrator/author feels over civilized or experiences a shattering misfortune or life problem. Then the individual meets an indigenous spiritual teacher who immerses the author in the ocean of spiritual wisdom. The author/narrator embarks on a spiritual quest and goes through stages of an initiation, which are usually accomplished by difficult physical or moral tests, which the candidate generally passes. The end result is the total transformation of the apprentice's conscious. Eventually the shaman/spiritual teacher tells the author that he or she has become a chosen one endowed with a certain esoteric wisdom that should be shared with the wider world. After this, the newly minted spiritual teacher/author goes into society to help solve the problems of Western Civilization, which faces perpetual spiritual and ecological crisis."[1]

The authors generally claim that they are taking old practices and updating them to be used in a modern context (which is simply another way of saying that the practices are made up). They miss the key foundations of what the old ceremonies were based on: connection to the whole of manifested reality. To just make up something new and claim it has an ancient lineage is, quite frankly, insulting to the wisdom holders of the last 100,000 years. Why did the authors go to so much trouble to make up a fantastic story about meeting with the so-called bringer of knowledge? It is likely because if they told the truth, no one would buy their goods—so they created a fanciful story to make themselves what they narcissistically wished they were -a wise and important guru. In both types of books, the author claimed to be a very materialistic person before they had their "encounter," but now afterward, they are "spiritual." However, when you examine how these people run their current lives, they seem to have become far

---

1   Znamenski, Andrei, *Beauty of the Primitive.*

more materialistic than they originally described. Especially as they peddle workshops, cds, dvds, crystals, healing baths, psychic readings, nature schools. Some even go so far as to sell ceremonies such as sweat lodges or sun dances. And it saddens me to realize just how prevalent this is. Fairy tales sell. The bigger the promise offered—the bigger the following. Only a very few seem to write in an honest and open manner, not looking to get anything or convince anyone, but just to put down some ideas on paper before they die. These are the texts and people that I hope you will seek out.

I want to be clear. My book is not a book about me. It will not portray me as an ancient master, or list the tenets of my modern mystery school, or detail my revelations as a shaman, Tibetan monk, Gnostic priest. It won't even necessarily portray me as a nice guy. This is the presentation of my fifteen-year attempt to understand the bizarre modern world by looking back to the ancients. Theirs was a past that built pyramids (which cannot be done today), by raising and placing 200-ton blocks of stone like they were Legos. Ancients who built monuments that thousands of years after their abandonment, still resonate with an energy unlike anything in the modern world. A time where sacred geometry, mathematics, astronomy and nature intermingled—creating a giant soup of knowledge, art, architecture and daily life. However, within the remaining symbolic texts is something quite magical, something that most modern spirituality glosses over in a New Age covering of sweet sugar. Attempting to unravel what they knew became my obsession.

The ancient world (continued through various Native, Eastern and Alchemical Hermetic traditions) held two key pieces of information. The first was that this world that we experience is nothing but a description based on erroneous perception, and that perception has been/and is conditioned and manipulated by an outside force that they described as a parasite. The world we think that is here and solid, is not really here or solid at all—that we are born, live, and die in a kind of dream world. We, too, are as much of a dream as the world we perceive. Secondly, that there is a doorway to move past much of this, but to reach the gate (that paradoxically turns out to be gateless) becomes the task of a lifetime. Their art and architecture were not to look nice, but were to reveal their message.

A spiritual vacuum exists in our modern word, which is getting more "spiritual," yet more distracted and delusional. No one is really going within, just playing a game of pretend happiness staring at their I Phone. It is the reason that I kept working on this manuscript, which began first as a series of notes twelve years ago, kept during my research on Ancient Civilizations. As my own experiences in these realms increased, the notes got more detailed—while more spiritual texts and teachings were seen as misleading. Perhaps I could put a few things down in a way to help save a few seekers years of wasted effort. Or at least to use my own mistakes to not fall into similar traps as I did. Each path one takes must be individual because each person's egos, personalities and past traumas will be packaged uniquely. People can only share what they did and what they passed on the road, with hopes it can be useful to another. Delusion sets in when someone thinks they have a specific formula (often believed to be the only way one should walk the spiritual road).

∽

"People should think less about what they ought to do, and more on who they ought to become." (Meister Eckhart)

I have meet several powerful and very direct people in my life. One was Bjung Chul Park (who we called Mr. Park), a Korean Zen teacher that I met in 1998. While Mr. Park referred to himself as a healer, he claimed that he was not interested in fixing the physical, but what he called "healing the soul," to cleanse what he called "darkness and poisons from our heart." Doing so would allow us to come to a place of knowing that he described as "nothing but nothing." Richard Rose also claimed that miracles come when the mind is thinking of "nothing but nothing." Of course, when we were studying with Mr. Park we all tried to "think of nothing," which just caused him to laugh at our foolishness. This statement is like one attributed to Socrates, whereby the word Nothing that is being used, is not anything what our normal egoic mind believes it is. Such statements can only be understood or entered from beyond the normal mind. I also was lucky to encounter and spend time with several Native Indian medicine men. I will share stories of all these people as this book continues.

Several authors were extremely helpful in my seeking, foremost are the writings by and of Richard Rose. The honesty (and in fact shock) of his writings felt like a gift when I came upon them after the canyon. He was about the only one out there not trying to seduce the masses with false promises, so they would give him money, prestige and devotion. He was just saying things as he saw them, knowing most were not going to like his message. He concluded early on that his life was not worth living if he did not know who was living, why, and who dies. How could either life or death have any meaning without knowing these answers fully? He used every second of his life to search for these answers in any group, idea, or avenue he thought could be of value. The results of his search can be found in such books as *Psychology of the Observer*. Rose was also unique in not just being able to present this material, he lived it. Totally and completely. Rose was so enticing to me in that he is the closest representation that I found to the teachings of Mr. Park.

However, I find Rose much more clear and direct in his recorded lectures than his writing. Other members of the group Rose founded (TAT Foundation) have a wealth of pointers and insight in print. The Ph.D. thesis *The Path to Reality Through the Self*, by John Kent,[2] that overviews Rose's system, I consider the best and most accessible spiritual work published in the last 100 years. No matter the problem or challenge, a good place to start a spiritual examination is to first read the work by Kent. Other books (and lectures), by people like

---

2   It can be found for free at the download section at searchwithin.org

Art Ticknor, Bart Marshall or Shawn Nevins may help to bring the message presented by Rose into easier to understand language. My book is but an addition to these texts.

I found that Rose's message was also remarkably similar to the famous Gnostic writings known as the Nag Hammadi Codex. This group was not an early Christian organization as usually presented, but more the opposite of modern religion—like a hardcore Zen or Advaita. I feel that sharing the Gnostic viewpoint through this book will help give Western seekers an ancestral foundation in this spiritual material (the appendix has an overview). Rose named his first book *The Albigen Papers* after the Gnostic Cathars (Albigens) of 12th century Southern France, burned at the stake in the Western World's first genocide, for believing that average men (and shockingly at the time, women) could reach the Truth of oneself without the need of a priest or saviour as a go-between. It is likely the Cathars were a last remnant of Ancient Egyptian Mystery Teachings, direct descendants of the Nag Hammadi Gnostics, and perhaps even held the sacred mystery known metaphorically as the Holy Grail. Their home area of Southern France is the focus of my most recent study. Both groups (Gnostic and Cathar) compared reality to a trapping holographic simulation, and that one needed to gather all of one's energy with their inner guide (called a Christ) to break free of it. They both claimed that people in the dream world were asleep (Rose called us hypnotized robots) for we believe a false reality. Only by turning away from this false could one begin to see what is "not-false."

Interestingly, I found another modern writer saying similar things, and that was Carlos Castaneda. Castaneda, though presenting his encounters through the interaction with a fictional character (Don Juan), had access to deep teachings on the makeup of reality. Unlike the writers who came after him who used his basic format to make up a story for themselves to justify their un-earned specialness, Castaneda was not following a blueprint, he was creating it. It was first book that made him famous, *The Teachings of Don Juan,* which I feel is not only the worst book of the series, I rank it as one of the worst spiritual books ever written. That it is held in such high regard (mostly by the 1960's drug culture) is a reminder not to blindly follow what the majority believe is good or of value. However, something it seems happened to Castaneda after writing that dissertation. A few years later he published *A Separate Reality, Journey to Ixtlan,* then *Tales of Power,* now dropping the need for drugs in the spiritual search. Somehow Castaneda came into the ancient wisdom that he had been pretending to know in his first book. How this occurred, why, or from whom is still unknown. What he did do is take his new found understanding and fuse it with the format of his first book (his fictional teacher). If one does not take the writings as literal, but as pointers within a novel (the same as found in *Moby Dick, Portrait of the Artist as a Young Man* or *Sherlock Holmes),* then the value within can be unearthed. Castaneda did not seem that he was able to live what he wrote personally, as his life became quite strange over time. Like many people who touch wisdom, if the egoic structures are not dealt with, they can boomerang back with devastating effects. But his work was a catalyst for me to ask a very powerful question, "If the world around me is just the way I think it is, then what would happen to the world if I stopped thinking?" Not to have a nice mind or happy mind, but no-mind. What happened when that occurred will make up a chapter in this book.

The more I studied Rose, Castaneda, and ancient manuscripts, the more they strangely confirmed each other, and (or at least partially) my own experiences. As such, I felt that my small contribution within this field was to present to those interested how these related sources, separated over thousands of years of time, point to the same subjects, just from slightly different angles. Each was not afraid to discuss as much about the dark half of duality as they are the light side. That to me is why their teachings become even more valuable, you can't hide from a part of reality just because you may not like it.

"There is no coming to consciousness without pain. People will do anything, no matter how absurd, in order to avoid facing their own Soul. One does not become enlightened merely by imagining figures of light, but by making the darkness conscious." (Carl Jung)

Part of what has taken so long for me to finish this book, was not just how write and present clearly, but also to determine what made it into this book or not. To put in all of the details, personal stories, and exercises would have made the book over 500 pages. I had to choose. As such there became a primer book, of around 80 pages (chapters 1-4) in which I attempt to present my viewpoint as clearly as I possibly could. Next comes 5 later chapters of around 100 pages, which is my attempt to provide a depth to the work. Lastly in this book is an appendix of useful information that might have disturbed the flow of the reading if it were placed in the book proper. It turned out to be around 70 pages. Finally are 150 pages that did not make this book, but which I have collected as an add-on work that can be ordered called "Additional Material." Hence the story of what you now are holding in your hands and reading.

↝

"So what's your point with all this?" I look over at my editor now finished reading the first chapter. "You know, why did you write this book?"

"My point was to waste your valuable time, and keep you stuck on the back porch for a whole afternoon." He frowns in mock disgust. "The book comes from years of the search to see just how most of spirituality is—well not of no value because there is some—but let's just say very limited value. That the teachings and the teachers are really grade two or grade three, but they pretend and sell like they are at the university level. The spiritual world out there is a kid's game of basic math compared to how the few who have really gone past present it. How the canyon presented it to me. That modern spirituality and religion are there to keep a hypnotized population hypnotized, not snap them out of it as it claims."

"So spirituality is just sleepwalking through life?"

"Pretty much."

"Then what else is there?"

"Going from a sleepwalker to someone who gets tired of the whole movie and theater and popcorn stand—and decides to finally go outside and see what's under the sun. Along the way to do this we have friends and helpers, but in fact the only real teacher or helper that we ever learn to trust is ourself. But who exactly is this "self" that we should learn to trust? What if the self we are listening to is a false self? Then what good is any of the information we get from a self until we are sure if it is true or false?" I smile.

"And that is what your book is going to explain."

"I guess. Slowly." I grab a full bowl that is beside me and offer some to Anders, "want some popcorn?"

Now it is his turn to smile.

Chapter 2

SEEKING

What do You Know?

"One cannot know God, until one knows the self who is seeking for God. You must be prepared to find What Is, not that which you wish to find, even if it is oblivion." (Richard Rose)

Something is wrong...desperately wrong. You feel it. You may not be sure what it is: yourself, your life circumstances, your family, society, the world, the planet, the universe. But something is off. The way you have been told to believe things just does not hold water anymore. There is a crack in the container. And even if you can't see the leak, you sense that what is leaking away is your life force. Your vitality. Perhaps even your very soul. That is why you are seeking. You have questions. The problem is that there are not many real answers around.

Only promises.

I don't have a lot of answers either, but I do have a few "anti-answers." Any type of truth is found by searching for what is untrue—and then removing it. At the end, whatever cannot be further removed—no matter how odd, shocking or pleasant the remainder may be—is What Is.

ᛒ

So what, then, is a spiritual search? That should be the primary question.

By definition, anyone seeking is looking for something. The problem is that most on a spiritual search already believe they know what the end result is or will be. Usually it is pictured or imagined to be something warm and happy. Love, bliss, perfection, control, importance, power, immortality. But a self-motivated search towards feeling better is not the same as a true search for answers.

> Of course, if most are honest about it, the start for anyone was not looking for God or some high ideal or condition, but to get away from deep discontent and pain. Thus the spiritual path will really begin when someone finally gets tired of trying to get something better "over there" and instead tries to look closely at what it is we are attempting to flee. (Eddie Traversa)

Spiritual seeking usually occurs as a bargaining. And the bargaining tends to take on a familiar, self-centered tone. For example, if we become nice, peaceful and wise, the universe will give us what we want. In other words, simply another tool to get cars, houses, or relationships. One of the key reasons that teachers say seeking is a problem is because people, even on the deepest level, still habitually seek to obtain some sort of material reward, or for the fulfillment of a personal egoic want.

Seeking, by default, then becomes a means of distraction away from the very thing that truly needs to be looked at.

We need to keep turning the attention back to the one seeking in the first place, to genuinely and directly ask why we are doing what we are doing. That is why the spiritual search will not really begin until we are no longer able to run away from ourselves. Everyone wants it to start with a wonderful vision or an inspiring feeling. However, a real spiritual journey rarely tends to get underway until some great loss, suffering or disappointment has become infused into our existence. The actual moment of beginning to study ancient wisdom teachings in my case started in 1997 (as will be discussed later). However, the path first truly began to be walked in 1994. That is when a former girlfriend, Joan Heimbecker, was murdered in what became a high-profile Canadian homicide case. A friend called me just before 6 PM to warn me of what I was about to see as the lead story in the news. I recall standing there, in silent shock, as I watched the story of someone so meaningful to me whose life had been tragically ended. I zoned out for a few hours. My mind was processing.

Something changed in those moments. Her death began the shattering of a whole host of fairy tales that I had been holding onto without even realizing it. One had been the belief that if you worked hard, gained some university degrees, and were a relatively nice person, that some force would then provide you with a good life. But suddenly—one of the brightest, kindest and most beautiful people I had known had been cut down at 23. The inner beliefs I'd kept could not withstand the actual experience of chaotic reality. A reality in which it was at once obvious how those beliefs did not determine anyone's success or failure. What did determine those things? Inner exploration had exploded unexpectedly within.

However, there was no reading of spiritual texts, and there was certainly no meditating. In other words, nothing that would be classified by the spiritual community as "spiritual" took place. All that happened was an intense, deep inner questioning of so many of my long-held hopes and beliefs. That, which I've just described, is a big part of the search; and it is the part that is generally ignored by just about everyone on the path.

ɔ

"In order to be effective, truth must penetrate like an arrow, and that is likely to hurt." (Wu Wei Wu)

It is about 7 PM. The seats are slowly filling in. What am I doing here? I could have lied and said I was busy, but here I am. "Here" is a Satsang talk given by one of the big names in the spiritual world. This personage is a favourite of a good friend of mine, who asked me to come along with her. I am always excited by the possibility of hearing someone speak who is rooted in knowing. Yet finding one is like getting asked to play a round of golf at Augusta National—it requires an extremely lucky break. There are about sixty people in the room, mostly sitting and smiling. There don't seem to be many 'rookies' here like me.

"Are you excited?" my friend asks me.

"About what?"

"Being here, to hear this talk."

"Indubiously," to paraphrase Michael Scott of *The Office.*

I am sitting on the end seat of the row, to have the possibility of an easy getaway. I am not writing about this event to show how much I know. Rather, it is to get all of us to ask, "How much do the people we are trusting to be our spiritual guides actually know?" One of the fastest growing businesses in the West is spirituality. The woman I am waiting to hear tonight just had a four-day, $500 a head retreat. Sixty people attended. That is $30,000 for those of you doing the math at home—and doubtful that fee covered room and board, which would be additional. In other words, that hefty fee most likely went entirely to the teacher. Good work for a weekend if you can get it. However, if you make awakening a business, then you need a product to sell. Is what is sold what is True? Or is it simply what people will buy? What is the Truth anyway?

Truth is a big word. Everyone has truth—my truth, your truth, etc. However, these small "t" truths about how to live life are based upon individual perceptions and views. As a result, they are really beliefs. Perhaps a strong emotional belief, but a belief none-the-less. Yet Truth is not about believing, or even knowing or understanding. You become Truth. Truth is not somewhere over there. Nor do we have to figure out how to get over there to have it. Truth is right here. So instead of moving anywhere, we must turn our awareness around to finally perceive it. Truth is not Truth until there is no separation from it. One knows Awakening not when they become Awake, but when the only thing perceived is Awakeness.

Awakening, especially for Westerners with money, has been presented as compassion, love, unity, happiness, no mind, and a dubious host of states supposedly containing no more problems. It has also been fused into a mindset of acquisition, like so many other wonderful sounding things that I can get (like a raise, Porsche, or new boobs) that will make my life better. But for centuries there has been another, albeit less popular message: that Awakening is simply the revelation that there is only One. "If you seek with a perfect seeking, then you shall know the good that is in you; thus you will know yourself as well, it is apprehended by that One, and by the very one who is comprehended."[3] Not as in "we are all connected" or unity. But One. Absolute. No second—thus, no time or space. There is no "we" in One. There is no "me" in One. It is the shocking realization that there is not a higher self, child self, true self, better self—but no self. The Buddhist term Nirvana does not mean happy—it actually means cessation or obliteration. Suffering ends when it is realized there is no one to suffer. "Me" and "the world" are illusionary. So WHO is going to improve by buying what this seller is selling? Shouldn't that be a fundamental question? Yet, paradoxically, at the same time there must be no ignoring of the world or the challenges therein (illusionary or not). For to do so (which is called spiritual

---

3   Allogenes

bypassing) can be just as destructive as it would be to completely focus upon the material world exclusively.

౮౩

"Truly I have attained nothing from total enlightenment."
(Buddha)

All are equal (a rock, a tree, an unseen entity, me or you). When I finally understood why everything was equal, then, at last, I was able to get somewhere. However, I also found there was nowhere to go! The price of truth is everything, as the saying goes. However, no one really knows what everything is until they are at the toll booth and have to pay it. Truth is available to you right now, wherever you are—no matter your current situation. Are you willing to take the step forward? What can make this tougher is that, generally, taking a step forward never seems like it is happening while it is happening. Instead, it often seems like we are taking two steps back.

I was what Castaneda called "Touched by the Nagual" (when the Spirit manifests and descends upon us unexpectedly) for the first time in 1997. It took me years to understand what this phrase meant. Yet I assure you, there was no forgetting the event, as well as the feeling that sent me searching for something more. It was March 1997, around the time of my twenty-eighth birthday. At that time, I had little knowledge of spiritual matters. I'd graduated university in 1993, afterward taking a year off for a business failure and family upheaval. Then, following Joan's murder, I ran away for a year to Australia—only to return to Canada in 1995 to suffer two more years of trying to be a comedian in Toronto. Nothing in my life was bringing me any joy. All of my "titles" and "identities" were powerless. I found, worst of all, that over time I was getting meaner and more manipulative. My relationships went from bad to worse. I treated the last woman I had been dating (Diane), as well as one of my best friends (Holly) so poorly that I wondered "What has happened to me?" Everywhere I turned, I saw people who looked stressed out and unhappy. I myself was broke and angry. I was at the lowest of the low—yet without realizing it, the conditions were perfect. My great transformation was only a day away, but how could I have known?

I came back to my mother's house in Ottawa, feeling like a great failure. On my birthday, I was flipping channels on the TV in my room. The time was around 8:10 PM, and I turned to a Nova documentary on PBS "This Old Pyramid." Even though later I would write a book that would dismiss most of what was said in that documentary, I will always hold a sense of gratitude for that program. It saved my life—or, more properly, it gave me back my life. Watching it, I knew without a shadow of a doubt, that ancient wisdom was to become my life's focus. I felt but one thing: I had to get to Giza inside the Great Pyramid—fully ready and prepared with knowledge before going. I had made a commitment. I was ready to sacrifice everything for what Egypt had to show me. Anything that seemed helpful for knowing Ancient Egypt was moved towards. Everything that would not was dropped. Seven years later—to the day, on my thirty-fifth birthday—there I was, inside of the Great Pyramid.

"You had a meeting with the Spirit," Brad, a Native man I sometimes visited, said to me later. "Spirit gave you one last chance with that television show," he continued. "It was up to you, up to your spirit, to find it, watch it, and absorb the feeling. That feeling would flow through you to activate your Intent. You intended at that moment to dedicate your life to learning ancient wisdom. Every cell in your being agreed and sent you on your way. Good thing too. Spirit had set you up with a great illness, depression, as a sense of shattering your world, to get you to stop rushing, to go searching inside. Even death halted to watch your decision. Would you close the door and move on without a backward glance? And then you made your decision, and your life as an average man, in an average world, wanting average things, came to an end. Ceased to exist. However— you, too ceased to exist. But you still don't understand that…yet."

The trick is to see depression and despair as a part of the process—which, admittedly, is hard to do when you are in it. Most, when living through this particular stage, go on some sort of spiritual search. However, they have no commitment when it comes to truth. What they really want is to be soothed and made to feel like everything is ok again. Instead, one has to see that this reality is a nuthouse. Not with the goal of fixing it or making it nice. But rather, to honestly examine why this world is the way it is.

Taking the First Step is making the unknown our moment-by-moment existence. Carlos Castaneda called it jumping into an abyss. This move is symbolized by the Tarot Fool, striding happily into oblivion. That jump into the abyss is not the end like people think (or hope) that it is—rather, it is merely the beginning. When you are having a wonderful dream, you don't want to wake up. We only want to wake up while in the midst of a nightmare. But seeing reality as a nightmare goes against everything we have been conditioned to believe about it since birth. To move toward a path of Truth, one must leave behind peace and happiness. As a result, for a long time one's life will likely become more difficult. To look within is where all can be found, and then personally realized. At this point, we should be asking, inside where? Inside what? It is assumed what is meant is the body. That our skin is, somehow, a form of dividing line. But am I this body? If not, what does going inside mean? All mediation practices will fail until this little pointer is grasped: "The 'I' is not me."

Everyone has the mistaken belief that awakening experiences, glimpses of the Absolute, are nice and pleasant (filled with beauty, love, light, or whatever). That, however, is the realm of the mystical. Mystical experiences (exploring the dream) are often nice and pleasant. They can even be transforming to a degree. However, that is not Awakening.

Going beyond the dream is about death. The death of everything that you believe is real (which, of course, is everything). THAT is awakening. And that is not fun for the ego, in fact, it is downright terrifying. One should come back from a glimpse of the Real partially with a sense of love and compassion—but they should also be both spooked and freaked out from the direct experience of emptiness. This empty part of spirituality is what most seekers are trying to hide from. What they want instead is the sweet enlightenment they have dubiously been promised: becoming Light (happy, nice, full of love, immortal, or whatever). Most choose a path that is nice and easy, so they never have to look very deeply. On the actual path toward Truth, however, the moments of peace we experience will be just that, moments between our challenges.

Death will come and take us all; all that we believed ourselves to be, all that we believed to be our own. It is the only 100% guarantee in this dream reality: We are all beings who are going to die. What good is greed, self-importance, pride, titles or anything once we are dead? For the last 3,000 years, humans have turned away from this fact, to work instead on making themselves look good, and to have power over others. The results of following this fear-based logic in action is quite evident; we are nearing the total destruction of this world. This, of course, is not the only "world" that there has been— but it is still a good and viable world.[4] We do have enough "time" to change—if we, as a group called humanity, use that time properly. Not that the destruction of this world would be bad or wrong—it simply doesn't have to happen. Or maybe it does?

All spiritual teachings and religions might be false. Just because one billion people are convinced something is the case does not make it good enough for verification. Lots of people were convinced that throwing a virgin into a volcano was a good idea for a while, too. "Hope" is not the best foundation for who you are, or for what happens after you die. All spiritual goals (God, bliss, power, peace or what not) are meaningless if the one seeking for them is still unknown. If we are not a form, then does it matter what our form

---

4   In 2012 we may have shifted into another world, parallel reality, or some
    other odd force impacting this dream directly. This is the subject of my new
    research.

achieves or fails at? We must go and find the answer to this out for ourselves—through experience.

Thus, to be honest in our quest, and to truly begin on the right foot, we must start our journey toward Truth with the firm conviction that "I don't really know anything about anything—and maybe nobody else does, either."

෨

"The Great Knowledge would be found if one should begin to pull down and destroy all the old ruinous buildings, and then enlarge the forecourt, afterward bring lights into the lodging, and then change the doors, stairs, and other things according to our intention." (*Confessio*—second Rosicrucian manuscript 1615)

By November 1997, I had researched Ancient Egypt a great deal, especially the writings of alternative archaeologists such as John West and RA Schwaller de Lubicz. There came a key moment about six months in when I concluded that I could never understand what the ancients were building and doing if I was thinking like a modern human. To understand the ancient past, I had to think like the ancient past. I began to try implementing the practices of Eastern religions, Native Indian ceremonies, Zen dynamics and even metaphysics. Anything that I felt might push my modern mind back to an ancient time. At this point, I had not met any real teachers.

I must admit that I gained a great deal of mental understanding and a wealth of information through the process to that point. I also thought I was hot shit. Then, I encountered someone who changed my thinking entirely—and I am eternally grateful for meeting him. He was the first to show me that I didn't know very much. Being in his presence proved that instead of being hot shit, I was merely the manure part.

His name was Omri. I ran into him only three days after I moved to Calgary in 1997—having relocated on a sudden whim. On that particular day, I'd had an urge to go down to a series of shops and restaurants, and I'd followed my hunch. Omri was working at an Egyptian shop selling statues and wears from the Middle East. Of course, I had almost immediately tried to dazzle him with my amazing knowledge of Egyptian pyramids and temples. We agreed to meet up again the next day. At lunch, he began to talk about what the Ancient Egyptian priests knew, how they practiced, and what they could experience. What he was conveying was so mind-bending that the front part of my head began to pound. At one point, I thought my head would explode. For all I knew about Egypt intellectually, I had extremely little knowledge practically—and absolutely none experientially. Information that I thought was of great value, he showed me was just grade one—a long way from university. He then took me to the New Age bookshop nearby. There, they had a poster board for people promoting events and lectures. He said something at that moment that has stayed with me until this day.

"See all of these people promoting themselves? If someone really has wisdom—the old stuff—you won't find them on a place like this. They will just be living it. You will have to go out and find them. Or, if they do happen to be on a wall like this, you can bet that seeing them will cost basically nothing."

Like all of us, Omri had his ego structures to work on—but for that lunch alone, I am grateful beyond belief. Within time, he introduced me to Taoist Qi Gong and Mr. Park. Through those meetings, I went seeking out Native Indian medicine men (those who I felt might be closest to the wisdom of the ancient world). For a while, they just sort of appeared wherever I turned. My book learning began to become practical. Consequently, I found that the words in the books often did not match the actuality of those who were truly living it.

Religions promise that if you just believe them, and follow their Saviour (Jesus, Buddha, Elvis), that you will receive a "get into heaven free" card. I soon found that the New Age spiritual community simply repackaged this. They compressed the same belief into saying that you can have your heaven right now while alive. This heaven idea is the spiritual carrot dangled before the masses, ensnaring them in a rope of confinement with no proof of what is promised. The Gnostics were not interested in heaven. Rather, their focus was in finding the power within, "to save that which does not need to be saved."[5] Thus, the great call to go inwards—for that is where any saviour is found. One wants answers to our deepest questions, not to uphold a tradition, or to blindly rely on what someone else said. Jesus and Buddha (assuming they were real people) were just guys who got tired of all the bullshit. And there were lots of girls who got tired of the bullshit too—they just never had long stories written about them.

If the Saviours can do it, then so can you and I. Something made them get serious and become spiritual warriors, committed to finding the Answer. Even this dedication is common to various cultures. The way of the warrior is found in the myth of Horus in Egypt, Arjuna in the Bhagavad Gita, and Hercules in Greek mythology.

The main attributes required are honesty, courage, and commitment. Honesty to look at the truth of the way we have been living (often for the first time). The courage to not run from what we may find. And the commitment to not stop until, finally, we know. The process is not fun. Most spiritual people do not have enough courage and honesty to examine their garbage. Generally, they will only do so when outer reality steps in and bursts a fairy tale or two right in front of their faces.

෫෮

The lecture has yet to start, but everyone has taken their seats for the first phase of the night. For the last fifteen minutes we have been bombarded by silence. I use the word "bombarded", for it feels like

---

5   Allogenes

we are in a military operation. The standard explanation given this evening is that the meditative music is being played so that we can all leave our "worries and fears" outside. The result will be an audience present and calm for the teacher's talk. Sounds nice. Yet I suspect that, knowingly or unknowingly, what is really being set up is a hypnotic trance state. It is easy to get people to act and think how you want them to. Just see some YouTube clips of UK hypnotist-magician Derren Brown for proof. And to back this hypnotism suspicion up further, the teacher even begins with a very slow speech pattern. It is as if the words are being directly inspired as she smiles glowingly at us. Hypnotic speech. This will set many minds up to have no questioning filter guarding the doorway when the big spiritual implants come in later: "All is Love, there is nothing to do, you can live your purpose, you need my $40 DVD's and $500 retreats." It may not be conscious manipulation. There may have even been some type of realization with this person. However, egoic layers run very deep. Ego's involvement in anything will be at the very least distortion—at the worst, a mess. We are already hypnotized enough by the dream, and the shadows on the wall of Plato's Cave. We don't need more sleep. We need sharper awareness.

She is now telling us how lucky we are today.

"It is good there are so many spiritual teachers out there, so you can act like you do at the grocery store and just pick one out."

I lean over to my friend, "Yes, buying spiritual teachers and buying apples. Nice 'logic.' And yet, how can you know what they have been sprayed with?"

My friend stares at me.

"People don't try to go after the Truth. They try to adapt society to fit their desires. And they go where they can get favorable answers, and they associate with people who flatter them." (Richard Rose)

The lecture continues. She keeps presenting the standard spiritual routine. "Ask yourself, do you feel peaceful? Is your heart open? Are you living your purpose? Are you bringing light to the world? Are you...."

All read like a robot off a cue card. Never once were the suggestions made to examine WHO has the open heart, what a heart is, what is closed, or whether there is even a world to bring more light to. Self, world, mind, desires are all presented as automatic things we must accept without any questioning.

"You are all the spiritual likeness of God." (Really, God looks like a lot of different people then—schizophrenic maybe).

"This world is a wonderful beautiful experience, full of awaiting joy and love." (Tell that to the government torture victim in some Middle East country, or the mother of a 6-year-old child killed by a drunk driver. Quite simply, Truth must be universal, for everyone, during all experiences. And these airy-fairy hopes do not have any meaning to the experiences I just mentioned. Truth must be the same for those who experience love or horror).

I have had enough of this. I stand up to leave.

છ્ર

One of the biggest fallacies about Awakening is what I call the fairytale idea. Awaken from the so-called dream, and then you will live "happily ever after." First off, such a concept as waking up from a dream is not really the actuality—it is merely a metaphor. The process is quite unique and somewhat indescribable. To therefore create ideas based on the words "dream" and "awaken" is to create a box. There are two distinct parts to the process of Awakening (or Realization): one process on the way there, and one process that happens afterward. These two parts are best presented utilizing the symbol of the spiral/labyrinth. The first process is a spiraling inward, going into the center of the labyrinth. This is done to see all the conditioning that has shaped our view of the world and ourselves. Like any spiral, it moves faster at the outside than in the center. Therefore, the few people who do make it to the middle feel as if they are in a great state of calmness and peace (at the eye of the hurricane). Given that most people are not actually looking for the Truth of their being, but rather are trying to find an escape from pain and suffering, reaching this center seems like such an amazing place. It is. So much so, that they have no interest in leaving it. They think that they have finished the quest. They stop, write a few books, gather some followers, and live somewhat comfortably for the rest of their lives.

However, they have only gone half way.

That can only be known when someone at the center stays honest with themselves. This honesty causes something deeper to rise. The Totality of the Self is not found at the center of a labyrinth, and thus, one must return. In the return process, all that dark stuff you shone your light upon during the down has to be revisited. One sees it all again not to determine how to be rid of it or how to change it—but to learn how to accept it and use it. And spiraling outward can be much harder than the spiraling inward. We may have come to see that everything, including our form, is an illusion—albeit a persistent illusion. So as a result, we need to understand ourselves in a new way. Getting to know the fullness of the light also requires getting to know the fullness of the dark. Being in light is one thing. Hiding in the light is something else entirely.

☙

Remember that those who have reached the answer of "Who am I," say it is so unlike anything they ever thought of or considered before as to be shocking. No book or talk could prepare me for the moment in the canyon when I was confronted with not being who or what I thought I was. Realization revolutionizes everything. While the body, mind, self and world are found to be unreal, shadows on Plato's Cave wall—and always have been, it seems you can't simply jump right into that realization with a body-mind unprepared to handle it, due to the shock involved. Odds are, among the ranks of hospital patients or homeless people walking around muttering to themselves can be found those who had a glimpse of their true nature, but did not have a container able to handle such a vision. Rose and Douglas Harding referred to the need to be vaccinated for this higher dimension. Since this higher realization is opened through the force of death, part of the vaccination is to have as many small tastes of death as possible. That way, the body or the mind will not short out from the shock of an Absolute Realization (ultimate death). Real meditation is not the forcing of a quiet mind, but in truth is an exercise that has two key functions. The first function is to get ourselves directed enough to focus upon our past traumas. This is done to see how they have, and continue to, shape our entire psychological outlook. Secondly, this is also done to take some time to experience being dead—in other words, to practice moments of non-existence. This helps to prepare us for when death really comes.

Awakening is characterized by breaking away from your old life. This is not subtle. Not a little movement at all—but rather, a death. Only from dying can a new thing be born. Death to your world does not necessarily mean losing the job, wife and kids (though it sometimes does). However, it does mean the death of the world that exists in your mind, the foundation on which everything else gets placed. Castaneda called this foundation the Island of the Tonal, and it represents everything which we believe ourselves, as human persons, to be. In the shifting comes the realization that most (if not all) of what we thought we were, is nothing but a costume. Once the old costume is seen through thoroughly and is known as truly being nothing more than a costume, there is a confusing period of limbo. But in that limbo, a new thing can come alive, and it can do so in a "Brave New World."

We have to create a physical and mental being capable of handling the immense energy that comes from a glimpse of Absolute Reality. No matter how pure the water is that you pour into a container, if it is full of holes and cracks, that pure water will leak out. The Hopi claim that the path should be an emptying of the vessel (body) of all its thoughts, beliefs, values, and traumatic memories. That way, we become an empty tube that the Spirit fills. This emptying out is not just about seeing how fast we can fly to God—but also about truth seeking in small things. It is done in finding every one of those cracks and leaks and mending them. A broken part of the self is not going to want to be seen through and dropped. Paradoxically, you must heal something that you will later see does not exist—but then again, a main feature of the path is paradox, itself. Every small thing we let go of is a step closer to true. Is the food we are eating good for us? Are our friendships toxic? How is our sexual life? Our work? Our habits? In what areas are we lying to ourselves? An inventory, in other words, of who we are. Everything found to be false, we back away from. Thus, the path is not actually towards Truth—but backwards (away from untruths). Until finally, as Rose describes, we bump backwards into God. This is another reason why enlightenment might be classified as an accident.

"I'm nobody. Who are you? Are you nobody too?" (Emily Dickinson)

The answer to "who am I" is not found in a lineage, a guru. Nor is it located in meditation, Satsang nights or kissing lotus-strewn feet. The real path is truly a battle of cutting through all of the bullshit to find out what's left. It is not about re-ordering your mind, or making it more positive. Rather, you are out to shatter the mind. Enlightenment is not some kind of construction project: building, ascending, rising, getting better and nicer. It is a demolition project. The process is about seeing your fears—and this is done by walking right into them. Seeing is to shine a light on that which is hidden. And to shine a light on any darkness is to dispel it. Of course, shine your light on anything in the dream state, and you will find that it was never there. We don't need faith in a Saviour, heaven, or another person. Instead, we require faith in ourselves. That no matter our shortcomings, we have what is needed to walk the path. And that if we are honest and sincere in our seeking, some force will offer us assistance. It seems logical to speculate that if we can learn to be more truthful and honest with ourselves on the mundane physical level, that we will have a better chance to be honest about the Totality of the Self.

To do this work requires a great amount of available energy. As a result, much of what is called spiritual practice really involves activities designed to store up or save vital energy. The marketplace is flooded with these grade 1 exercises—which is fine. Everyone needs to know and do them. The problem is, they are being sold as the university physics course. This trick is keeping the masses continually learning their ABC's, while never graduating. Meanwhile, it never even occurs to them that there may be far more on the horizon.

☙

I am walking to the door at the back of the lecture room when I am greeted by one of the people who was accepting the money for the talk, still seated behind the large table.

"Going out to get some air?" she asks.

"Nope. Going home."

"But you will be missing out on all the wonderful energy that is being generated."

"That's ok. Not an energy that I need."

"Well, this planet is a wonderful school of learning," she instructs me. "So, maybe you are just not advanced enough to see the great.... "

"What if it's not? What if this is not a school, and there is truly nothing to learn? What if what we call learning is just finding ways to walk in circles, pretending we are getting somewhere, acting like we're becoming someone? What if nothing is going on here except for our own hypnotized enslavement to a false reality? Wouldn't that be a kick in the teeth? All our best hopes and dreams that our suffering is getting us somewhere might all be crap. Instead of a school, this might be prison—or even better, a mental institution. What if this is where the universe sends all its nuts. Believing you are in school when really you are in the psych ward—THAT truly would be a reason for being in the psych ward in the first place."

She stares at me with utter disgust. She's rather young, 24 or 25—so perhaps not old enough to have invested too much into anything. Hopefully, she will see what she has gotten herself into before ten years have passed—her bank account empty as she sits in a white robe. Donning an Indian-sounding name whilst wondering why nothing in her life has really changed. To soften some of the blow, I smile and respond as I walk out the door.

"Then again, the only one in the psych ward might be me. What do any of us really know?"

ↄↄ

"No self is true self, and the greatest person is nobody." (Chuang Tzu)

For the last few decades, big money has been made through telling people how to manifest their desires and wishes, simply by focusing enough on those items. And on examination, thoughts, actions, and even ceremonies can—in fact—change elements of this theater production that we call life. John Kent calls it "making prop changes in the show." However, this little skill can easily blind someone who should be asking, "Who is creating these things, and whose desire is it for these things to change? Does it really matter if we can make more shadow objects in a shadow world? If the self is false, would anything a false self creates have any value in an unreal reality? Or is it all just a projection of our own vanity and ignorance—hurling more useless shadows onto the walls of one's cave?" The spiritual search takes us to such nihilistic questioning.

"If it's a spiritual thing, don't do it halfway, because you will only get halfway. And halfway to eternity is nowhere. That is still ignorance, because you know nothing, until you know Everything." (Richard Rose)

&

Now, outside of the Satsang building, I take a long deep breath—and really let it out on the exhale. As if trying to push everything from inside away. It is always hard to know how dangerous such events can be. I know two different people, both seduced by popular gurus, who within only a few months were no longer thinking for themselves. Each walking around in a zombie-like state, repeating words from the great teacher's books. It is easy at the beginning of our search to get seduced by all sorts of happy promises.

As long as someone is focused on having a happy mind, they will be limited as to the depth of their study. Yet as soon as one wonders, instead, what it may be like to have clarity or sanity of mind, the search truly changes. And to see our mind clearly only happens by finally observing the mind from a vantage point beyond it. That will open a fundamental question, should such a view should finally occur: What is the mind if I can observe it? And who, then, am I, if I observe the very thing I believed I was?

Just because something feels good does not necessarily make it good in our search for answers. That is why (beyond simple faith in ourselves) we make habit of doubt our chief ally and our best friend. Not as a wall used to disregard everything. Rather, as a tool that says, "I don't know, but I Want to Know." People say they want to discover the Truth, right up until the moment when they realize that it may rob them of their deepest hopes, desires and dreams. We have to want the ultimate answer far more than our desire to feel good. For if feeling good is really our goal, we will stop once that is attained—never questioning if there could be more. It does not mean that feeling good is a bad thing, it is extremely useful sometimes—especially if the body or mind has been sick a long while. We must get that into a sort of stability of energy to go forward. But we do that to move forward, not simply to feel better, because even feeling good cannot be allowed to act as a temptation, or turned into a false harbor for stopping safely during the often unsettling search for Answers.

"When they have acquired it (Truth) on their own, they will no longer be a Christian, but a Christ." (Gospel of Phillip)

Chapter 3

MAGICAL COMMITMENT

The Doorway to Energy

"Once a person steps on the path that is no path, they will always be tempted, always challenged. Unless you have an unshakeable commitment to this work, you'll get sidetracked by everything that comes along, and there are lots of pretty illusions out there. The path to Truth is very simple. You make a commitment for Truth, and then whenever you come to a crossroads where you have to choose between the Truth and something else, you chose your commitment to Truth. That's all." (Richard Rose)

It is Sunday, around noon, and I am arriving in a car with three other "white folks" from Calgary to an Indian Reserve in Western Alberta. Every Sunday for the past four months, I have attended sweat lodges given by Bruce, a local medicine man. He is one who is comfortable with whites joining. When we arrive, Bruce is standing outside. There is no fire burning, which should have been lit two hours ago to have the rocks ready. "Hey, there's no sweat today," he says, "I have to take down and cleanse the lodge." The Calgary group, many who have been coming for about a year, are visibly upset.

"What do you mean there is no sweat today?", one of the women asks Bruce. "All of us have come out here, given up our Sunday. We come for the healing. Just clean it tomorrow, we're here, we're ready, one more day won't matter." Another car drives up, and two more whites come out to join the conversation. Most Sundays have about 16 people at the sweat—half native, half white. It was a beautiful early September day, and like everyone else I was looking forward to the feeling of cleansing, and clarity that one feels after coming out of a sweat lodge. I just simply stood by quietly watching the scene unfold.

"Hey, sometimes the sweat needs to be cleaned, you know," Bruce responded.

The conversation ends. My white friends decide to go for a walk along a nearby lake instead and enjoy the nice weather. "You coming?" they call out to me.

I ask Bruce if he needs help. He nods.

"No, it's ok," I reply, "I will stay here." With that they got in their cars and drove away.

※

While both Advaita and Zen focus on what can be called non-duality, they see it in different ways. Pure Zen wants complete commitment and practice on answering one's koan (deep life question). This will exhaust the seeker, which can create a mini-death and allow the Absolute to reveal itself. Pure Advaita has less a focus on personal doing. It is but more aimed at trying to back away from the small self and dying to all objects of creation, until one is only in Big Self. The Native Indian teachings are about living in harmony and balance with one's surroundings. Yet those who get the call to be a shaman, are the ones who have learned how to cross death and return to be of service.

All three have death as their central doorway to knowing. And as such, all three pathways are related.

Yet these ancient traditions are not what is sold in the spiritual marketplace. New Zen, New Advaita, and New-Age Shamanism are not really about the ancient practice of Self Knowing. New Shamanism wants us to feel good; New Zen wants us to be peaceful; New Advaita, to imagine we are perfect. In each, no commitment is needed. Instead they claim we are already enlightened; we just don't remember it. Yet as John Kent wrote, "that is like saying we are all rich millionaires, we just we don't have the money, and forgot where we buried it."

While it is claimed that the final realization is a complete giving up (total surrender), one cannot give up as an action. Thinking you can surrender, or that you can be detached as an act you can do or not, is not really surrender or detachment. Both happen when there is no other choice but to surrender. As Rose claimed, "while Enlightenment is an accident, we still have to find ways to perform committed action to make us accident prone." Tremendous effort is needed, due to the forces trying to keep everything unchanged.

While practice is one half of the spiritual path, it must simultaneously be done while seeing the fallacy in our actions. It is very paradoxical that one must work like hell, to find there was nothing to work hard about. Many of the current spiritual teachers now claim that since all our breakthroughs and advancement will come only from grace (which is true), it is our very effort that is the problem. As a result, we should just stop everything. This is a misleading teaching.

To start with, it is not our seeking as such that is the problem, just that we are seeking in the wrong direction. Rather than looking for answers, people seek to find ways to get egoic needs met. This includes acquiring toys, happiness, or importance, in the dreamworld. Thus, such seeking never leads to realizing one's nature.

"When grace comes, most people try to run away from it. They don't expect it to be so merciless, so relentless and overwhelming. Grace gives you nothing, and takes away everything." (Karl Renz)

Secondly, the word "grace" must be addressed. To use this word makes the descent of the spirit on us sound pleasant. It also makes it sound like we have to be some specially chosen individual for it to happen. While this is true at the core, the problem comes from telling students to just give up trying and wait for grace. There is a specific moment for that, but it has to be executed at the right time. Do that too early, and it will just be an egoic strategy designed to remain lazy. It is why I prefer Castaneda's term "descent of the Spirit," a very ambiguous phrase to describe when a doorway shows itself. His description (in *Power of Silence*) shows that the experience is not something we are wishing for or acting on. It just happens—exploding on us without warning. When it does, we must take immediate action to not miss the doorway placed before us. Even in surrender, there is still a doorway that requires a choice: enter or ignore it. Action and surrender constantly interact in a cosmic dance of spiritual seeking.

Real practice takes us to surrender, while real surrender eventually takes us to practice.

&

The one teaching that I wish I knew at the age of 16 was how to become a master of commitments—no matter what the commitment is. To say we will do anything becomes a promise to ourselves to carry it out. Making a commitment, and sticking to it, is in fact equivalent to powerful magic. Why? It's simple really. We don't take the time to truly look at what we say yes or no to, often saying yes to everything and everyone. [Usually to avoid feeling guilty for telling someone no.] As a result, we overbook ourselves and stay constantly drained of power. Rose suggests that by following a path of commitments, it undercuts this very dynamic. For example, if someone asks us to come to a party, we can no longer say our usual "sure I will come," even though we know we really have no intention of going. To say you will do *anything* is a commitment. Therefore, we must start choosing what we say yes to very carefully. That is because once we say that we will do it—*we will have to*. If not, we will lose the magic such a path produces. Captain Ahab had that sort of commitment when he responded, "Swerve me, ye cannot swerve me, else ye swerve yourselves! The path to my fixed purpose is laid with iron rails, whereon my soul is grooved to run."[6]

The ego will test any commitment, especially if we start to walk a real spiritual path. It will do this to see just how sincere we are. Since ego layers are made up of nothing but fear, the deeper we go, the more fear gets thrown back at us. Or in another scenario, it may offer us something we have always hoped for—like when a game show offers $50,000 if the contestant will quit and not go for the million-dollar prize. Any possible trap can be used, and it will stun you just how many traps and fears we have. Commitment says you don't care what the dream throws at you. Instead, you are going to go through every one of them and do what you promised yourself you would do. When Richard Rose first began to teach, he had a group that met every Friday night. Lo and behold, each Friday either his wife or his kids got sick, forcing him to cancel. Finally, he told them that he didn't care if they were dying on the floor of gunshot wounds—every Friday he was going to go out and do his teaching. Guess what? The illnesses stopped. In a sense, the universe tested his commitment. Since his commitment was firm, the blocks ended. Do not think that the path will be smooth and easy just because we have commitment. Some tests and trauma must come to us, or else

---

6   *Moby Dick*

there will be no dismantling of the ego. Commitment only reduces certain tests.[7]

The problem is that one is not that likely to have the drive to complete our biggest commitments right away, so we have to start small. For example, a simple thing such as a commitment to do stretching every morning for four days, or walk to work for one week. Then do it. It seems simple, but to finish one small task we committed ourselves to, proves we can complete what we set out to do, and gives us energy and self-confidence to tackle bigger things: eventually taking us to our biggest commitment, to know ourselves

∾

Bruce, his son, and I, walk over to the sweat lodge. "These people... they come just to get. They think like white people. What can I get for free from these Indians. You don't just come to a sweat when you feel sick asking for help, you come when you feel good, so you can help others. You have to give to get. This sweat right now is full of their old sorrows, fears and illness. It must get cleaned, so none of it can come back and hurt them anymore. I did this today for a reason, so each person could clean away their own pains. But I guess they really like their pain. So you see, it's good that you stayed."

With that we began to take down the sweat lodge. As we do, Bruce for the first time, begins to inform me on the symbolic nature of a sweat lodge. What the door means, why it is a certain height. Why it faces a particular direction, what the ties mean, what the wood means. I learned more in those four hours than I learned in the previous four months. In short, I had made a commitment that day to

---

7   One extra piece Rose feels as part of the commitment, is to also make a vow that while currently helpless, if you do find answers, that you will take time to share what you found with others. You will become a helper. It is like your willingness to be a helper later, draws like a magnet those forces, beings, and people who wish to offer help right now.

be at Bruce's sweat, and make myself available in whatever capacity to help: fire starter, rock carrier, water getter, simple participant. Just because there was no sweat itself, did not mean I was not there to help. Keeping that commitment that day opened a door to learning about the door of the sweat lodge.[8]

ℝ

"If you are trying to take a vacation from nature in order to find your essence, the forces of adversity will attack you in any way they can. And that usually means finding the weakest link. It can be your wife, kids, job, importance—anything you might be attached to. If you let these adverse forces slow you down, you are just going to encourage them. To have a chance at really doing something you have to set your psychic shield in place, that is a state of pure commitment. No exceptions. That way you are protected because nothing can be thrown at you that will sway you, and even though they may not know it, so is your family [protected]." (Richard Rose)

Once you examine the matrix reality we call the world, it becomes clear that this place is not set up for anyone to leave. Instead it is set up like a giant perpetual wheel, to keep everyone running for the carrot dangling before our eyes, where all our efforts only keep the

---

8   I should point out, that just because someone has a sweat lodge, does not mean they know how to use it. It takes years of training in the old ways to be gifted by the spirits to have the responsibility of leading sweats. I say this as there are many white people, particularly in Europe, claiming to have been trained by some Native Indian medicine man, and now are running sweats. They usually do so for a fee. Bruce has never asked for one cent for coming, but has appreciated all gifts given to him, usually quickly given away to someone else.

great wheel spinning. If one wants off the wheel, each sleeper must make a mad dash for freedom. Few make it, most never try.

> "Seeing all colours of meaning bleached from life, all gods exposed to be humbugs, and then looking inside and seeing one's presumed identity devoid of substance leaves one empty and aching, with the resolute desire for an answer being all that remains, echoing within the heart. One's prayers disappear into the void." (John Kent)

The Gnostics used much of the Nag Hammadi text to discuss this world being an artificial simulation (called Hal) influenced by shadowy-like figures that they called archons. These beings implant into humans a parasitic mind, which John Last has translated as "the virus." To recognize this, and counteract it, was one of the main steps to rise from the chains in Plato's Cave. I will discuss this parasite more in the upcoming chapters and present a vision directly related to this discussion. For now, part of commitment is aimed at one hand not to ignore the way the game has been set up, but at the same time not to focus obsessively on the source of the adversity itself. To angrily dwell on overcoming the forces of adversity head on is a trap that sidetracks the seeker into a futile waste of energy. Study HOW the delusional influences may affect our mind and actions. The study of hypnosis reveals important clues about how easily we can be programmed and fooled, and in a sense how to deprogram and unfool ourselves. This will help us move to a more witnessing vantage point to determine what is "my own," and what is coming from an external/internal parasite. The search and work is always an internal one, going within one's own psychological condition and correcting the errors found in our own functioning.

It is a journey of discovering the false, and the only way it can be discovered is by honestly going to look for it. As you can see this book will be filled with stories, here is one. The Korean Monk that I spent much time with, Bjung Chool Park (Mr. Park to all of us) was in Hawaii when a number of girls flew over from Germany to meet him. While at times being one of the kindest and most compassionate humans I have ever been around, he too was like Yoda in Star Wars, totally unpredictable. When these girls arrived at his house, Mr. Park came out of his room to meet them. The first one extended her hand to say, "Hi I am Anna from Germany." Mr. Park immediately recoiled and began screaming at them, "Germans, all of you Hitler, Germans, evil, you should all be killed." Then turned and walked back into his room. Needless to say everyone in the room was rather speechless. Of course, the traveling German girls wanted nothing more to do with this "crazy man", so they went downtown to have a coffee and plan the rest of their Hawaiian experience.

While at the coffee shop the same woman introduced herself to someone she met with the similar, "Hi I am Anna from Germany." This time, she noticed her shoulders dropped and head bent down as if to say, "I am from Germany, please don't hate me." Upon noticing this, the women immediately came back to the house and called Mr. Park out of his room to which she stretched out her hand again, this time keeping her back straight and head up to say, "Hi, I am Anna from Germany." Mr. Park now shook her hand and said, "Welcome." He saw the victimhood of her false self instantly playing out, and he was not going to pretend or play games, but honestly call it out right there. It was either going to get worked on or not, but no games, no hiding. That is a great thing I can say about this work. The further you go, the more honest you have to become in order not to get swallowed whole by the process. Honesty with everything inside and out, and such events like the one above simply reinforce that "dramatically."

Instead of suggesting we are divine, Rose claimed we are beings lost in a maze of mirrors in a madhouse, and he suggests we look at all the ways we fool ourselves from facing the truth of our condition. Honestly examining reality—inner or outer, can be terrifying. Therefore, most people instinctively never risk turning their attention inwards, but would rather remain as puppets on a stage, never questioning who is pulling their strings. Since the ego-self does not want to die, that energy is needed to push us to the death experience; to go past the ego and the parasite that is behind it. Castaneda said much of what Don Juan was doing was to "make his head bigger, so it would feel safe when being destroyed," while Rose reminds one has to fatten the head before chopping it off. "The person who becomes enlightened, first has to become the sanest person on earth." (Rose)

The Allogenes call the seeker a "Perpetual Youth," seeing the world and self in an ever-fresh outlook, as a child sees before conditioning takes over. And while someone like Mr. Park or Rose agrees with this, Rose also suggested the need for people to be old as well. For in old age as one is getting close to death is one of the few times people see the foolishness of their lives, and all the games they wasted their time on. Unfortunately, this comes either just prior to death, or with the person so old they have no energy to do anything about it. Rose said part of his job was to "Age a few young people," to have this death understanding at an age when someone still has time and energy available.

❧

"The preparatory condition for enlightenment is trauma. Indulge in it while you can. You will have enough peace in the cemetery." (Richard Rose)

Perhaps our suffering is there just to show us the next egoic layer to drop. However, we don't have to go out and try to make our life hard, or cause trouble, life will do it for us if we are serious. Trauma is what happens to us when we turn our attention back on ourselves. To finally spiral within to see all of the old pains usually only happens when someone gets exhausted from their outer search through illness or failure: when one has tried a guru, time in India, vegetarianism, climbing the corporate ladder, having the perfect spouse and kids, but sees that none has worked. Only when all our efforts have failed might we finally decide to look to the only place we have yet to look—where we currently are. John Kent summed up how difficult the path is for those who turn within:

> The path Rose describes is not easy or pretty. It does not promise immediate peace or comfort, social betterment, a loving God, or eventual celestial delights. It promises work at self-understanding. The anxious uncertainty of doubt. The dissolution of the mirage of "enjoyment" and egotism that we have used to justify continuous living. The tension of existing in conscious ignorance. The challenge of countering adverse forces. The increasing loneliness. The quiet frustration of being stuck between heaven and earth yet having a home in neither. The pain of an awareness that is as yet inadequate to answer itself. And, finally, the inescapable appointment with Death that mercilessly exposes all of our lies and makes a mockery of our dreams. Unless one's desire is for the unembellished Truth, regardless of price, one will have little motivation to continue on this kind of path, as long as more attractive side roads are available.

To pass through the eye of the needle, one needs to be as light as a feather (as in the test of the Egyptian weighing of the heart). It is why we have to clean out all egos, false beliefs, identifications, and projections, otherwise we will stay attached to the illusionary realm. To awaken in a dreamworld we know nothing about, turns dreams into nightmares. And there is no guarantee that we will not wind up trapped in an after-death state that is nothing more than another projection—either a wishful heaven, or a scary hell. Both may be another delusion in Maya's giant dream. Perhaps as Rose says we (living people) are the real nuts, for we never realized that we could have been better off by staying dead, and not narcissistically having to get another body and get back on stage and play another game.

A great ball of energy is required to get us over each hump that we come across, and that is where our commitment comes in. Yet, as we continue through the adversity we begin to notice another element. Help. Just as there seems to be beings and an intelligence there to get in our way, there is another that seems to offer us what we require. Learning how to spot and be open for this help is another part of learning the path to Truth.

As such we have to work very hard while at the same time being what Gurdjieff called sly. To work hard to awaken, but not disturb the other sleepers, who will lash out at those who try. Spiraling inward takes courage, and one tends to only have real courage when we have nothing to lose—when we see we are boxed in with no way out. Can't go back, but only continue forward. Death is coming. This is a special mood, one that at first looks like defeat, but is in fact, the mood of the warrior. It is from this mood where transformation takes place, where a Silence from beyond us is also seen to be us.

"There was within me a stillness of silence, and I heard the blessedness whereby I knew my Proper Self." (Allogenes)

Chapter 4

JACOB'S LADDER

Rising Alone

"The great path has no gates, thousands of roads enter it. When you pass through the gateless gate, you walk the universe alone." (Mumon)

I have decided to sit alone while I write this chapter. No Anders. No anyone. Just me and an empty room. The jury is out as to how empty I might be, however. Symbolically, alone was the best way to do this. The material this chapter is based upon hits me very hard. Almost every time I began to write, a giant headache would form. It almost paralyzed any attempt to generate anything readable. The pain felt like a nail being driven into the center of my forehead. [This might actually be backwards: Perhaps a nail was getting pulled out of my head. Going in or coming out can hurt just as bad. Time will tell which side of the hammer I was using.] Rather than just take an aspirin, or chew some willow bark—the stuff aspirin comes from—I will go on with this presentation, alone.

Awakening is a very misunderstood—I was going to write achievement, but it's not an achievement. Just a happening. It is like making a long, steep, tough climb up a mountain, only to get to the top and go, "Mmmm, nice view." Then you walk back down.

That's it.

Nothing special.

But it revolutionizes everything.

At least that is how it looks when it first happens. However, one discovers that there is a whole new process which is about to start.

Awakening is the shocking realization that there is only One. Not one thing or "all is connected". Just One. It sounds like a simple re-ordering of words, but the deeper meaning of that word order is profound. Everyone has the constricting belief that Awakening, or God, is over there somewhere. Their job in life, they feel is to find it. The problem is that we are "here" and will always be here. But if Awakening is over "there," how can it be found? Actually, it is always here, but what it is, is not what 99% of seekers really want. Seekers want the Enlightenment they have been sold. Being happy. Important. Full of love. Having no more problems. Enlightenment as a continuous orgasmic drug high. That is the reason they are seeking in the first place: the wished for blissful finish-line. If anyone really understood what Awakening was, no one would want it. That is because there is nothing for "me" in Awakening.

A true encounter with the Absolute/God reveals that no one is doing the experiencing. Only the Absolute—revealing itself to the Absolute. Nothing exists, yet there is the appearance of existence. Realization is alone (all-one). But everyone fears alone. So as a result, they run to spiritual practices, patterns, lovers, food, booze—in other words, any distraction to avoid the only true fear. The fear of no self (often called "emptiness") is not the fear of death. Rather, it is the fear that you, as a human being, do not exist at all. That is where all the spiritual groups get caught. They look for what's in it for "me", or "us." Awakening is one and alone—for there is no second. The initial glimpse of this is so terrifying to ego, that it responds with corresponding emotions of meaninglessness and despair. This is done to try and get us to turn back to the dream. But when the mind falls away, those emotions go also. And all that is left is the marvelous curiosity about the dream, and a genuine interest focused upon what is going to happen next.

> "Each person blossoms from a different catalyst. The only thing that enlightened people have in common is that which they find, so it is better to encourage the inward search, without demanding the student find an exact formula or discipline." (Richard Rose)

When talking about the exit door to Plato's Cave, no matter how many groups of people band together spiritually, that door must be walked through alone. For a while, we can walk with others and share the journey, but there comes a point when continuing onward means having to follow the metaphor of squeezing through the eye of a needle. Nothing can go with us-not even ourselves That stops many seekers right in their tracks, as everyone has something special in the dream which they do not want to give up.

There are a few odd things about the exit door from the cave that should be mentioned. The first is the well-known Zen reference to a "gateless gate." The door seems to be locked or barred, until we pass through it—then we see that it was never locked at all. Similar in theory to the chains latching the prisoners in their seats, (i.e., the locks that bind are not actually locked). The second part of the exit door metaphor is that, generally, it seems few go all the way through the first time they come to it. Most stop part-way. Some get a glimpse of the hallway beyond the door. Some turn around and view the entire theatre-cave. Others just turn and rush back without seeing much at all. Yet, if they manage to return to that doorway a second time, they tend to linger far longer. If the cave can be classified as the Greater Mind, then the doorway itself is the viewpoint where one can turn back to see the mind and dream in its complete entirety.

Taking this to the next step, the hallway beyond the door would then be the funnel or vortex leading to the Totality of the Self.

℘

PYRAMID ONE
Umpire-Horus-Nigredo

Richard Rose symbolized the entire spiritual process as a ladder—which he diagrammed more as three triangle/pyramids one of top of the other. Each pyramid represented a complete stage of the work. Jacob's Ladder is the map utilized in his book *Psychology of the Observer*, (the text where Rose outlined his spiritual system). It is named Jacob's Ladder in reference the story in the Old Testament. That tale tells of Jacob—who, as he slept while on the way to Harran, climbed a ladder to have a vision of heaven. On returning to reality, Jacob commented, "How dreadful is this place."

After years of studying this material, one day a connection was made. It was an inspiration about the number three. In sacred geometry, three is the digit that acts like a door—where the non-moving two can become the many (four or greater). The main Ancient Egyptian pyramids at Giza (and secondary pyramids) are found in sets of three, which personify in stone the religious trinity of Osiris, Isis and Horus. Handed down through Persia (Mithras) and Greece (Bacchus), this eventually was translated into the Christian trinity of Jesus, Father, and Holy Spirit (Mother Mary and Magdalene). The three stages of alchemy are symbolized as well through a three (or four) step process of Nigredo (Black), Albedo (white) and Rubedo (Red). Upon completion, this process led to the Philosopher's Stone (total knowledge). It was hard, for a while, for me to see these specific connections with alchemy—aside from the basic principle of three main stages. The ties, however, were strengthened when I came across the alchemic manuscript *The Mutus Liber* (Silent Book).

First published in 1677 in New Rochelle, France, this work contains almost no words at all. Instead, within it one finds 15 images. The first plate of the Silent Book shows a sleeping man with a ladder beside him—while the last plate depicts the man risen and the ladder cast aside. I believe this book to be the symbolic rendering of climbing Jacob's Ladder.[9]

Finally, when listening to Adyashanti present his view that there are three main qualities in an Awakening, it was like a tumbler on a lock fell in place. Each trinity is a similar pointer to the process of going from seated in the cave, to walking through the exit tunnel out of it. Could Rose, the medieval alchemists, Ancient Egyptian priests, and Adyashanti all be explaining the same thing?[10] And more importantly, what help would any of it possibly be for someone on the path to Knowing?

Rose's map of Jacob's Ladder—while simple and functional—can be confusing. There are a couple of things that I really like about the metaphor. As mentioned, his ladder is symbolized as three pyramids, each on top of each other. The lowest is the physical realm (body, thought); the middle pyramid represents the mental area of Higher Mind, and the top pyramid is the Essence or Self. Yet each of his three pyramids are purposefully not meant to be equal—in fact, they get smaller as they rise. Mirroring similar principles from Gurdjieff, Rose felt that everything in our reality was pyramidal in form. There are more people on the lower stages in any area than on any of the higher ones. Similarly, there are far more amateur golf

---

9   The *Mutus Liber* plates and my interpretation are presented in detail in the Appendix.

10   The ladder metaphor in Ancient Egypt was symbolized by the Djed (pronounced TeT) Pillar. This pillar represented the spine of Osiris and was often worn as an amulet or talisman (suggesting ladder work is protecting). It is called a TeT pillar today because the Ancient Egyptian language was written only with consonants, and Egyptologists—to make sounding a word easier— add an "e" between consonants. But this is not necessarily the correct vowel. Thus, in even greater connection to Rose's organization, this talisman might have been known as a TaT pillar.

players than professional players, more students to professors, and so on. It is much the same in spirituality. I think that this is an important point to bring out. If someone goes from seated in the cave-theater to walking around, by default joining a smaller area of the upper part of the pyramid. That is the key reason for the gravitation of seekers toward spiritual groups. Less people makes it seem like something different, but it is still the same pyramid, just compressed to appear different.

Rose's pyramids are each, of course, triangular. Each is made of a baseline of two points, such as A-B. These are opposing forces that create the dual reality. For example, in the lowest pyramid, the two ends can be labeled pain and pleasure, good and bad, high and low, etc. We spend our lives trying to move away from the negative pole of experience (pain) towards pleasure. However, it continually seems as if life itself is pushing back. As a result, a tension exists. There is a great chance that we may never even realize that we swing back and forth like the pendulum of a grandfather clock.

As soon as we fall away from the center point-the string we are attached to yanks us, but always too hard, thus thrusting us to the other side of center. This process repeats endlessly. That is where the idea of between-ness comes in: being in the magnetic center point which has all the power. Power that can then propel us up the pyramid. Advancing is accomplished by implementing inner processes on ourselves—ones that move us eventually up to reach the third point of the pyramid—the top.

In each pyramid, essentially it is this middle basepoint which rises upward to become the new higher pyramid point C. This is my best explanation for the use of between-ness in ladder work: it is not that we go up, but "pull" the central point between A-B up. I saw this in a documentary once on pyramid building, the base must be stable, and the center point gets raised up as it grows to not allow twist to the shape. This point C becomes the high point which Rose labeled the Umpire. At the same time, we also perform what Rose called Ladder Work. This is to help someone below you to move up a step, while simultaneously gaining help from someone one step above you to aid your own upward progress. Thus, in a sense, all participants will move up the ladder together.

Reaching this unifying higher point will reconcile the two opposites below into a clearer point-of-reference. One where both sides of the line are seen as equal. It is not about bringing the opposites together, or balancing the extremes:

> "Rather, it can be likened to the sky that incorporates the alternation of day and night; the Tao that incorporates the Yin and the Yang. It sees that a zebra is neither white with black stripes nor black with white stripes: it is transparent–with black and white stripes." (John Kent)

We don't fix the duality; we see it clearly from a much higher place—a vantage point where both are false, but necessary. In simple terms, to reach the Umpire and to integrate what it shows, leads to optimal human functioning thereby facilitating living as a human being was intended to. This higher third point (such as point C) is then found to be the base of the next pyramid (C-D), where an entire new process begins, with the new goal being to reach the top of that new pyramid.

The second pyramid is topped by point E, which Rose called the Process Observer (Greater Mind). The highest point of the third pyramid is G (the Absolute). Each point is a higher, more refined observation post for what is below. In other words, the Umpire watches the body's experiences, the Process Observer watches the body and Umpire, and the Absolute watches all Awareness. While there are only three pyramids, Rose did not mean to imply that there are only three steps. Rather, each pyramid is a complete stage, yet one that is filled with multiple smaller steps along the way.

Rose also commented about something called the invisible current-the finger of God stretching back to us. We can use this current, via between-ness, to touch the finger, as presented in the Sistine Chapel ceiling. Rose suggested that spiritual work is not just about us doing personal work (where we more clearly see all areas of adversity and expose oncoming traps, so that we can thereby step over the holes). Rather, it also involves being directly aware of this higher force that is looking to help us. The point may be, no pun intended, that the finger (or ladder of God) may not be easily seen. In fact, it might even be thought of as something we would want to turn away from initially.

The finger for the adults in the movie Pleasantville, was the arrival of David and Jennifer. The adults saw them as troublemakers creating rebellion in their young people. Thus, they were taken as something to confront, rather than messengers from a realm beyond the bubble. The message being presented within the story was to take a step out of their closed black and white static reality and into a world of colour possibilities. We must hone our own intuition to catch similar messages arriving for us.

With the ladder metaphor, most get the idea that spiritual work is climbing upwards like a religious movement to heaven in the sky. Given that all of this is a paradox, we may find Truth through falling rather than from climbing. Falling into Truth means that rising up the ladder generally comes from some form of dropping (of attachments, egos, addictions, and beliefs), trauma (which makes us fall over ourselves), or surrender (where we drop to the ground—as Arjuna did—from realizing our inability to make the dream behave as we want it to). Yet each time something falls off us, we get lighter. Hence, the inevitable rise. Herein lies a reminder from one of Rose's key pointers: that the path to Truth is really a path of backing away from that which is untrue. Most of what is untrue consists of the very things we hold onto the tightest. As a result, there is the feeling of falling as we let go of our hard grasping to all these makeups of self.

This, therefore, is not guiding us to look outside of ourselves. Rather, it is a call to go directly inward. Most spiritual work is built upon the assumption that if we do exercises from the highest point of the ladder, we will then reach the top faster. That is not necessarily true. This is because the work in lower (i.e., the more physical) areas will by default have been ignored. It is more important to see exactly where we are right now and work specifically with that area. To not do so would be akin to blasting off for Pluto without first taking the time to build the spaceship. This entire realm of thought and inquiry was one of the main areas that first drew me to Richard Rose. These precepts encourage a very practical, grounded and self-directed focus towards Self-Knowledge.

The challenge for us is not to get drawn deeply into anyone's metaphor of the spiritual search. Instead, we want to examine the pointers from various people—individuals that we think offer us honest insights about the path. From there, we sort through it all to take into our worldview the pieces and ideas that are most helpful to our search. We use these pointers specifically to go further. In other words, looking where the finger is pointing, and not falling into the temptation to get stuck looking at, or even studying, the finger. While this chapter is more or less an overview covering some of the main pointers that I came across which matched my experiences in these areas, I leave it to you take on for yourself anything that might be helpful—before going off and finding how best to apply those items to your search. Our walking must be individual—the path we actually require—as opposed to the one we wish to have. (Which, more than likely, will just be another way of finding a group and staying cozy somewhere within the cave.) The ladder is about locating sanity. It is definitely not about increasing personal insanity. As such, that journey is personal both and unique.

☙

The Umpire and its three pathways

"Please don't shoot the umpire, he's doing the best he can."
(sign in Kansas City ballpark 1880's)

Work within the first pyramid can be classified as the areas of modern religion and spirituality. Included as well can be self-help, psychological therapy, alternative healing, breath exercise, connecting with spirit realms and divination. In short, all things designed to allow "me" to function more easily within standard reality. These all can serve an important purpose. In the ancient world, such subjects were the fabric of the entire society—encompassing the world of adults and a part of every child's instruction. Our world is missing even the most basic of human instruction in these areas. On one hand, it makes sense that the modern spiritual marketplace is all about first pyramid work, because it is where almost the entire human population resides. The problem is in the formatting: in other words, the way that this set of basic instructions is presented as if it were the whole package. Someone who manages to reach the Umpire will, in comparison to these opening elements, come away with the sense that they have truly taken a step up in their functioning. And rightly so.

Rose compared the top point of the first pyramid, the Umpire, to a computer program. If allowed to run, it will help us (individually and as a species) to be safe. Allowing us to not die off before our basic purpose has been fulfilled. (To spawn, and then raise, another group of children).

"Something in us urges and inhibits. Something within encourages bravery and fear. Something within makes us enter joyously the game of life, and at times long for death. And yet, all of these things seem to form a pattern which makes for some kind of destiny, something within us, if we allow it, will make decisions for us, take care of our children, and condition one for dying when the time comes." (Richard Rose)

Rose chose the word Umpire because it connotes a deciding mechanism. It is the English name for a referee—a moniker still used in tennis and baseball—whose decisions are generally very cut and dry, or black and white. For example, in tennis: in or out. In baseball: ball or strike. Within our world, Rose's Umpire chooses what to eat, what habits to have, as well as nearly the entire spectrum with regards to the use of one's time and energy. For everyone planted in the seats of Plato's cave, this is mostly a lost (or unused) function. Rose claimed that the problem for most in the physical world was that the obstructions and distortions in our psychological make-up prevented the Umpire from functioning properly. People keep eating poorly until they have a heart attack, for example, or keep smoking until they contract cancer.

A functioning Umpire instinctively knows what is needed, as well as what activities should be moderated. Moral codes were created hundreds of years ago because so many Umpires, for some reason, no longer were functioning properly. To discover the Umpire and get it working effectively and efficiently may be interpreted by a religious person as "salvation." Meanwhile, a New Age person might call this finding their higher self. The conscience is another name for this feature—a voice inside that is trying to steer one away from actions that create harm for the individual. While this utility is not necessarily a spiritual aspect (being simply a programmed robotic function), to have this utility operating properly will by default lead to more vitality and mental clarity. To a prisoner, having spent their whole life to date without such a function, (especially considering the depth of mess they create for themselves without it) this would indeed appear akin to a salvation-type realization. That in and of itself showcases another reason why it is hard to get past this level: The fear encountered when pondering whether to lose the Umpire would mean returning to the chains of ignorance. We are not trying to become perfect, but see ourselves in clarity.

"This is not a school. Why would some omnipotent being create a bunch of ignorant people and then torture them to make them better?" (Richard Rose)

There is little need to present the traps and chains of modern religions within the context of the material being presented here. If you are reading a book such as this, you likely turned away from those ideas long ago. For most seekers, the turning away from a Western religion happened when fairy tale being presented was exposed beyond repair. But that leaves such individuals with a distinct dilemma: What happens when one has seen through religion, (a supernatural explanation for where we are, and why we are here) but finds themselves still searching for ultimate answers? If recent history is any indication, one turns toward what has been broadly labeled "spirituality." Yet spirituality is much more of a religion than most people tend to think. On the one hand, as a system it is freer than standard Western religion. However, instead of offering a future paradise in exchange for following moral codes, spirituality promises that we can be happy, all the time, right now. As soon as a tradition or way becomes for sale—as so often is the case in the spiritual marketplace—it must be made attractive to the buyer. There is nothing wrong with the study of various practices—from psychic connection to alternative healing—to create an organism that is healthier, more intuitive, and more efficient. However, the modern spiritual lifestyle requires money and is a way to show the masses that they are one step above based on the goodies they showcase. It is difficult to explain in words, but once you look for it with these people, it is easy to spot the dynamic.

Rose felt that most people moving toward spirituality did so as an attempt to compensate for unhappiness, suffering and loneliness, rather than as a means for seeing who was suffering and why. The bulk of the spiritual crowd is searching for a "feel good" answer. But to ever have a chance to finally know—we must first understand our own minds intimately. In other words, to see all the psychic pollution that is in there. Even ideas we have of God, spirituality or society can quite often be little more than pollution.

"Yes, I am dismissing spiritual aspirations within the sleeping dreamstate, quality of life issues like happiness, peace, health, prosperity, and so on. And salvation and life everlasting to take it a small step further. Greed, vanity, ego, all arising from fear. Yes, I categorically dismiss all of that. It is the muck and mire in which mankind wallows, and from which sincere aspirants must extricate themselves. Now the valley is the mountaintop, and everyone is enlightened, if they go along with the switch. The new goal is right here, right now, and need only be recognized as such. Voila! Total failure is now total success." (Jed McKenna)

❧

One challenge is how people use words to describe the spiritual. What one means by the word awake, may not be what another person using that word means. It gets very confusing if we substitute our meaning of a word with what another means by the same use. Especially in this field. Since I am mainly discussing Rose's ladder, I can comfortably keep utilizing his three coined words for the three pyramid levels. I could have used Egyptian terms, alchemical concepts, or simply made up three words. The word used itself is not that important, just a marker to show what area is being discussed.

The first stage, the Umpire, can be characterized as an ah-ha moment. A small example of one would be remembering where our lost keys are; a larger one could be encountering a shift in control. Becoming a full functioning adult could be another way of seeing it.

The second stage, the Observer, would be to no longer believe who and what we thought we were. This, by default, results in a shift of identity. Most of what is classified and labeled in books as Enlightenment, is really describing this second Observer stage.

The third stage, or pyramid, is reaching What Is. In other words, encountering the Absolute as the only reality.

Adyashanti wrote of how what he calls Awakening (i.e., meaning reaching the Process Observer in the second stage of the work, in my opinion) is composed of three qualities. I feel that this idea of qualities which he discusses should exist at the top of all three pyramids. (This would then actually mirror the Hermetic process as each pyramid would then represent one of the three qualities.) This also makes the ladder holographic—wherein each part both contains and mirrors the whole. Adyashanti labeled these three qualities as mind, heart and gut. Here, I have taken the same basic principles, but I have renamed them mental, emotional and philosophic. This is to give less of an idea that these qualities are tied specifically with any part of the human body. They each, instead, are elements of the universal makeup. In summary: every one of the pyramid tops is made up of a conglomerate of these three qualities or aspects. Given that every pyramid contains the three qualities, it would therefore make sense that one can find three distinct pathways to reach the top, representing each aspect.

I have a new diagram that shows a pyramid with the letters MEP (mental, emotional, philosophic). These letters represent the three pathways—which we use distinctly to spiral inward (i.e., walk the ladder). While it is possible that we may touch all three paths along the way, typically, one will tend to be the main focus of our ultimate direction. As each pathway has a different set of methods, so, too, does each distinct path look unique within the diagram itself.

Interestingly, I believe that each pyramid-stage also reflects one main quality. The first pyramid is climbed with an emotional edge. Therefore, for most (as the general mass of people are in the first pyramid) their main goal is to feel better or improve themselves. Emotion is the driving force; thus, we must use some type of emotional-devotional base to rise. A mental or philosophical approach in the first stage is going to be much more difficult if there is not a matching emotional element to the process. Should someone naturally follow an emotional path, they will be more in tune with the work of the first pyramid. An emotional seeker has the most likely success of reaching the Umpire, but on reaching it is most likely to go no further, as their main focus is to feel happy.

The second pyramid is mental, as it is topped by the Process Observer (Greater Mind), hence all approaches in some way have a mental aspect to them (looking at our mind and thought) even if the pathway is mainly emotional or philosophical. A mental approach is more likely to reach the Process Observer, and a mental seeker is more likely to stop there, as they wanted most to know their mind, which is a main gift at the Process Observer.

The third pyramid is the philosophical pyramid, and thus requires a primarily philosophical or existential approach to maximize the work for that stage. Again, one can travel the third pyramid with a mental focus, but without philosophical examination as a main element diving into hopelessness and emptiness, one will stay trapped at the height of the mind and never find the between-ness point to begin rising.[11]

Is it clearer to you now why the presentation of love, joy, and being happy as the basis of the spiritual marketplace? Most who have taken a step up have done so in an emotional based first stage and are thus presenting what they know. Most cannot fathom that there are stages beyond what they reached. To present love as the answer for everything is true from the context of the first pyramid. It also becomes a main stumbling block when trying to communicate with someone in the second pyramid stage who has moved into a more mental examination of self and reality.

A mental focused path (M in my diagram) will move up the left edge of each pyramid to the summit, thus appearing as a continuous sloped line. That makes the mental path generally the most direct, but it is also the most treacherous as there are no stopping points. There is also a long slide down if we slip. The emotional direction, for a while, follows either the mental or philosophical side depending if

---

11   This mirrors ideas of both Rose and Gurdjeiff that there were 4 types of people on the spiritual ladder, discussed in the Additional Material.

our deepest draw in our identity is toward pain or pleasure. At a key point, the emotional seeker will plateau (usually from an experience designated as a psychic or mystical) toward the center, and then rise straight up (similar to the image of floating). Thus, the emotional path does have work involved in the original slope, but it is the most enjoyable path to walk due to the plateau moment of rest, and the floating like aspect of being raised, and the shorter drop to the plateau point should one fall.

The philosophical path is symbolized on the right slope, indicating a driving force of pain and challenge, and is usually the most difficult of the three on the body-mind. Here there is a slope similar to the mental but traveling in a zig zag fashion or a lightning bolt. This path comes less from clear defined practice and is more of a haphazard life pushing you here and there. Then out of nowhere, a bolt of lightning occurs, and a level jump. The examination of hope and despair is a key aspect of this path, hence the resulting zig zag pattern. This path can raise someone the quickest, but carries the most confusion for one is not sure what happened, how they got there, or where *there* is. A long integration period is needed for the philosophical seeker.

Each quality is unique and could be thought of as its own special viewpoint from the Umpire. If it came via the mental path, it is the realization that "what we think shapes our world." It is often brought about through self-help practices, psychological counseling or contemplation from various amounts of reading. This person begins to focus more on changing thoughts, positive affirmations, or ways to limit negative thinking. There is a dropping of fear when we see that we, as well as the world, have an interactive element. We seem co-creative.

If the realization came through a devotional path, (generally through the giving of oneself to a religion, organization, nature or even the care of a child), the view causes the wants of the self to become secondary to the perceived wants of something else. Our wants come as a reward for helping this other attain their wants, thus the focus is no longer completely on ourself. This emotional realization can also occur through a mystical moment, such as connecting with a dimension beyond this one or a near-death experience. Generally, one where an angel or dead family member comes and tells them they are loved and protected. The result of the emotional rise is to operate in a more selfless way.

For those who came existentially, via a lightning bolt type of the philosophic path, they see the world around them as a type of dream. The need to control will drop when the world is seen as less real, thus not as important. They soon find that the less their egoistical wants get in the way, the easier it is to shift the dream. However, due to seeing the world as a dream, this type of realization can also lead someone to a great deal of paranoia and hopelessness (if it is not tempered with humour and a compassion for the dream itself).

Each quality presents to us that life gets easier if we give up some of our personal control. This follows Rose's description of the Umpire as a feature that helps us and looks after us if we step out of the way and allow it to function as it was programmed. We rise from the chains in Plato's Cave, and we explore the cave reality—but generally only have one flashlight.

Given that reaching the top of the first pyramid, and having a new mode of operating in reality is such a big thing, why do so few venture beyond that step? A major reason is that this experience is what is presented by many teachers and books as the outcome that someone should aspire to. It makes sense that if everything one comes across points to the very thing one has accomplished, there is little reason to think there might be further steps to take. As such, many Umpire-realized people become teachers and authors— prescribing their how to feel better formulas, while never thinking they are bunkering in rather than looking to go beyond.

The Umpire is all logic. Even someone with an emotional realization, if you look carefully, will just display an emotional logic. If I pray x number of times, give x number of gifts, then the deity will feel so moved and loved by me that it will give me y. This is a sort of mathematical emotionalism. The Umpire is still the ego, or still greatly influenced by the ego, and still in Plato's cave, but with more movement. In no case is there a complete shift in identity (the clarifying factor of the second stage). Here, the person who was Jim Smith on planet Earth "still thinks" he is Jim Smith on the planet Earth, just living more selflessly.

A big reason why any Umpire realization will not take a person too far into Knowing themselves is that the seeker was mainly seeking to escape their problems. If the problems that started them searching come to an end, they stop seeking, and simply live out their lives at this more comfortable level. Secondly, the Umpire may be never fully integrated because one generally sticks to that single part of their realization that comes from their specific path, while ignoring the other portions. Each path has its own built in trap. One with a mental realization will in time see that they cannot force the dream to give them all their wishes just by thinking about it. Where is their million dollars? Why as their wife left them, or their dog gotten run over in the driveway? They must be inferior because the books say they should be a god. Most will take more courses, or read more books with the thought "if I just know more, I will get more." The trap is the idea that wisdom can only be accomplished via mental knowledge.

The emotional-realized (though seeing they are more than just a body and are protected) have mostly ignored the philosophic and the negative sides of reality. They are not able to handle it when tragedy strikes. They think the helpers are upset with them, so they try to find more rituals and ways to pray and appease the gods. In other words, some attempt to float away from mundane earthly problems, as a result they lose touch with their own life and everyone else, except to tell them how blissful and happy they think they are. A push up the ladder comes when someone begins to wonder if this help was coming from an outside source, or if it had always come from inside. Have I only been praying to and getting help from myself?

That question, if followed, will produce a radical shift from looking outward to looking inward.

The philosophical-realized person sees the world as a dream, but they lose the ability to see how they relate as a human being within that dream and lose empathy. Others, due to the lack of conscious understanding of what has happened, and with no one around to guide them, decide they must be crazy and try to just forget the whole thing.

To step beyond the Umpire requires one to question if the realization, while useful, may not in fact be true, or complete. Rose claimed that The Umpire is limited, for it only has its built-in programming and only sees things in dual concepts (much like a computer that operates only through 1's and 0's). It is very good for choices being made in the mundane world. But without seeing the master plan of the entire universe, it makes choices based upon what it thinks is best for the survival of the person/species without seeing the overall story. It is good in areas it is programmed for, but does not work well in others. What should be surprising is that if there is a computer-like feature built into us to make basic living decisions (for our best interest), then who or what is constantly over-riding this inner voice?

❧

PYRAMID TWO
Process Observer-Isis-Albedo

"I suppose that the same will happen to me, namely that I will suffer great difficulty, grief and weariness at first, but in the end shall come to glimpse pleasantries and easier things." (alchemist Michael Maier)

Work on the first pyramid started when someone saw they had problems and wanted solutions. One wants to be healthier, have more money, be more attractive or have an easier experience of life. Upon reaching that Umpire apex, a human running in good optimal fashion will correct many of these problems. People (especially those at the Umpire stage) find even more ways to distract themselves from the gaping emptiness of reality (often by digging into a glorified spiritual ego, or by acquiring more worldly objects). However, a constant low-grade inner anxiety, that one cannot really place, continues no matter how many external goodies arrive. The big issues (death, meaning, reality) are not being answered. Rose commented that most at this point go to a therapist who will try and help them to ignore the subliminal messaging coming through; reminding the patient that:

> "He can do anything he sets his mind to, and that society will no longer like him if he becomes inactive in the social-commercial game...The person wants to stop at the Umpire, and bask in the new freedom this rational knowledge seems to give—which will guarantee them a good career, good health, and a good marriage. But then the person gets sick, or the relationship stops going well, or society begins to ignore us that we begin to wonder what went wrong. A few people become obsessed, possessed, defeated and destroyed enough to go looking beyond." (Richard Rose)

First off, we should not look at this like a step by step process, such as the first pyramid work needs be completed before starting second pyramid work. There can be overlap. There is a point where one moves fully to the next stage—but often multiple stages take place at the same time. Those who move into the second pyramid are no longer interested in feeling better; they want to know the internal cause for their dissatisfaction. Instead of focusing attention outward on the objects and experiences of the dream, we must turn our attention within to try and see who is having the experience, and why.

ↀↄ

"Go to the woman who washes her sheets and do the same as she does." (Atalanta Fugiens)

The second phase in alchemy is known by the name Albedo (sometimes called Solutio) and leads to the Awakening of the Greater Mind. This is revealed in the *Mutus Liber* plates 8-13, and the quote, "burn your books and whiten your latten." This is meant that the answer will not be found in any book, but within the seeker's own mind. Latten is a word play on two words. The first being Latin—the language, thus burn all of the works of the modern (at the time) enslaving Western World. It also references Latona, the woman of revelation—Isis. To know Isis one must become one with her, or experience her directly.

Albedo begins at the darkest part of the Nigredo, when we think we have reached the limit. As long as we do not give up at this point, a whitening begins. It is here that the feminine principle (Luna-Isis) comes into its own. Dreams are exceedingly relevant at this juncture, signifying that the information we need at this stage is more intuitive. A woman is depicted washing sheets. This is humbling and grounding work that we might rather not do yet are routines that strips us of our defenses and forces us to look at all we have suppressed, just as the dirt from the clothes is stripped away in the washing. Through the humbling work we are washing out our mind. Through this pain, the white rose is shown blossoming. This symbolizes a pure spiritual substance and becomes the White Queen—Isis. In the myth, Isis searches for the scattered parts of her dead husband Osiris, requiring a commitment to the intuitive feminine side, which comes out strongly in stage two work. She finds all of the pieces (but one), builds a temple on each site and then reassembles the parts long enough to impregnate herself via virgin conception to produce Horus. The concept of lost or misplaced parts and the need to regather them, was something I recognized as a metaphor for inner process. Parts we must place together in jig saw puzzle fashion, as we find one misplaced part at a time rather than all at once. I later found that this idea of finding lost pieces of oneself is a cornerstone of another modern California teacher's presentation.

 ↵

"I have lived on the tip of insanity, wanting to know reasons, knocking on the door. It opens. I have been knocking from the inside." (Rumi)

That teacher is Jed Strauss. He describes second pyramid process as *the rot*—letting us know it is not going to be simple and fun. It is difficult because our entire spiritual search in the first pyramid had been about trying to get somewhere else, or be a better "me," as we looked to perfect how we felt about ourselves. The rot is the willingness to face all that we have run from our entire lives, because there are no more options of escape. We must accept our reality as it is—probably faced with disappointment. Once we surrender to the confusion, and start to honestly examine our mind, all that is false begins to rot. Don't push away the rot. Allow it to happen, then utilize what comes from it as compost to fertilize your inner garden. For as the false rots, what is located are the misplaced parts of ourselves that were covered over with egoic sludge.

The rot shows that much of what we thought we were, we aren't; and that many things we forgot or never noticed are actually what we are. In the middle, our worst fears surface. One needs trust. Fighting against ourself is nothing but exhausting. It makes us prematurely sick, tired and maybe even dead:

"The only thing that burns in hell is the part of you that won't let go of your life, memories—attachments etc. They burn them all away, but they are not punishing you, they are freeing your soul. If you are frightened of dying and you are holding on, you will see devils tearing your life away. If you have made peace, then those devils will be angels freeing you from the earth." (M. Eckhart)

The Awakening process will not make you "better," rather it dismantles you like Osiris, or more correctly stated, you realize just how dismantled you are and have been most of your life. You find yourself in pieces. This is a good thing because we must first realize that we are disassembled before we can begin the work of reassembling ourself into our natural form. In our childhood we became fragmented, like a giant jigsaw puzzle shattered into a million pieces. We tried psychology, self-help, religion, spiritual practice (first pyramid work). But all our efforts couldn't fit these pieces together completely. Only by relaxing into our pain do we begin to see this fragmented jigsaw puzzle of *me*. We can then look at the pieces honestly and do the real work to remodel our being to match the original, not what our ego has continually forced us to be. Thus, we are calling on the force of death in the Osirian dismantle. Not an actual death as in the third pyramid necessarily. But one that forces us to tear about all that we felt was solid and secure—about the world and about ourselves. For the Awakening process reveals everything was not as solid and stable as we had previously believed.

One of the traps in this stage comes from the keyword self-observation, now packaged with two modern spiritual sounding ideas: being in the now and mindfulness. Second pyramid spiritual work has nothing to do with improving oneself. The idea of the need for continuous self-improvement is a way of staying stuck in the first pyramid. What rots, of course, is the same egoistic mind that keeps telling us we have to keep improving. Real self-inquiry sees all parts of ourselves and tracks back to the foundation of each part to see how it originated and acted. It is designed to exhaust the mind by watching it internally so what is behind the mind shines through. Most will do anything to avoid the process: find a religion, go to a psychologist, a healer, get married, even run away to India to fall in a guru's lap. However, if we follow where this process is leading us, and go within to the only place we have ever needed to go, something revolutionary happens. To walk the path and finish this quest, the commitment to it must be of the highest order, symbolized by the Knights searching for the Holy Grail.

> "Rose insists that one's philosophy has to be one's life, if that philosophy will ever blossom. One must determine to fully manifest the teaching one now professes to believe, and not only admire it from a distance, or worship it as an idol." (John Kent)

What waits for us at the end of second pyramid's inner self observation? Rose called it the Process Observer (Totality of Mind). This is the Mind at its highest capacity. It is interesting that Rose chose the term Process Observer. He called it that for it observes all the "processes"—everything we do, see, think and experience. The word "process" also relates that the Process Observer is an Observer that is reached through the "process" of observing. Once we know we can observe a thought (or feeling) from somehow beyond it, we begin to see that anything the body or mind does cannot be as real as what views them. No longer is the body the division between "me" and out there. They are all outside of this new Observing Witness. It is very hard to explain this shift in words, and the experience of it will be totally different than how it is imagined. You see everything you always believed to be you—thoughts, opinions, memories—from a place far beyond any of it. Yet the place you are observing from, you recognize as a more real "you" than any of these other aspects. That is the best way I can describe it... almost like there are two of you, but the more real you is formless, timeless and still.

> "The person who has reached the Process Observer becomes a very real creature. This is where a man is no longer living

[solely] a somatic life. He is watching his own mind. He has risen to the point where he is concerned not so much with the body as he is with consciousness and the workings of the mind. He becomes obsessed with this—this is the center from which he works." (Richard Rose)

Most of this book is about the process through the second pyramid, to show the traps of spirituality and religion (which lock someone to the first stage) and ways to seek beyond this. As such, I feel no need to go into more detail on this subject here. Simply put: stop looking outward and turn all of your attention inward. What is needed next is a bit more explanation concerning what happens should the Process Observer be reached. That requires a very unique, and confusing integration process, and is something almost never presented in spiritual literature.

❧

When I use the word Awake, to me this means to have reached the Process Observer, the place where once can view their own mind from beyond it. But this concept of being Awake has come to confuse and stop many seekers. Many get fooled either by a first pyramid realization or mystical experience into thinking they reached the furthest part of the Mind. However, just reaching it does not mean one is living in the Awakened state. The entire Awakening idea today is sold on the fairy tale "happily ever after" concept—marketed as an achievement, another item on one's to do list. Yet It is not that simple. If Awakening does happen, it is not an end point at all, but the beginning of an entirely new process. In his lecture *Different Qualities of Awakening,* Adyashanti helped me to understand this idea of a non-complete Awakening, and the confusion it produces. I will attempt to combine his insights with my own struggle.

To recap, it is a first pyramid realization when there has been a seeing of the dream-world in a new way to give us more ease of operation. We are essentially still the same person, but we *feel* different. In a second pyramid Awakening, we no longer feel different. Now our perception is different, seeing from a much deeper Witness, which causes a radical shift in our essential identity. We are no longer who or what we *thought* we were. Reaching the end of the second stage results in this shift in identity, because the "me" thing is no longer classified as "me." I am none of the things I defined myself by previously. That is radical and explosive as an understanding. Awakening does not bring God or love into our life, but reveals that the box of my life is not really "my life." It has been a lie.

Awakening is not going to look exactly the same as someone else's, for like Adyashanti describes, there appears to be three qualities about it. Again, this is a metaphorical way of describing a change that occurs with the Process Observer, and it has a different edge depending on the specific pathway used to reach it. Mental Awakening results from seeing that the mind is false, and that no belief is true, Emotional Awakening results from the experience of Unity, thus separation is not true, while Philosophical Awakening results from seeing No Self, thus "me" is not true. That all three qualities are found together is a myth, no matter how much books try to present otherwise. That becomes one of Awakenings great traps, it looks like a complete package has happened, when in fact only a part has happened. It is an odd thing on one hand to gain a great clarity (especially mental clarity) of self and reality, but meanwhile missing the need to integrate it.

> "On an Awakening, the manual we were given about how to live life (from parents, religion, culture, society) is blown out of the system. That manual is what you wake up from. You find from Awakening that it was not a manual of how to live, it was actually a manual on how not live. It was a manual of how to be sane, written by the insane. But as that disappears out of your system, you don't quite know how to live anymore. Because everything has changed. You are

not given the Awakened manual. You have to treat the new (paradigm) like learning to ride a bike. Keep getting back on each time you fall off, but once you find your balance, then it's on its way. It runs on its own then, but you first have to find a whole new balance." (Adyashanti)

What Adyashanti calls a mind Awakening (reaching the quality of the Process Observer that is primarily Mental) he describes as an Awakening of space. Previously all mental activity was somehow individual and personal (limited to our own head). But with Awakening we are no longer only a mind, body, thoughts, and personality. Instead we see we are infinite. One gets a great amount of clarity as we see through the limited knowledge of mental thought, and all the ways we have been creating ourself through beliefs and concepts. Something in us has done as Rose suggested, seen the mind from beyond the mind. It sounds like a simple thing, but if it happens it changes everything about who we thought we were. I am not my thoughts or what has happened, but the nothingness of a Greater Mind. At first this is very wonderful and freeing, as we know that no matter what we believe, it is not true. This creates a space where due to a lessening of focus on our thought, it can stop more often on its own leaving a gap. In this gap a more Direct Knowing (Gnosis) can now arrive suddenly and answer that which we have been pondering. In some cases, this new insight will come immediately, for others may take time.

If the Awakening occurs from an Emotional path, generally there is what is called the experience of Unity or Cosmic Consciousness. The experiencing of the universe as an undivided whole, of its being alive, conscious, perfect, eternal, and beautiful. It is usually considered the ultimate spiritual experience in most metaphysical teachings. Adyashanti refers to it as a Total Intimacy with all of existence, since you see, in fact, that you are all existence. It is not just the feeling safe and protected of a first pyramid heart realization. This shows that the one doing the protecting must, in fact, be Myself.

It provides overwhelming love, openness and calm. One has escaped separation—as my Self is everyone's same Self.

As Adyashanti suggests, the Philosophical Awakening is the awareness of an existential form of Nothingness. A grasping at a personal self, likely since childhood, stops. We see we never were that self, we are in fact not a self at all. It is the realization that not only is the world a type of dream (first pyramid realization) but that, I too, am nothing but a dream. This brings an incredible detachment to one's experience. This Awakening will result in a great lessening of desires and wants such as success and achievement, which are seen through as ego-created concepts.

As one can imagine, any of these Awakenings will be transforming for a while. But then, like lotus flower that opens to the light, it begins to shut back down on itself, and all we had viewed clearly becomes murky again. There is much work left to do, because all honeymoons eventually end.

"In the honeymoon you are beautifully stuck in the naive sense of total completion. I am totally awake, it is done." (Adyashanti)

In one sense it is true that all of Awakening has come complete, but in the hologram sense where a part contains the whole. Awakening is a part that contains the whole, we glimpse the whole while seeing with just a part. It sounds confusing but that is the best way that I can describe it. The withdrawing egoic mind tricks us into thinking that the Awakening itself was total, as opposed to a clear view of a part which contained the whole. No matter, the ego does get weakened by the Awakened view, and for a while there is a clarity and vitality— similar to falling in love or being on a honeymoon. A place where there is great freedom, relief and ease due to ego's retreat. Since the Awakening seems to arrive complete, we feel this is how we will be forever living—in this clarity and vitality. It can last for days, weeks, months, and in a few cases for several years. That is what happened to me after the canyon. For 4 to 6 months there was great mental clarity and an amazing ease to life. I didn't think the clarity could ever be lost. I should have taken "cave time" to allow the body and mind to integrate what happened, but I walked back into the world right away. Then the honeymoon clarity began to fade, and the return to normal sensing reality was hard. Back in the everyday world, all that appeared was confusion because while the old beliefs were blown out of the system, nothing new had come to replace them. I got ill and confused. I wondered if anything really happened at all, or if I had tricked myself. Was I still asleep, or perhaps had I gone back to sleep? One can never really go back to sleep, though, for there is always something in the background that sees the delusion of certain actions or thoughts, only "it" has trouble stepping in to stop the action.

Oddly the culprit after Awakening is still ego—which is not killed from the view of the Process Observer. It is more correct to say the ego gets wounded and leaves in retreat, hence the ease and clarity. But ego has not run away. Like a good general, it retreats to re-organize. Ego is the greatest chameleon in existence and will rally to morph itself into something new. Some say there are way more places to get stuck in AFTER Awakening than before. I would have laughed at such an idea until I saw personally how true this is. The way to stop the re-organization of ego is to complete the integration of the Awakening by recognizing that there are three qualities (mental, emotional and philosophical) that define and make up the Process Observer. This small understanding (that Awakening will appear as complete, but likely is not) will help us avoid thinking we are done. Instead, look carefully at where we really are, what has happened, and what we might be avoiding or denying. This can bypass a lot of problems and avoid good intentions getting mixed with distortions and errors—ones that can create some really odd mistakes.

"The thing is: I'm certain it takes years to incorporate the insight. The somatic mind is what has the experience, but it takes years for it to come to terms with it and gradually alter its whole psychology in accordance with it." (Mike J, from John Kent)

To sink into Awakening requires nakedness, vulnerability, and a total defenselessness, as there is no longer a protective shield (masks or armor). That requires a state of freedom. Not the idea that one is now free to do or get anything they want. But instead a freedom to let everyone and the whole world be just as they are. It can take years to allow that need for control everyone and everything to drain out of our system. Years to let that different non-personal definition of freedom arise and act in our lives.

> "Post Awakening is a transition from oneness back to duality. During this phase you will be disturbed, every genuine account of Awakening has the disturbance aspect to it. Many mystics talk about enlightenment in glowing terms, all bliss, love, ecstasy. They can only talk about it in those terms because they did not take the whole trip. Awakening is the whole trip: darkness, horror, confusion as well as peace, joy, comfort." (Eddie Traversa)

✂

Life after Awakening will show where we are still caught in our conditioning. We will experience failure after failure and put ourself into places where our self-image is tested. These challenges must happen, as what we are still hiding from cannot be seen alone in a room meditating all day. We need to interact with the world to test the cleanliness of our inner condition. It is telling that young priests in training in Egypt did not spend all of the time in the sanctuary of the temple. They spent six months of the year in the normal world. This was done partially to bring a more spiritual knowledge into the community's daily affairs, and partially to test the student. Being still in a quiet room is easy; doing it in Times Square during rush hour is the real test. Such tests are a key part of the work.

Spirituality is more challenging than people would like to know, that is why they go to teachers who reassure them as to how wonderful everything is. If a real Awakening occurs, one can run from it forever. But the more we try to push away the integration if it, the more challenging the adjustment is for the form and small mind. You could say that learning how the mind really works, to circumnavigate it, is part of what Rose refers to as using the mind's tricks against itself. I don't want to go into more detail on this here, but you can find in the appendix information on the process of integration of Awakening. It would be quite helpful if you are at, or close to, this stage.

> "After realization, everyone will make mistakes—big blunders—you know, but it is like something does not really want to believe it. You start to do very dumb things. It is not ill will or want for harm. Actually, the intention in all the dumb choices was usually very good and honourable. But being drunk on emptiness, and with egoic structures still in place—the actions that come out can be very distorted. And the only way out of it was to let go of all this (ways I wanted to perceive myself, the person I wanted to be) and just get honest." (Adyashanti)

Fully integrating the Process Observer can take many years. One's entire body and mind has to get stabilized to this new way of seeing self and reality. Anything no longer aligned with the spirit's intentions is likely to feel unpleasant and uncomfortable. Some will have to make many changes, others few, depending on how aligned their life was prior. The main reason someone will go back to egoic mind after Awakening is that, due to confusion, they attempt to maintain structures that no longer work. Usually someone only does this for so long before life gets too painful, and they must set these structures down. As fear diminishes, what comes instead is gratitude. Gratitude for the fact that something wrong has vanished. We become very thankful for what we know. Even though challenges and problems don't go away, we are grateful for how we now perceive them. For everything that comes to us that we like, our heart begins to swell for the surprising way the Universe found to bring those elements into our existence. For anything we don't like, it is now seen as a challenge—a way to find one more block in our subconscious. Things are less a blessing or a curse, and more like openings from the Spirit. Some are fun, some are not, but we have changed our perception on life's experiences.

An entire document in Ancient Egypt, the Pyramid Texts, was created to help with this stage. That is because if an Awakening has really occurred, it will begin to open all the areas within that we have been hiding from. Old pain and trauma will surface, as will odd facets of our personality or strange desires we had pushed away. Even though it can create tremendous amounts of problems, it is a good thing, for something is forcing us to look fully within in order to finally acknowledge our totality. To draw out all the hidden parts of ourselves will demand a total honesty. The good news is that while someone can run from this process their whole life, if Awakening has occurred and inner honesty will eventually take them over and they will have to look at all they have attempted to avoid. It may take 20 years, but it will still occur.

Recall that what I am calling Awakening is reaching the Process Observer in the second pyramid. This is also the Greater Mind, thus there is an aspect of the mental as part of any Awakening, but that can cause problems if there has been little work done on any old emotional issues along the way. After an Awakening, issues can become very messy for yourself and those around due to this emotional baggage not being cleaned. We can do some crazy things if the ego is still around and unchecked, for it will flow to one's deepest delusions. Generally, the intention for any action has an honourable foundation with the intent to help or make a difference.

It is the remaining unseen egoic structures that twist it and gets us to act in misguided ways. This will continue until these hidden inner emotional pains are walked into and transformed. Some may need professional counseling (more first pyramid work) if they had traumatic experiences in their past not yet cleaned up. Knowing that such distortions can happen will help us be more aware too see the traps earlier and move through them more smoothly. Doing so will hopefully cause far less damage to ourself and others during the balancing period as possible.

Rose was asked once, "Does the path get any easier after an awakening?" Rose responded, "No, but it gets funnier."

One of the strangest challenges that can come with Awakening is a loss of personal will. That means the basic source of what drives and motivates us (getting things for "me") starts to go away. As such there is almost no motivation to do anything, even eat. It comes as a shock. More and more you lose your references of what you want to do for the next five minutes, five weeks, five years? It can be strange. There are times I only have the urge to sit still. Not to meditate, read, contemplate—literally just sit there. It is hard to describe. The egoic mind is not demanding any action be started as a way to accomplish something, hence the call is to just sit still. Like I say it's really odd and can't be known until it starts to happen to you. Most will try old activities and behavior even if they never really liked them to break it: doing something seems better than doing nothing. Just because one set of wants leaves, however, does not mean that something comes right in to fill up the space. Almost like it is waiting for the entire space to be empty before it comes in. This results of this are living for a long time in a limbo zone, a gap between the disappearance of one thing, and the coming of the next. And for some this limbo can last years.

One of the beliefs is that Awakening will create ways to live life more deeply or enjoyably, the world somehow becoming one's playground. Rose confronts us that it is quite foolish to go rushing for Awakening with the idea we will then return to life in some sort of wonderful superhero state. We may in fact find out we no longer have any interest in the game of life at all. That is because a major part of Awakening is to see that there is no real world, and no real people. All are fictional shadows cast on an also fictional cave. That does not mean one goes out and tries to hurt others, as there is no reason to do so. There is no reason for ANY action. All one can then do is decide to stand fully within the Truth as has been revealed without worry. Something that can help with this process is to look over an idea from Carlos Castaneda in his early books that he called controlled folly,[12] which caused a great amount of misinterpretation by his readers. People believed this description was some sort of practice to drop the ego, but Castaneda was describing the state that comes after an Awakening where one action is no longer better than anything else. Everything is equal. Controlled folly is a specific reaction to this revelation, which is to pretend like we still want things. This tends to make one like an actor on a stage. We allow for the unfoldment of whatever What Is wants.

> "I am pretty much the same person I was before, but I don't put much value on stuff. I admit I am a spectator in the audience, I am not trying to change the script. Before I was always trying to change the script...." (Richard Rose)

With an Awakening the body goes through a profound physical transformation. Energy is getting turned from its normal outward focus to acquire, to just being still so the body can be cleansed. This is often leads to a lot of insomnia, as the nervous system is not used to that much raw energy inward. Awakening can be a shock to the body, combined with an energy surge (kundalini force released) in response. So strong was it that some likely died within a few hours of Awakening and might give a whole new idea to the unknown

---

12   This was mostly laid out in the book, *A Separate Reality*. For someone going through this loss of personal will may be helped by reading the pertinent chapter in that book.

phenomena called Spontaneous Human Combustion. The body must clean out the conditioning, and for some this can be an agonizing and burning-experienced for weeks following the Awakening. For others such burning comes later, and often manifests as an illness in the post Awakening experience. In my case the illness began seemingly from nowhere one and a half years after and lasted for about five years. I saw twenty experts in all aspects of healing and medicine, each who gave a different diagnosis and cure. None of them worked. Then one day, it just stopped. I still have no idea exactly what it was, but it not only made life difficult for the body, but it was very difficult for the mind. The time the illness left was at a time I had made some major life changes that I had needed to make and had been putting off, as if the illness was some sort of beacon based on the ways I was living. But when we finally acknowledge that we don't have to be that old person anymore, in fact is just a mask, that grasping part of the identity can start to fall away. Others conversely can find they may sleep day after day, catching up on years of no rest. This of course begins to tear at the mental concept that "I should be doing something, I need to be working hard to get ahead." It too can be a very confusing experience. The old identity does not leave peacefully.

One has to watch ways the ego tries to reform itself after Awakening. A standard one is try and gain superiority from the experience. To no longer work on ourselves but go out and tell others what they should be doing via talks, or just with everyone they meet over coffee. They now believe they know everything and want to make sure they tell everyone. It is something I went through facets of and seems like it hits in some way for everyone. It is ego trying to redefine itself in the identity of an Awakened person. But of course, there cannot be an "Awakened person" and that is what makes the trap so bizarre. Sometimes called "spiritual drunkenness," the period can be mild and harmless, or seriously destructive. Others turn this into a belief that the planet and all humans need to be saved, and that they are the only one that can do it. This type of delusional person will crash hard when it finally gets revealed that they cannot save the planet, or humanity—and maybe not even one person. It can lead to a long post Awakening depression until they sort out exactly why they needed to turn Awakening into a job.

Adyashanti points out that another trap is the attempt to run away from the process, either by traveling or finding a relationship, and avoid focusing on all that is not complete right here and now. Since either of these actions are based on the need to run away from oneself and one's remaining shadow parts, the relationship or travel will generally be messy. And that is going to get pointed out to us over and over until we get it.

For some there will be odd desires that they always wanted (bungy jumping, marshal of Mardi Gras parade). All of those want to come out and be acknowledged and allowed to leave on their own. Not being conscious of the process can mean that a lot of odd things can be brought into our actions trying to fulfill these unheard desires, hopes and fears. The more we can be aware this will happen, the better chance we have to see and acknowledge them, without needing them to be acted on. Some act the other way and just try to hide from life all together, and this sort of running away is called "Zen sickness" or "spiritual bypassing." These people often say phrases like, "I don't really exist so it doesn't matter what happens, ha ha ha." One is avoiding the actual experience of being a human, and not bringing in what was revealed in the Awakening down into form. A few who came from a place of deep pain before can re-organize around a state of what can best be called a stupor, where a sense of great bliss comes over them. But not a true experience of the Absolute, but an ego induce covering of their inner emotional pain still not worked through.

An emotion focused Awakening can leave one totally vulnerable at the level of feelings. And ego does not like to be vulnerable at any level. To Awaken here will be wonderful for a while, for all appears to be love, happiness and joy. The problem here is that there is no Awakened mind to help the heart discriminate where to go and be. Thus, the Awakened heart person can do some really strange things, for the willing to open is not tempered with logical thoughts to ask, "is that really a good idea?" Others can get lost in a semi-blissed out stupor that makes them incapable of functioning in the normal world, as they sit glossed in a personal almost drug created state of love and bliss that they never see is all just an egoic cover to keep them from looking within at all that is being pushed into the hidden corners of the self.

If the destruction of Self is a main component of the Awakening, the loss of personal will can hit very hard. Seeing there is no self, thus no choice or free will, the egoic mind distorts itself on the concept of nothing to do. They get bored and just sit around all day in a sort of depression. Susan Segal went through five years of that, what she called "the wintertime of the experience." The ego is no longer in charge, thus sees emptiness as empty therefore boring. The flip side of seeing one does not exist as a form, seemingly means no consequences for any actions, so just do what you want. Phil Connors' actions after driving the car in *Groundhog Day* has this delusion. Though he has no consequences for any of his crazy actions the next morning, none of them brought Phil any contentment. It is not happiness he was missing, but being at ease with where he is right now. This changes when he stops trying to get what he wants, even stops trying to kill himself, and decides he is stuck with it so sees how he can use the time for something more valuable. Having no fear is only valid without egoic conditioning to mess with it.

Karl Renz reminded me that the experience of Unity (even pure white light) is still a mental experience that needs an experiencer. That means a separation between the experience and the experiencer. It is so subtle it is missed, but there is still someone here having the experience of Unity. Any second pyramid Awakening is a MIND based quality. It will seem either more mental, emotional or philosophical depending on the path one was walking, but it would still be and "emotional mental" quality for example.

☙

PYRAMID THREE
Awareness-Osiris- Rubedo

"What you conceive and imagine about the process of dying, and what you fear as death, is actually the process of discovering the only thing about you, or connected with you, that is alive. (Bob Cergol)

Once one has a good view from the doorway there are two options. The first is to do their best to integrate and solidify the Awakening in order to deal with dream reality in a new way, as a new thing. But sometimes, even in the midst of the most deeply felt gratitude, something is still whispering—maybe this is not *it* either, maybe there is another reality or awareness out there. Even possessing an integrated clarity within the cave, some still have a need or even an anger to know who or what is Dreaming. The lure of the long tunnel out is too much for them. While it may appear as though one walks out of the cave down a tunnel, or that Truman Burbank sailed the sea away from Seahaven, the pathway really is in the other direction. Within. The exit door demands we walk into the very depths of every self we've believed ourselves to be. This cannot happen anywhere but where we are. The most uncomfortable and difficult places are right where we are right this moment. Hence oddly, to take the first step out the exit door, the final alchemic stage of Rubedo, is a trip into the deepest recesses of the Self.

There is no geographic region for Truth. It is not in India, China, or with the Navajo. Truth exists within. Traveling all over looking for it can be helpful, but can also become a substitute for being still. Beyond a look at the alchemic symbolism presented for this stage, there is not much that I can personally say about walking to the end of that exit tunnel. At least, I don't think I can. This stage can only really be talked about by someone who has finished it. That someone is not me. All I can do is provide a framework for examination of what this stage might look like. To reach the Process Observer (the open exit door) is to reach the totality of the Mental realm, yet is still not complete:

> "...the witnessing of the outer world as a projected illusion and oneself as that witness. This is near the top of the Ladder, but is still an incomplete experience. What is lacking is that one does not yet realize oneself to be the Totality, but is still identified as an individual center of awareness tied to a lamenting human mind. One is stuck in a tragic Twilight Zone dimension: dead to all meaning in a world that no longer exists, yet not having found Life. One's remaining days are haunted, until the final key for release can be found." (John Kent)

Rose also called the Process Observer the Manifested Mind (that which creates). At the base of the third pyramid is a complimentary point on the opposite end, which Rose called the Unmanifested Mind. The Unmanifested Mind can be considered the place where the objects created come from (the place of all possibility—past, present and future resides there). To fully know Totality of Self, one will have to go beyond even the Mind to What Is. Going beyond all of this is an experience of being "out of one's mind". Or, as Mr. Park used to tell us, "You must go crazy to know God." It is not about finding God, but rather realizing that God, and the seeker (me), are only mental concepts. Something lays beyond all that, but it is not "my" Self, for it is not personal. The Process Observer (witness-consciousness in Advaita) is a keyhole to see this deeper reality, but we still must become formless to pass through. The eye of the needle concept.

The third process is known in alchemy as the very mysterious stage of Rubedo (reddening) and was rarely mentioned in the texts. It was likely thought that so few people would make it to this stage that presenting it would just be confusing. What *is* presented describes

Rubedo as akin to a leap in consciousness, where everything comes together. Symbolically, above and below marry. Rubedo is very hot like a kiln, the stone (essence) being perfected through heat and pressure. It is a redemption through sacrifice, and what is sacrificed is the dearly held ego-centric idea of life. The alchemist who manifested the White Queen in Albedo, gives birth to himself as the Red King. It is the Red King rising up in the Final Plate (15) of the Mutus Liber. While Jacob was asleep in the first plate, here he is on the ground dead. The seeker ends. The death of the old self occurs. The objects around suggest the dead figure might be Hercules, the Greek hero version of Horus (Heru). In the distance, the ladder is laying sideways on the ground, while a new Jacob moves up from it. It is interesting to note Rose said that to make the shift from the second pyramid to the third pyramid, one makes a 90 degree turn. The Process Observer turning around to stare with Direct-Mind into the ultimate source of one's own I-ness. One goes through the plug of the TV screen, to find where the pictures on the screen originate.

> "Consciousness isn't a journey upward, but a journey inward.
> Not a pyramid, but a maze (labyrinth). Every choice could
> bring you closer to the center, or send you spiraling to edges,
> to madness." (Arnold, *Westworld* TV Series)

We reach into the third pyramid less from desire, and more because something unknown pushes us through the door beyond the Mind. Rose suggested this is not a linear pathway like things seem to be through the first two pyramids. Instead, it is a 90 degree turn. Which, means not a turn to go inwards (which was the symbol of the second stage), but a turn away from everything we have ever known. In a sense this would be the point where we realize that the ladder metaphor is incorrect. We are not actually climbing, going higher. There are no people above, or people below. There are only people in ignorance of Self. Can one robot really be classified as further ahead spiritually than another robot? As such the turn creates an even-ness or equal-ness to the search, no longer are we trying to rise to be better than another or group but to see what WE all are. This symbolizes a philosophical mode to living—turning from life to seek the Answers about who is living and why. The walk out of that exit doorway is, at some point, a walk into death. It seems that the only way one reaches the Total Self, is to die to all that is false.

By turning towards and not away from the great fear, we leave ourselves open to be brushed over by "The Great Accident."

> "The path Rose describes is not one that encourages peacefulness and joy, and thus may repel many prospective seekers who insist upon a path that promises serenity or delight as its primary characteristic and sole criteria for determining the Truth. Rose instead promises years of effort and aloneness, the hardship of confronting the many facets of one's ignorance, and restless wariness in the uncertain race between becoming and death. Rose regards the Albigen System as one of artful sobriety, rather than presumptuous celebration." (John Kent)

☙

To move beyond the Process Observer, this baseline (E—F), is where Zen meets Advaita. Specific practices end here, as advancement comes from something spontaneous. While Enlightenment is an accident, one must work to become accident-prone. All we can do is vaccinate ourself for this new dimension, because to go through the exit door is going to take all that we have.

> "Why is my friend behaving so unnaturally (spending all his time alone meditating)? His purpose is to find the meaning of life, and how birth, suffering, old age, and death itself can be transcended. And his method is that of vaccination and

homeopathy; cure like by like, give yourself a mild attack of the disease now, and thereby build up antibodies that ward off the real disease when it strikes." (Douglas Harding)

The idea that we need to be vaccinated to handle the third pyramid is one of the best phrases I have come across. And since the third pyramid is walked through via death and going within, the way to vaccinate is to work with our death. We must begin this vaccination procedure as early as possible. Douglas Harding in his *The Little Book of Life and Death* suggested that one's mediation practice is to sit motionless and thoughtless—not to be quiet or happy but to have a taste of death. Not death in the sense of heaven, after-life wonders, or reincarnation; but total non-existence. Since death is the mind's great fear, we purposely walk into the fear. What is it like to taste death? The death experience may come suddenly, without sufficient preparation (accident, drugs, unwise kundalini-raising practice, or unexpected trauma). This can leave a person a wasted wreck the rest of their lives (in an insane asylum or wandering the streets) if nothing was done to prepare the mind for the encounter. Thus, we have to work hard now to prepare for the unexpected, so that, you might say, "we" will be able to handle it. We want to be death-vaccinated. "All the while I thought I was learning how to live; actually, I was learning how to die." (Plato) [13]

We don't like to think that death may come in the simplest moment, such as when I went for a hike in the Alberta mountains. Whenever death comes to us, it opens hidden potentials. Any survivor of a near death experience gains a new interaction with life. The problem is that this new awareness slips away very quickly and becomes a memory, like the death experience itself. Yet they fondly

---

13 A good exercise for studying one's death was done at an Ireland TAT meeting my wife attended, where the participants were asked to go to a graveyard, find a headstone they liked, then draw it, but with their own name in the stone, to give a chance for the conscious and unconscious mind to deal with mortality directly.

remember the aliveness and energy of that time. The movie *Fearless* with Jeff Bridges demonstrates this well. But because death was only touched, its impact fades. What is needed is to embrace death.

What scares people most about death is that within its grasp, nothing we have ever done matters. We are going to die, and it will be as if we never lived. We keep trying to spin this in a different way. Those trying to get their name on a building or a yearly award are somehow attempting to keep their life continuing. Religion fosters this idea of continuation with a magnificent paradise waiting for us after dying—thus the ability to keep "me" alive for eternity. Since the egoic "me" does not want to come to an end, it projects an afterlife—its continuation. All the accounts of the afterlife could be nothing but mental projections created by an egoic self not ready to face its non-existence. When we realize that our normal day to day reality is a projection, it makes us wonder if we move into to another projection once we die. Why not drop our beliefs, hopes and fears instead, and see if we get a real answer? This follows the famous Samurai motto, "Whenever faced with the choice between life and death, always choose death." And paradoxically when one chooses death, what they actually choose is life—or a complete immersion in the current moment.

Western medicine does people a disservice by equating death with failure. Because it presents death as bad, it needs to be avoided and postponed as much as possible. But death is the only 100% guarantee, so why is something that is certain seen as a failure? People think that to examine death is somehow naughty or a sin. As long as they have their life insurance paid up, and a burial plot, all is fine. Much of everyone's time is spent in some form of distraction (from a crisis to television) to pretend that death is not getting closer and closer each second. What we should be doing is living right now. The biggest part of the third pyramid process is to stop being afraid of death, and head towards it. This examination will be unique, yet at the same time common to all seekers. The process of second stage Awakening uses the transformative power of death to bypass the normal mind, while third pyramid process maximizes it to cover all aspects of the small self, through philosophical examination, and the opening of oneself to between-ness so a still gap is present for the grace of the Absolute to enter.

Castaneda hinted that at death a doorway opens—but we need all our energy, all our awareness, to not miss this tiny crack towards Total Knowledge and get sucked back into the dreamworld via whatever fears, worries, or hopes we may have. One of the reasons Rose suggested a celibacy path was that it was a key way to store energy, and we need a lot of energy to cross the threshold of death, and cross back to normal life again. If death gives us a doorway, some figured to see if such a doorway could be found while still alive. This is walking into death before the body gives out, or as Bunyan suggested, "Die while you are alive, and be absolutely dead. Then do whatever you want, it's all good." The idea is to go through the door of death, without dying physically. Imagining or simple reading about this won't work. Ego's don't crack unless they feel threatened. For this to happen one must go beyond such ideas as white light, protective grandparents and other projections of the first pyramid, is something the mind could not previously prepare for, which helps to validate the experience if it occurs. Death is nothing like we imagine it.

Those who reach the top of the third pyramid talk about how much of an explosion there is at the end, which relates largely to how much of the seeker is left to die by the end of the path. The more one dies before one dies (or drops what one believes to be themselves) the less there is to die at the end. Once we drop something false, it does not help us to pick something else up in its place, as an effort to fill the void. That is not emptying, but replacing. Through allowing real emptying to take place, it is no wonder some find less stable ground as they move along the path. There was no great welcome after years of intense and focused searching:

"Instead, what Rose found was death–absolute negation of all that he had known and all that he was. He claims that a mood of despair and oblivion precedes the death experience, as all of one's efforts and hopes seem to lead to nothing. There is even the sense of being on the edge of insanity; of losing one's mind. God remains silent and aloof.... This can be a rough period in the search and will test the seeker's commitment to the truth to the fullest, as well as the resolve to resist grasping at straws of attractive make-believe." (John Kent)

This is the real Dark Night of the Soul, rarely mentioned properly for it is not some sort of grief or depression. Rose stated: *"You are on the verge of Enlightenment when you see yourself in your totality and futility."* Something must die for Truth to be found—the artificial entity "me" and its beliefs about reality that has been in charge for as long as we can remember. The only koan we ever have to work with is our own current life circumstance. Working our way through to see in a new clear and honest way, is the work. [14]

ℰᴈ

"No possessor of Cosmic Consciousness would wish to change anything but his own erroneous view of things." (Richard Rose)

---

14 "I have looked on death and lived, but my life is as empty as death. I have been dumbstruck, and crawled from the sacred unknown, bearing the look of horror, regret and pain; for I went in, and another man came out...The final trip is inside your Self, and you will find God. You find God inside yourself, and you are One with that.... The task of the seeker of eternity is to die while living, to know death so that the seeker will know of all the secrets of life. To affect this enormous task, the seeker must produce a great amount of energy. And to create that energy, the polar mechanism must have a large gap...a gap as large as death itself." (Richard Rose)

We can be in a room full of people and still feel alone. The deepest truth is that everything is a dream or a movie, nothing exists, not even you, or me. Waking up is willingly drifting into that fear to see what will happen, doing it because we can no longer stand the alternative of not doing it. The road to all of this is a most solitary thing. Even if a few people walk together for a while, each one knows that they are alone and that they cannot expect anything from the others, nor depend on anybody. The only thing one can do is share their path with those who accompany us and know that accompaniment could end at any moment. It is normal to look for silence in the mountains or forest or the desert. These periods are like a lover's retreat, to be with one's own inner silence. Silence becomes our lover.

Religious and spiritual teachers direct their students to practice detachment, yet it seems no one really has an idea of what exactly it is. People believe that detachment is somehow linked to how many desires or objects they have. On a basic level it is good to find where we have made our life more complex, and to bring simplicity into those areas. It might be our work, or diet, activities or hobbies. But detachment has nothing to do with possessions, and it is not an intellectual thing. It is not about losing our desire for a BMW, finding Mr. Right, or giving away all our stuff, because it won't be long until your mind is thinking about how to get it all back. Detachment is about the possessing mind that uses the energy of emotion to make us believe we will be better and more complete with the object or experience. Look to rid yourself of the thoughts and mental states—objects will come and go as they come and go.

> "When you start out it is a wide path. There is all sorts of garbage you can get rid of. As you go on, the path gets narrower, and the things you have to let go of get very precious to you. Finally there is no escape, you go through the funnel and that's all there is to it." (Richard Rose)

Ego is about finding purpose, a reason it needs to be here. Most people's purpose in life, has only been to find their purpose in life, which never gets found. If it were found that there was no special purpose for our existence, ego would have nothing to do. This is why the search for meaning never ends, for the end of searching would be the end of the very ego that is seeking. As always, Rose confronts our egoic search to prop up our false self. He claims we, as form, do have a purpose, we just don't like to see it—to be born, live, have kids, and raise them before we die and get stuffed in the ground. That is our purpose and the only thing this place wants from us. All of our supposed seeking of meaning is to hide this fact of our robotic puppet-like existence. "The purpose of mice might be cats; the purpose of worms, birds. Any spiritual thing you get comes by real hard work—ruthless interrogation." (Richard Rose lectures) Perhaps we are but insignificant extras in an epic cosmic production. Maybe our life is like that of lab rats, placed in an artificial environment by another species to watch our actions and reactions to various events.

"The longest journey begins with a simple step." (Tao Te Ching)

The famous first step of the Tao Te Ching is the moment something causes us to start walking from Plato's cave towards the exit. There may have been many actions previously (to break the chains and get us to stand in our seats). But from the standpoint of Awakening to one's True Nature—it is this step that one crosses over from being a spiritual seeker (something for me) to a seeker of the seeker (who am I). The Tao reminds us that it is a *simple* step, not a *single* step as sometimes translated. Carlos Castaneda described the step as jumping into an abyss—the Tarot Fool striding happily into oblivion. It is the moment Arjuna stands up on the battlefield. Before he could stand, he first had to fall. A fall due to hopelessness and meaninglessness—from seeing the untruth of the world as previously perceived and believed.

Seeing the possible utter hopelessness and meaningless of our existence is an important part of the path. Depressions are typically from touching the void, the vacuum, the emptiness. Grief is another common reaction, as is anger or rage. But that is only the ego's perception of emptiness. The problem is we see Absolute Reality with an individual mind. That relative mind experiences meaninglessness in a glimpse of emptiness. What happens is that the ego begins a slow destruction. Most spiritual work is the very act of keeping someone FROM the first step. Certain types of depression are powerful moments, especially when the depression is linked to seeing the meaninglessness of existence. Thus again the reminder not to destroy the mind, but to back away from it—in order to see more clearly and deeply. Meaninglessness is also just a stop one must make on the way to Totality.

"I am a mirror that madness looks upon, and sees hope surmounting foolishness." (Richard Rose)

The story of the Bhagavad Gita is not so much about why Arjuna fell (meaninglessness), but why he got back up. Krishna shows Arjuna the truth of reality, then explains why he should rise and play his defined role in the stage production. In a sense Krishna represents hope, the outside force that comes to our aid. Even if we are not asking for it.

You may call this help angels, guardians, power animals, helper spirits, or inner guidance. There seems to be something that helps us overcome obstacles that are in our path. When we get frozen, hope can be the very thing that gets us to take the next fearful step. The reason most never experience this hope properly is that people keep trying to package it in a particular way. David and Jennifer brought great hope for the people of *Pleasantville*, Sylvia to Truman—just not in the package that they imagined. The more we turn ourself over to some aspect of nature, something inside of us helps our finger move to meet the finger of God coming towards us. God's finger is always there. But we must work as well to not leave our outstretched finger waiting aimlessly by our side. Here we are waiting for the cosmic accident. Where no practice can move us there, only by the lightning bolt of grace can we finally experience that which is beyond body and mind, and always has been. Right here, always trying to penetrate us—just we have been blocking it for our entire life. In a sense spiritual practice is only a tool designed to weaken the defense against the Absolute we have been throwing up our entire time. Hence the statement, "enlightenment is an accident, but practice makes you accident prone."

This is not a call to "love ourself," or to make ourself moral and perfect in order to receive this help. Instead this is seeing that we *already possess* that which we need to bring that help to us. We must learn less how to say thank you and accept its arrival—even if in a different package than we wish it to be in. While on the one hand we are programmed robots, on the other—magical creatures of possibility. It is a paradox that to gain our full magical ability of between-ness, we must see our robotic state and realize there is little that we can change. We look for the small part of the robot that allows for alteration and learn to follow the original design. We are not looking for happiness, or to manipulate and control—but for places where we can take a rest. We welcome these moments of calm, laughter and relaxation. They heal our wounds, sharpen our sword of discrimination, and peacefully prepare for the new battle ahead. A battle where the more we realize that we are alone, the more help we receive.

It might seem that by reaching the top of the third pyramid we have finished our work. But the written reports indicate what we have really finished is ourselves. Extinguished the belief that we are a separate, special person, living a meaningful existence in a real universe. One has become different, yet keeps the appearance of the old thing. Caterpillars get the new form when they transform into the butterfly. But when a human reaches the top of Jacob's Ladder they change—even though their form remains as it always has.

❦

"In what concerns you most do not think you have companions, know that you are alone in this world." (Thoreau)

"The Absolute is a very lonely place. You are the only one there. Of course everyone is the only one there." (Richard Rose)

The world for the Awake is a rather solitary place and learning to be comfortable in this state takes some work, because our conditioning to be social is strong. Once one learns to enjoy themselves just as much with a group of friends as when totally alone, that is when they have reached a new plateau. Most people are social because they feel so alone. Loneliness is the ego's way of responding when it touches the empty core. With a deeper perception of what we are, this loneliness vanishes. There is still the appearance of other forms, and still interaction with things—yet one tends to enjoy their time alone more than previously. One can then interact with anyone, for they know they are only interacting with their Self.

The beginning of such an experience can leave one in confusion and shock for some time. Even this, too, is eventually integrated, and a new awareness arises that includes an equal combination of detachment and love. They do not necessarily become a nice person; their love may shine, even in their ability to be a jackass.

I can only guess at all of this. If it happens to me in this life, fine. If it happens at death or after death, fine. Perhaps it will never happen. Such is the unknowing that one must take into this work. We know nothing for certain until we Know. All we can do, is our best to walk the path of Jacob's Ladder as is right for us, and to turn our attention away from that which is laid out to tempt and trap us. To look for guidance along the way, and to be of help for those with whom we can help—be they human, plant, animal, or unseen being.

Intermission

Generally, one only finds an intermission in Broadway theater or at sporting events. Never in a book. But I feel that an intermission here is fully warranted, for two reasons.

The first reason is that the beginning chapters of this book contained a great depth of material. And even more was said between the lines. In fact, I consider that basically all I feel the need to say in this book, has in fact been said in these opening four chapters. They stand in a sense as a holographic image of the whole.

After reading them, everyone should take a short break. A small contemplation period. Have a coffee, go for a walk. Allow what is there to work to your subconscious. Let it percolate.

Yet there are still some 170 pages to go. While on one hand I could end the book now, and on another I can not. That is because there is a large missing piece to all I have said to this point. What specifically did I do, feel, experience, and be challenged with that produced what is in the first four chapters. What does observing the mind and self mean in hands-on terms? For me or for you.

The structure will change going forward. I have included conversations with my editor and his wife, hoping that more detail of my experience can come through to you. More information, more detailed personal stories, things less symbolic but more direct. More focus on my time with native medicine people, suggestions of early teachers, Castaneda novels, and personal inner seeking. In a sense this is a break point between two linked, yet in fact unique types of writing.

I figured that, yes, an intermission was in order. For you to take in what has come so far, reposition, and get ready for the new type of presentation to follow.

Please take your seats, the show is about to continue...

Chapter 5

MIND GAMES

What is past thought?

"And so the robot saw motion in that which did not move, and began to love things which had no substance, and to develop reactions which it called thoughts...and being so immersed in his thoughts, the robot did not realize that his thoughts only apply to relative experience, and that relative experience admits opposites in matters of reactions or direction. So that in choosing the realm of thought, and overlooking the possibility of no-thought, the robot passed the door of the Absolute, wherein thought is only a distraction." (Richard Rose)

It is said that the task is to know thyself. That sounds easy; like a self-help exercise where we write down all of our traits on a piece of paper, then figure out how to get rid of all the bad ones. Yet seekers rarely wonder about step one. What is a self? Who or what is it that has these so-called traits? We are told to be true to ourselves.

But if we do not actually know who this 'self' is, we might wind up as John Kent describes: being true to a false self.

We are tricked into believing we are some sort of constant entity. In other words, the thing here today is the same as the thing here yesterday because it uses the same name and wears the same shoes. But millions of cells die, and new ones are born during this one single day. In seven years, every cell in our body will be replaced. Thus, what is here right now is only a copy of what was here seven years ago. Where did that old thing go? What if I am not really the special creature that I always thought I was? Rather, what if I'm simply a bit of rather unimportant skin and bones—one who has as its only destiny to be placed in the ground before it decays? The body changes, ages, and most importantly—it dies. As a result, meaning or wisdom must be somehow beyond the body to be of real value. Our body is so important to our identity that an entire pantheon of religious wishful thinking occurs. Musings such as the body being projected into an afterlife, where all are supposed to possess duplicate personalities and bodies (perfectly healthy ones, of course). Where is this new body supposed to come from, especially when the old one is in the earth? Why would a personality (the "me" and its memories) need to continue, along with the exact same body? Why not have different bodies and personalities in the afterlife? Alternately, we can have a happy story of reincarnation, and hope that somehow this soul grows over countless lifetimes. Or, instead of playing fantasy games with all of this, we can turn our attention toward seeing things honestly. No matter what that might mean.

We have learned to use the body as the main defining point into what is me and what is not me. We, as the body, seem to be solid and real. But are we truly the way that we believe? Rose wanted students to ask themselves some very bizarre questions around this topic such as;

"If I weigh 300 pounds, then diet and lose 150 pounds, am I only half a person? If my body (including the brain and its

memories) were exactly cloned and there were now two of
me, which one would I be?"

These questions make us take a closer look at the body we attach to so
strongly, and the material world that we never question. The Gnostics
and the Cathars saw the material world as, if not evil in and of itself,
at least evil in the beliefs which we are conditioned to hold regarding
it; "Fear not the flesh, nor love it. If you fear it, it will gain mastery
over you. If you love it, it will swallow you and paralyze you." (Gospel
of Phillip—NHC) What is constant and never changing? These are
the underlying questions.

Perhaps digging through our ideas concerning the body may
not take all that long. The part that generally takes a long time for
people to process is the part that makes up so much of our identity:
thoughts. Thoughts that connect with beliefs, which then connect to
personality and memories. In short, that which inter-connects with
everything we point towards when we use the term "myself." To
unravel the self, we have to go within and examine the very roots of
what is a self? What is thought?

 ∽

"It's one thing to study war, it's another to live the warrior's
life." (Telamon of Arcadia, 5th century BC)

It is 2002, and I am out walking in the Canmore mountains with my
new friend Brendon. I consider us friends, though he sees me as more
of a spiritual teacher. I was doing much more of that sort of thing
back then. He was a young guy just starting university when we met
earlier in the year at a talk I gave. Then again I was rather young
myself, just past 33. We had been going out in the woods around
Calgary that summer to do some stalking exercises (such as walking
without making sound, or walking blindfolded to use other senses to

not trip over rocks and roots). But I had suggested we get into the mountains to do some deeper practice. That is what we had done, and we now walking back down the trail to his car.

But for me this day was not over. I kept rolling an issue in my mind. Brendon is really nice guy...but underneath there is a lot of anger there. And I could see there was no way to just tell him that, he would deny such a thing up and down. The mind is very good at not seeing what it does not want to see about ourselves. How could I point this out to him in such a way he could see it? The opportunity soon presented itself almost by accident.

He began to tell me on the walk down about a new spiritual book he had just read last week. He expressed on and on about the incredible way it was written and how amazing this teacher must be. The way he was gushing, you would think he was talking about a new girlfriend not a book. And there was my opening.

"Oh I've read that book Brendon. Worst piece of trash I have ever come across." Of course I had not read that book, never even heard of it until he mentioned it. But I thought it was time to see how his mind would react to this. "Boring and uninspired."

"What do you mean boring? How can you say that? It was brilliant," and he began presenting something about some chapter or whatnot. Actually, it didn't sound too bad, but I was on a mission here.

"Really. That is the worst piece of junk ever. Come on, only an idiot would actually like to read a book like that. Are you really an idiot?" I continued this barrage. Anything he presented was constantly met with a wall of disbelief and countless ways for me to say that not only was the book idiotic, but he too had to be an idiot to like anything about it.

But it was starting to get dicey. His anger was rising up. And fast. I had been in enough hockey games to see that look in someone's eyes. Soon I wondered if he was now going to come at me. I began scanning the side of the trail for a giant tree limb I could use as weapon, for Brendon was young and in real good shape, and now full of rage.

Just as he was about to strike I stopped walking and replied very calmly, "Brendon, I have never read that book before. Didn't even know what it is. I am just saying stuff. Look at you. Why have you become this way just because I disagreed about a book you liked?"

He took a few deep breaths. Got a good look at his surroundings in the woods, then at himself. "Wow," he replied reflectively, "I have a lot of anger in me."

"Yes Brendon, you do. I am not sure why, maybe you are not even sure why. But this is real good news. Once you have seen a truth about yourself like this, you have now gained the power to make a change if you wish. The only way to change thoughts, emotions, states of mind, even the self, is to see it in total shocking clarity."

And in a year or so he did just that. In that game the score turned out to be Brendon 1, anger 0.

❧

Anders has been helping me look into this chapter because on his first edit of it he claimed it was a mass of information that didn't flow all that well. I saw and agreed with him. It's a tough series of topics for sure: thoughts, ego, self, masks, all inter-connected yet each requiring its own explanation. In fact I realized, most of the writers I have read on this subject do not really do much more than present a few ideas and move on. Partially it is because to whittle down what should be 100's of pages into 10 or 20 is a task. Anders and his wife Liv have tried to help me do just that.

I got my first look at this "mind problem" some 20 years ago when I saw that my mind ran in constant rings what I labeled circular thought patterns. It was weird to see it in action the first time. I was making a record in my diary of what was in my mind at different points of the day. I had gone for a walk to get some fresh air and calm my mind down. That worked until I got home, when the mind seemed to wind up again all on its own. And then it follows a really odd pattern of linking to the previous thoughts—something like this, 'I really should go to the store...I remember Dave's corner store when I was 8 years old...I wonder how much muscle I had in my 8 year old body...Body Heat, wow that was a bad movie...why are they not making better movies today...' And on it went. A thought, seemingly linked to the thought before—yet always going nowhere. None of it has any value. And some of these patterned loops are big and sort of just keep coming over and over again, 'this won't work out, you're a loser, or you are the greatest person in the world or whatever.' These too just seem to come out of nowhere when an external trigger calls them up. And mediation never solved it.

Anders again looks up from the notes. "Are you saying meditation does not work? Can't you just stop the mind?" Anders asks. "Like just have no thought?"

"Thoughts begin just after you wake up in the morning, right? Yet you never consciously choose to start thinking. They just start on their own. You also cannot choose to stop thinking, except for very short periods of time. Ceasing thoughts—that is the promise of meditation. However, that is actually more of a trick than it is any sort of true help."

"I don't really understand that. Every spiritual teacher I went to wanted me to meditate in order to stop thinking."

"Did it work?"

"Did what work?"

"Did the meditation stop your thinking?"

"Well, no. I guess we all felt we weren't doing it right—that we were meditating wrong. It never occurred to any of us that maybe it simply couldn't work."

"You don't want to quiet the mind just for the sake of quieting the mind. Except maybe for a short 15-minute rest, like if you've been thinking hard at work or something. You aim to quiet the mind to get your first honest look at thought. This examination of thought is done not so one can label them good or bad, and then try to take away the bad ones. That is a control issue. A way of trying to induce self-hypnosis on an already hypnotized mind. Instead, you just want to see it, and try to get to know what thought is. And, of course, to start to wonder: if I always labeled myself as "my thoughts" but "I" can see thought, then who or what is observing this thing I thought I was?"

"Ya, that really clears it up," he says, shaking his head and rolling his eyes in a gesture of giving up. "But thought can stop, right? Like, stop." I nod. "What happens if it does?"

"Your mind will be dead. Thoughts do not stop from a quiet mind, but from a dead mind. In that space of a dead mind can come something far greater—the reaching of the Actual Self. But you can't really talk much about the Actual Self, since each one of us so mesmerized by a false self and false thoughts."

ᏃᎧ

The standard belief is that thought occurs in one's head. But does thinking really happen in my head? And why do I call it mine, take ownership of the thoughts when I seemed to have no choice in any of the thoughts that came up. Am I a possessor of thought, or possessed by thought—stuck to perpetually observe them with little influence in what appears on the screen of my perception? A hypnosis show reveals how easy it is to get people to believe they see or hear something that is not actually present, even that they themselves are a cat or a dog. So how much of our day to day world is nothing but a hypnotic suggestion and mental projection? Perhaps all of it. It is why in the Native medicine tradition, so much work is placed on challenging perception.

"Have you ever noticed that anyone driving slower than you is an idiot, and anyone driving faster than you is a maniac." (George Carlin)

Point-of-Reference (the center point that is used to filter through all perception and experience) should be a main topic of spiritual examination, yet is not. If it is 27 degrees Celsius out, and someone asks you if it is hot, it will depend on your point of reference. If the reference thinks hot is 24 degrees you say yes, if the point is 30 then it is warm but not hot. It is still 27 degrees, but all perceptions and beliefs around it are dependent on the point of reference being used as a baseline. We use baselines in everything we do or think about, without even realizing it. Usually the body and the planet earth are our main point of reference (dividing line) for what experiences are mine and not mine. The same in Carlin's joke, we are the baseline of all experience. But no point-of-reference has been validated.

The best tool we have to know ourself is observation. At the beginning we are told to go 'inside,' or go 'within,' and this is usually taken to mean inside of my body or inside of my head. But over time and practice, this line of the body as being the dividing point for what is me, and not me begins to become less static. When we start to wonder if everything inside of our skin, not just bones and blood and organs, but all our thoughts might be outside of our Self, a shift happens. This is another reason why Rose stressed that the primary issue in the spiritual search is precise self-definition, rather than the search for God, bliss, power, knowledge or love. That makes all spiritual and religious systems highly questionable as they lack a foundation of a valid and provable point-of-reference. We lessen our obsession with the pictures on the cave wall/movie screen and begin to see where the picture originates. The robot is looking for its programmer, the puppet is looking for who is pulling its strings so that it can move itself for the first time. Only then can thought stop.

The basic idea of Advaita is that we have no control over our thinking, and the goal is to end thought by ending the thinker. Without thought, the Self is revealed. Actually, if we ever get to the point of physical danger with the likelihood of dying, as I had in Johnston Canyon, the body throws all of its energy resources into the situation to survive and the normal thinking mechanism is not there. So just how valuable are our normal thoughts if they disappear at the time we are in most need?

The problem to our functioning within this reality is thought itself. The normal thinking process becomes an overlay that keeps from what Rose called Direct Mind, and Castaneda Direct Thought. You might call it a thinking that is not thinking, thought that appears to be thought, but is something much more dynamic, a link to a higher dimension. One way to re-open this direct link is to get back in touch with what we call intuition. As a child, everyone's intuition is strong. But as we got programmed to play in this stage drama, we lose our intuition, and become confused believing what others tell us. In this confusion we stop listening to intuitive suggestions and begin to trust mental thought more and more. That is one reason Rose had his students sit in what he called rapport sessions, to try and reconnect to an intuitive interaction with people or dimensions beyond their usual mind. In rapport his students would sit together and remain open, in a sense seeing who might be able to connect with another's mind in the room, then letting that connection happen. The hope was that this opening to another person could lead later to the opening to bypass thought and reach this Direct Mind connection to the Source.

ॐ

Recapitulation

I have been raising these topics with Anders and his wife Liv. I am spending Friday at their place, so I can take them on a weekend visit to some of Scandinavia's terrific stone circles. We are scheduled to leave early Saturday, so Anders thought that coming by Friday would give us time to go over parts of the manuscript, leaving the weekend free to discuss stones and energy.

After dinner, the conversation turned to our lives. Liv passed along some details of her childhood and some odd experiences that happened to her, and along the way I told her some of my life stories. Most of my Awakening talk has been with Anders only, so I had been keeping a bit of a guard on some of my answers. Then, for some reason, a question out of the blue really got the ball rolling.

"So how come she didn't work out?" Liv asks.

A standard question about one's past. I happened to be telling some stories in my life that revolved around a time of great intensity of practice, which was also during one of my longest periods of dating someone. I mentioned how we met and whatnot.

"Well," I offered, "it was a good relationship for a couple of months. But it first began to go downhill one Saturday night when I wanted to spend the evening in her closet."

Liv's eyebrows purse upwards, while Anders poked his head in from the kitchen.

"Is there something about you we don't know?"

All of us broke into laughter.

"Maybe. I was a lot different during that period than the person you know now. I really did want to spend the night in her closet—it was an honest desire in the moment. I recall that she responded very forcefully that. 'No boyfriend of mine is going to spend a night in my closet instead of my bed.' We probably talked about it for an hour. The relationship started to spiral downhill shortly after that. The problem was, of course, that while she was spiritual, and she had friends that were spiritual—they followed the kind of spirituality which demands little of anyone. Watch a few thoughts, do some yoga stretches, have an acupuncture session, eat some organic apples and voila: You are on the spiritual path. To actually see hardcore practice, as I was engaged in at the time, was scary for her. I think she felt that if she kept dating me that she might have the expectation to do the same: to get in the closet and see her life honestly. Which is one of the main things the spiritual crowd doesn't want to do. But she ended up marrying a really rich guy, who I am sure does not want to sit in the closet at night, so all in all I guess she got what she wanted. "

"But you wanted the closet," Liv asked perplexed. "Why exactly?"

"It was part of my practice at the time. Recapitulation. And you need a small space to do it in. The best space I ever found was a small underground area in a temple on the Giza Plateau, just up from the Sphinx. But a closet was the best that I had available. The recap is designed to relive your entire past, in intricate detail, in order to see all that has been hidden, lost, and forgotten. Doing so cleanses the past... well, energetically it does. And like I mentioned, this was during a period where I was ultra-serious with this stuff."

"How serious is serious?" asks Anders, wondering if the weekly workshops nights they were attending were close to what I am talking about.

"I had about seven or eight hard core inner practices going on every day. Only the most basic requirements of staying alive took time away from them—and often not even that. Recapitulation was one of my practices, that I practiced one week on, one week off. This particular week where every night was a recap session. So the fact I was at my girlfriend's place really didn't matter. Recap mattered. I spent the evening with her at dinner, then watching a movie, followed by talking. But then from 11 PM-7 AM it was inner work time. I didn't actually sleep any night during a recap week. I recall around that same time, I was at a work party with a good friend of mine. Well, maybe not a party. All of her workmates had gotten together for a barbecue at someone's house, and she'd invited me along. And all was fine, I chatted, even ate some burgers. Then 4 PM came around, and that was my time every day to start a 45-minute afternoon session of Qi Gong. I remember telling her that I was going to a small park that I knew was close by, and if she needed me in the next hour that is where she could find me. The fact I was at a gathering—even enjoying myself—was no excuse to not do the Qi Gong. Everything then was like that- there was something which I named practice that was calling me at any particular moment. Putting even a hint of it off until tomorrow was not an option."

Liv had been talking about some odd moments of her childhood earlier on, and so the idea of reviewing and cleansing one's past intrigued her immediately. She began asking about the process.

"Ok, so about this recapitulation thing. You mean you look over a few key moments of your life—like when you are in therapy?"

"Like therapy...no. You are not looking to fix your life, you want to relive it. Every moment from the time you were born up until right now."

"But that's impossible." Liv demanded, hands now folded over chest.

"Is it?"

"It sounds pretty impossible. How can you review every moment of your life? Do you stop time?"

"No. You want to redefine time."

∞

Most of what is called meditation (sitting quietly with our eyes closed, repeating a mantra, visualizing a happy place, or trying to eliminate thinking) is really a way of further entrancing an already hypnotized mind. The real idea, however, should not be to calm a turbulent mind by force or distraction, but rather to get clear enough of it to look into and resolve the root issues that caused the turmoil in the first place. That means our best meditation is the examination of our past. See how those events created the foundational layers of thought and belief that we then live out daily for the rest of our lives. Awkward. Rose called this early stage "garbage sorting". This happens to be the very part that everyone avoids. To step out of the past, we first have to come to know it intimately. To understand this story of me, once can use the tool of recapitulation.

Recapitulation is more than just an examination of the past. We can also see how much energy is still tied to people from long ago. This is because we either hold onto guilt for something we felt we did, or are still holding anger and resentment, and continuing as a result to energetically demand some sort of payment. The recap involves not just re-seeing, but re-experiencing our past. We do this to, in a sense, unwind the tape of our life. We look for the moments where we created both the egoic walls and the foundations that shaped our life patterns and choices ever since. Recap shows the moments that we betrayed ourselves and our promises—vows to never be happy, never be rich, never be loved. We then go on to take this hardened crystallized conglomerate of ideas throughout our life in what Rose might call "a state of mind." The process of recapitulation was my way of breaking through some of this. It is not the only way, but I can only honestly share what I actually did.

> "To recount events is magical for sorcerers. It is not just telling stories, it is seeing the underlying fabric of events. This is the reason recounting is so important, and vast." (Carlos Castaneda)

❦

Liv is continuing her questions. She is getting very intrigued by this idea of reviewing the past, where in a sense you don't learn from it, or fix it, or hide from it. You energetically through recapitulation cleanse the past and present of all your interaction and see the truth of each moment.

"Ok. Have you reviewed your entire life?" She asks.

"Yes. Twice actually."

"How long did that take"?

"My first life pass—the initial review—I started when I was 29. It took about three to four years. The next pass I did started about five years after that. It lasted for maybe a couple of months or so."

"A life review took 4 years?"

"Yes. There are some tricks that you learn along the way as you do it. It goes very slow at first. However, once you begin to understand what is really going on in those reviews, then the pace picks up rapidly. I know that to the mind it sounds impossible or crazy—just about anything really useful for us does. Hence, the need to persist no matter how strongly the mind protests. I give her the basic overview of how it is done, and the steps to follow to try it out. (The process of how to do recapitulation appears in the Appendix. Don't mistake something that seems simple to do, will be easy. Simple and easy are two different things).

❧

"To know yourself, you have to know your past. You have to honestly examine it. See the errors, egos and self-importance of it. Traumas are not there to break our spirit, but to break the ego. Suffering is truth calling us home the hard way." (Richard Rose)

"Actually Liv, I never really knew what recap actually did until I was finished. I spent four years where not that much happened, and not much was really learned about myself. Then a few weeks after I finished the four years—Whammo. I had the life epiphany."

"The life epiphany? So something important?"

"Oh ya, shattered everything I thought about my past. Something called the Usher appeared, where I was not just reviewing an event from my past, I actually was there. Reliving it again, and it sent me on a spiral of inner explosions that rocked my sense of self. Its a long story, but I can see that you want to hear it."

❧

My Recap Usher

(This is the collection of journal entries made between July and November 2003. They have been kept as complete as possible, exactly as were written down. All names have been listed by initials. The events here may seem quite dramatic, and they turned out to be—but I wanted to share it as a presentation of just how the work of recap can affect us at deep levels.)

It is July 2003 and I had completed my first life pass, even including memories of my first "thoughts" in the hospital room after the delivery. I had come to see some events in new ways, had gained some energy each time I recapped, thus felt I understood the process. I was wrong. The powers of recap would soon slap me in the face. Finally, after three long years of active recap, spontaneous recap and an usher pulled forth their truth.

The revelation revolved around two women in my life: PW specifically and JA marginally. J had been my first love when I was 16. At the time I had no idea what love was, thus I had no idea what I felt. There wasn't much love around my own home, so nowhere could I see this force modeled. Yet, still I felt it. I knew she was seeing another guy, who was a few years older, played in a better hockey league, and had his own car. Thus he was far ahead of me in every competitive situation. I tried my best to win her heart, but she wound up choosing "him." In time, J and I developed a friendship. I loved her so there was no need to condemn her just for making a choice.

In May 1990 I was in Olivers, the campus bar at Carleton University as I was back in Ottawa for the summer. This was one of those days when my connection to intent was strong. I felt sure that today was a day that I would meet "a very special woman and I would date her for a long time." I went to the bar with a buzz of inner knowing that "this woman" would be there. So who did I run into? None other than JA, but even though my heart has my senses on high alert and even though I still loved her, I felt that she was not the woman I was supposed to meet.

An hour or so later I saw her. PW. Every cell in my body told me that this was the girl I had come here to meet. Fear evaporated from my being and was replaced with a place of sureness. I went to talk to her. We talked all night, then went on a date, then two. We began dating. I felt something so special for P, but like with J I had no idea what I was actually feeling. Like most young men I had not been taught to feel, only to drink more and hide away from those feelings.

A voice in my head kept saying, "you are going back to university in September, there will be other girls there." For some unknown reason I listened to this voice, even though it sounded nothing like the "other voice" that led me to P in the first place. In September I went back to university and we broke up, but we didn't really part fully. While I chased other women, I realized that I didn't want to catch any of them. Each time I heard her voice on the phone, or the few times I saw her in person were feelings beyond anything I had experienced. Why was I so unable to acknowledge what I was feeling? What kind of society do we live in where men are not allowed to have feelings?

She came to visit for the last week of the school year in 1991, and then we would take the train back together to Ottawa. It was the most amazing week to that point in my life, and little did I know, the last week of "normalcy" in my life for a long time. The story I had kept in my mind all these years was that we took the train home, parted, wished each other well and that was that. That is what my mind kept telling me. That summer I would have a giant breakdown with my father, he stole all of my money from me and went to jail, and I ran away from my final year of university to start a business that failed miserably. In fact, I only went back to university that year to claim my clothes, all my furniture I just left. All this symbolism my mind ignored too all these years, but not my True Mind. The True Mind stores everything. P and I kept in contact for a while. I ran off to Australia for a few years after an ex was murdered, while P became a police officer. We lost contact in 1996.

In 2003 my recap sessions had ended. I had finished a complete life review, and I felt a sense of pride at actually having accomplished it. I did find many new events from past, but my mind still presented this story as written above as fact. For whatever reason I decided to make a journey to 1999 (the year I was supposed to die in the story next chapter). I wanted to see what my life would have been like in "that life." I drifted back until I was in a townhouse in southern Ontario (it felt like Oakville). I felt it was morning and I was dressed for work. I looked around "my" townhouse. In my actual life I have never owned anything. That alone was enough to fill me with a longing, even for a life in which I would already be dead. Two kids ran around the corner, my kids. At that moment I realized that for there to be kids, there had to be a wife and I was curious what she looked like. Around the corner stepped P. Even though I was actually lying down, I felt like I had fallen off a ten-story building. P had been the one. I had never realized it until "that" moment. But the clarity was unmistakable. Spirit had fated her to be my wife, and I turned my back on fate and her. I had been too arrogant, too self-important to see the omens. I wanted to cry but I could not find the tears. I thought back to the day I met her and realized it has a touch of great irony. My first love (J) had been there to introduce me to my wife. Yet this is but a small piece, the usher still had not yet found me.

The next day I was at a computer sending an email to, you guessed it, J, when the spontaneous recap hit me. I was in April 1991 again. I was back on that train to Ottawa with P. There was no computer store anymore, no 2003, I was on that train in 1991 in the moment. I remember thinking how amazing our week together had been and that maybe I was making a mistake by not having this woman in my life. As the train stopped and we gathered up our baggage I said, "The last week together was so great maybe we should think about dating again this summer." Her response was, "I don't think that's a good idea," and then she told me how she had no interest in dating me anymore.

My legs buckled, both back in 1991 and in the moment in 2003, it showed the eternity of time. That moment, like any moment, is always happening. I staggered down the train stairs, though I don't know how because my legs did not really function. My heart, oh yes, my heart. It was as if I had suffered a shot gun blast to the chest. I was numb, my world had been shattered, more than I ever imagined. Spirit had fated P to be my wife, but I had pushed her away long enough that she finally decided to follow my pushing. Her sister was waiting for us on the platform. Something happened, something shifted. I had to go on, but to do so, somehow I just eliminated the last 60 seconds from my memory. Sixty vital seconds were erased, and a different scene placed over top. That quick, that easy. Gone consciously, but never really forgotten. Something deep within kept wanting me to acknowledge and feel that pain, feel that loss. It made my life and relationships afterwards horrible, trying to get me to wake up, to remember what my mind had hidden. It was only the process of recap that waked it up.

When I said that it felt like my world had shattered, it did, it had to. The gods had to re-script a new fate for me, the old one was now useless for I had not accepted it. They started doing everything to put my "normal" life into the garbage can to show me that my life was now something else. But I held onto that old life, held onto it until my fingertips turned blue. P accepted her new fate far easier than I did. I did not really accept it at all until 2003. She likely felt and grieved properly back in 1991, and that change allowed her to become a police officer, something I am sure would not have been on her life path had she stayed with me.

I looked back now on all of 1991. I remember when I decided not to go back to university for my fourth year and finish my degree, even though it meant not being at 27 Fir St. with four of my best friends in the world. I couldn't go back to that house, it was the last place "we" were together. It was why I left all of my furniture, especially my bed, for it was the last place "we" had slept together. How could I ever sleep on it again? Of course, all of these things were buried, hidden under so many other lies, but recap was bringing them out. How could I have missed all this at the time? Now I understand just how much truth we all bury.

Several months later, on November 8, 2003 I took a dreaming journey to see P. She was sitting across from me at a table. I immediately apologized and asked her to forgive me for not realizing our fate. I complimented her on moving on with her life so well, to which she said that it had not been easy. At times I felt like crying, other times my heart felt warm just to be with her. She reminded me of the need to find more fun in my current life. We went for a walk on a path in the woods. She looked just like I had remembered her from 1990. P turned to me and said, "I may not look like this now." She finally said that it was time for her to go, and I kissed her. It was the "realest" moment that I have ever had on a journey. For a second, I even smelled her. I went to kiss her again when she told me that she was married and had two children (both things would be found as correct a week later). She told me that she was doing fine, her husband was a great guy, so there was nothing to worry about. Her life had turned out fine. I said good bye and watched her walk to the path when she hollered out, "How ya been jellybean? See ya later alligator. Maybe we'll get a chance in another life?" With that, she walked into the woods and was gone. As she left all I felt was sadness. It was finally ok to grieve my lover, and wish her well, with love and gratitude.

I woke the next morning feeling energized, but I knew it wasn't over yet. The journey was healing, but I knew what I had to do. Many "new age" teachers would tell you in a situation like this to write that person a letter and then burn it in a fire to release the feelings. Thankfully I have had true teachers, and they would want me to release those feelings in person. This was the not-doing to complete the recap. I had to do it in the physical world.

It had been seven years since I knew her whereabouts, as a police officer in a small town in Ontario. I called them, which was a rather fearful thing, phoning a police station to try and contact a female officer. I was a potential stalker or looking for revenge. But I had to do it. The receptionist I spoke to said P no longer worked there and passed my message on to her supervisor. I thought that would be the end of it, but at least when I had gotten off the phone I felt better about trying.

A week later I was in the Calgary airport flying out to do a show in Northern BC, and I had the urge to check my email before getting on the plane. There was an odd email from someone I did not recognize. P was right, as promised she would not contact me in the physical, but her husband did. The message had got from the police force to him, and he emailed me to pass on his wife's number. The trust he showed in her and me made me instantly like this man.

November 19 was call day. I had no idea what I was going to say. I was more nervous than at any time in my life. How would she handle my stories of journeys, recap, spirits and seeing events that never happened? Would she think that I was trying to start a relationship with her again? It was a moment of great advancement on the warrior's path. The true path is not all fun and games, it will take us to the depth of all that we are trying to hide. I know that no matter what PW thought, I had to call her and release the unknown burden I had been carrying for the last thirteen years.

I won't go into any detail of that phone call, that is one of those things meant to stay with her and me. Yet even so, I remember very little of the conversation, but I did what I had needed to do. It was one of the hardest experiences to hear her voice (the tone, pauses, inflections were all as I had remembered). The whole time my legs were shaking, almost as bad as on the train. When I had hung up the phone with her "don't worry about it, it was a long time ago, we were young," I realized that she did not fully understand what had transpired in 1991. At least not now, maybe in ten years she might, and I may get a call from her then. I felt a tremendous sense of relief and heat in my body. In an hour or so, all I felt was exhaustion. Yet I did it. I'm not sure how many other men would have done something like that. I was free, by finally honouring and wishing well a woman I had loved from the depth of my being, from the depth of my inner silence.

I was staying at my friend B's, but had trouble sleeping that night. No surprise. I thought it was due to the 100 rock sweat lodge I had been part of the day before, a sweat that had pulled a lot out. All night my stomach was in pain, like I had food poisoning. I hadn't slept at all and in the morning the pain was now in my kidneys. With B "too busy" to help me, which was odd him being such a caring person, I used the last of my money to take a cab to a healer to work on me. She claimed I was not having a physical problem, but that I had suffered several kundalini releases. So much was happening, my system was cleansing profusely. Afterward I felt better, a bit light-headed, but decided to walk back to the apartment. I got dizzier as I walked, sadness began pouring out. I made to a hotel on 8th avenue, and I went inside to sit on a bench. I had gone in to be close to a phone in case I had to call an ambulance.

I was short of breath and my left arm was tingling. I had read about this, a heart attack. I was having a heart attack…at 34 years old! I kept breathing and after 15-20 minutes I felt much better. I made it back to B's when I plopped down on his bed, he was not yet home. I couldn't move, even breathing was a chore. I saw a black ball rolling at me, just like I had read death looked like. I had paid little attention while reading, feeling it was a metaphor. Yet I was being slammed to death by a metaphor. It is interesting what you think about when you believe you are about to die. My number one thought was that the most important people in my life who I would want told of my death I contact by email, but no one knew my hotmail password so not one would get a message to them.

Somewhere in the midst of all these thoughts, I dozed off. An hour later B arrived and I woke up. I realized I was not going to die, the worst was over, but I felt horrible. I slept for two straight days.

Did I really have a heart attack? I'm not sure. I thought of it later as a symbolic heart attack. My heart broke on that train in 1991, but I had stuffed it down never feeling it. My experience that day was my body's reaction to the stored pain that I had blocked for so long.

ल

"Is that story is true?" Anders asks while shaking his head slightly. Liv is sitting quietly staring off into the distance. Something in my story has touched something in her past and I just let her be, so answer Anders' question.

"Yep all of it is true. That whole experience taught me more about what recapitulation, our mind, how we store memories, the effect of the mind on the body than any 1000 books I could have read. It was truly an amazing thing."

"Did you ever get to meet her again. Your friend P?"

"Oh ya. About one year later. We met for coffee and chatted. It was sort of the finishing touch. The phone call was the work to clean up the energy body, then the meeting in person was what you might call the finishing its mind-body connection of those events. It was so nice to wish her well in real life. When she walked out of that coffee place to her car I remember I sat there for about an hour. I was mostly in a place of no thought, the very hoped for experience from meditation. I felt content."

ल

Sex

"That is the way it is with people in the group. A person conserves his energy for a while, keeps himself clean and tries to rise above the manure pile. But what happens? The king falls off his throne. He meets a woman who is like the black paint on a mirror. He projects all of his desires on that woman, who is doing nothing more than reflecting back what the person wants to see." (Richard Rose)

It takes little to see that sexual union between people, is a form of between-ness. This is the act that can manifest a new human being into existence. The connection of opposites can also lead to pleasure, energy, and also manipulation and the loss of energy. It is the realm of the masculine-feminine integration, and as such links clearly into this topic. Rose's mention of the black paint on the mirror in the above quote is very important. I suggest you contemplate it very clearly, because so often we people we get into sexual interactions with- we are never seeing "them," only what we wish to see.

Most every popular song of the last 60 years is about love and sex, obtaining it (most rock and R&B) or losing it (blues or country and western). Relationships with good friends have their troubling aspects to them, but as soon as something moves to the inclusion of sex, things can become difficult. Once the pair becomes a couple, each usually projects the largest deficiencies of their 'self' onto the relationship partner to make up for all of one's shortcomings. How often have we seen that as soon as one partner begins to work on themselves, trouble ensues? Because a partnership is not often based on growth and change, but on stasis and inertia (to keep things in the exact energetic way as when the couple first met). One in the couple is fine with this, the other is not- and if so, that is where the block between them appears.

It is important is to examine the topic of partnership and sexuality—but not from the in-dream standpoint (how to have a better relationship or be a better lover) but from the viewpoint of Awakening. Where does all of this fit in for the spiritual search?

I have come to believe that much of our sexual foundation is created as a child. How things go in this area, then, is a main structure of what we will move towards or away from. I will share two events. The first happened when I was around the age of 9 or

10. I met a girl. She lived across the street from me and was maybe two years older. I have forgotten her name. I had not really had much of any notice of girls up to that point, but something about her was different. Maybe it was because she was older than me. It was the summer, and she the daughter of a single mother who worked all day. She may have been new to the city, or at least the neighborhood, and didn't know many people. She started to spend afternoons with me at my house. I am not sure why she spent so much time with me. I don't recall us playing much, like I did with other friends who came over—my memories of her are mostly sitting on the front stairs...just talking. There was no doubt this was the first girl I was attracted to—blonde, tall and a few years older. Is it any wonder that for most of my robotic life I was attracted to tall, blonde, older women, who were excellent at conversation? The main emotion I always felt around her was that of inadequacy. I never felt I could be good enough for the "girl across the street." Yet still the greatest moments of my early life were the few times she invited me to her apartment. Just me and the tall older blonde girl, sitting and talking. Even now all I feel are twin emotions of extreme excitement, and terrorizing fear. I think we kissed once in that apartment, but for some reason that has been blocked out. She moved a few months later—I am sure in a very messy family situation. But I have never forgotten her. I wonder if she knows how much she shaped my life, how in some ways I was looking for an exact replica of her—to experience what I was too afraid to fully experience then.

જી

My second personal story is from November 1979, and my tall blonde has been gone for a few months now. This afternoon is my last day of school in Sault Ste. Marie. My family is moving to Toronto the following day, and classes have sort of been stopped, as we are having a bit of a going away party for me. Funny, for all the leaving I have done in my life this is the only going away party ever thrown for me. It is also a memory of one of my most fearful moments—all psychological, all self-induced. My other crush of the time was a short brunette named LJF. It was something about her smile, and the way we would laugh together as I would walk her halfway home, before turning left and going to mine. Today, however, there was an unexpected twist.

It was around 2:30 and class was over early. Most of the class were going to go home like normal, but LJF had a different plan. "How about we go into the bushes and say good bye properly?" she asked. I froze. I mean I literally froze. Something I had been hoping for, was now being presented. The only images that could float across my mental screen at that moment was thoughts of how I would "embarrass myself" with her. I would be inadequate, and somehow give her a terrible last memory of me. My feelings I had from the blonde girl continuing. I made up some rather stupid excuse and if I recall correctly, went running all the way home. In some ways I may have not stopped running. If you want to know what is odd...around 1998 I took a close look at the girl I was on a date with right next to a wooded park area, and noticed she bore an amazing resemblance (short, brunette, cute smile) to a series of other girls I dated over the years. I wondered about their similarity, especially when I know my main attraction was for tall, blonde, older women. Then I tracked it back. They all reminded me of LJF. Somehow the rest of my life I was trying to create the situation to make it into those bushes; I had tried my best to find a similar likeness of the woman whose simple question sent me running. This is the sort of condition that is running our lives without us even knowing it, and why we must deconstruct every area in our life. The further back we go with our examination, the more valuable the practice of recap becomes.

∽

What is sex? We really don't investigate this question much and even attempt to hide it from children as long as possible with fairy tales of storks bringing babies. On the simplest level, sex is the biological mechanism to make more human beings, and is a similar urge is inherent in all animals on the planet. However, unlike most animals—who get an instinctual urge at one moment of the year, in humans this urge can come and of 24 hours a day. Rose wonders at what point in history did humans begin to change our natural mating urge for upkeeping the tribe, into something that is a "pleasure and relaxation tool," or "attempt to control and manipulate."

So hypnotic is the spell that sex casts over us, that just to examine it is one of the hardest parts of the process. That is because we have become programmed since childhood to have such great pride in having a boatload of children, to gain arrogance in our sexual performing, or create value in ourself based on the attractiveness levels of our partner. We are making decisions based on a sex-urge. The advertising and the media community know this. They say sex sells, by selling the idea that if we have a certain car, or tool set, or diamond ring, that we will somehow get more sex. One of the many subliminal messages on the subject is that we should be engaging as many times as possible, as the ideal method of tension reduction. Tension however is energy and is not necessarily a problem that needs to be eliminated, for tension is the main condition needed to create the gap of between-ness. To simply reduce tension might mean you are wasting energy that could be used somewhere else. At the same time, an equal programming is telling us that feeling this urge and engaging in sex is evil (a sin). On one hand they push us towards, then beat us with the other for going. No wonder we are so confused. However for anyone who has ever been an artist knows, sexual energy is in some way a bridge to their creative energy. For some they need sex to bring the creation to the fold, others to not have sex to keep the energy within to express in the creation.

"Meditation on sex is like lighting a match to see how much blasting powder is in the keg. You have to look into that keg without lighting a match. And when you do, you will see that you have been a robot, and that you have been doing things which were not your ultimate choice of behavior." (Richard Rose)

While Rose suggests that nature is our friend, and that we should do our best to live in accordance with natural law as much as we can, we must realize that following nature will not necessarily lead to a spiritual realization. That is why Rose suggested one of the most important things anyone on a real spiritual path can do is to take a serious, no-nonsense evaluation of sex. Mr. Park used to tell us, when we would listen to him on the subject, was that none of us should be having sex. Not because it was bad or evil, just because we didn't know what we were doing, thus we were creating a mess with our energy. He said once you learned totally this area, then you could have sex.

The Gnostics, and many other key spiritual figures, were at the top of heresy when they suggested that none of their followers should have children. They were not rejecting sexuality, instead they were seeing everything in terms of energetic expenditure. To them making a baby was the biggest expenditure of energy there is, not only in the making of, but in the raising of the child—and they wanted all their energy to be put towards Self-discovery and universal knowing. They felt there were (even in 200BC) more than enough children on earth, each a part of the Absolute trapped into matter. They felt the earth didn't need more children, but to look better after the ones that are already here. Family pathology is passed on generation after generation, and parents generally are the same as their parents in raising children. Since most come from dysfunctional or abusive families, it is no surprise that the mess keeps getting transferred from generation to generation. It takes much transformation to be anything different, especially in crisis. The best way to make it stop, is to have no children to pass it on to. It was the number one reason I chose not to reproduce in this life.

But open discussion about sex in our spiritual journey is not that big of a seller. People want the spirituality where we can give up everything except our precious sex lives (or if anything find how their spirituality can get them more of it). It is why the teachings of tantra (red tantra actually) are so popular. We get to screw as much as we want, and feel we are screwing our way to God. We do not see until it is too late what this chase for sex and relationships has meant to us—physically and emotionally. While young there is so much energy to use, it is hard to notice that it is being drained in the hunt and chase. Sexuality is often an attempt to fill a gaping hole within.

Another aspect of sexuality is what the ancients referred to as "the secrets of gender." In the ancient mind the interaction of not men and women, but masculine-feminine was important. Most ancient languages have gender built directly into the language. And there is a reason for that. It was a part of understanding this dual world was seeing how these two forces makes up every part of reality. Certain things and actions were masculine, while others are feminine. That does not mean only men or women could do certain actions, but something much deeper, certain actions need to be done in a masculine way, others in a feminine way. This has mostly been lost to our modern society.

In fact in the last 2000 years there was an attack on femininity and it has been systematically destroyed, with quite serious consequences for how society and government were shaped. But now I the last 50 years, it is now the masculine that is under attack and being destroyed, and that is and will also have serious consequences for the future. In the ancient world young girls and boys were taken away from the village for a year and taught by elders what it mean to be a man or woman, not just from the standpoint of the village, but that make up with in all of creation. This has been lost, so instead of a system set up where men and women can grow up to co-operate intelligently with one another, we have created a world were both are in confusion, competition and corruption together. A return to the ancient way is desperately required.[15]

> "It would be more compassionate to encourage people to fully feel the void they wish to fill with pleasure, and help them locate their misplaced souls that should fill it." (John Kent)

Any teaching of using sex to attain liberation from the bonds of earth seems clearly contradictory, like dousing a fire with gasoline. Granted tantra claims that its practice does rechannel this energy, and certainly results in altered states of consciousness, even ecstasy. But if someone is using their spiritual practice to feel blissful—even feel better, then they likely will have little chance of going beyond any stage that they feel good in. A state is still a state, and the work is really a continuous life quest to see what is beyond or prior to ALL states.

ϾϽ

Rose was a strong proponent of celibacy (at least during a crucial period of the path) as the best way to store the energy needed to make the final breakthrough into Knowing. This was not just the ending of the act of having sex, but also to have ended the thought and desire in the mind for a period of time. He has likened celibacy to coal, in that it represents latent energy, and by pursing this practice it causes the coal to catch on fire. The extra energy is what can propel us over the threshold of death, or as mentioned in Indian Yoga, can provide us

---

15   I have a section in the Additional Material on this subject.

with various abilities of the body mind that are normally dormant.[16] To him, celibacy is one of the most powerful acts of between-ness. Basically, he is saying, one does not need a lifetime of celibacy, one needs to be celibate to examine sex fully, and to finish the business of getting the answers that we have committed ourselves to. When that is complete, we will know who and what we are, and if sex and children are in our "life movie" then we can go down to fulfilling that in a natural grounded way. This is most hard at the beginning, when like backing away from any addiction, one will suffer the pangs of withdrawal symptoms. To try and turn away from sex can produce as big a reaction as trying to get off heroin or crack.

I have found, particularly for men, it is not so much the orgasm that is problem, but how that orgasm is being generated. If it is via sex with a partner that you have feelings for, then the brain and body will operate normally. If it is via masturbation, fantasy, and even worse, porn-induced fantasy, then not only is the body being depleted of vital energy, we are destroying the brain. The dopamine centers responsible for pushing us towards pleasure get rewired, for this new pleasure requires no effort at bettering ourselves, being of use to the world, or even of being useful to ourselves. It is an addiction like any addiction, and the addiction is the effect on the frontal lobe and dopamine centers. An entire new phase of sexual revision has appeared on the internet, known by the code NOFAP, by which thousands of young males and men all over the world are working to get off the addiction and regain their mind and life. For most it takes at least 90 days to allow the mind to return a normal state of functioning, and for others up to a year of this work. I suggest you look more into this and see how it could apply to you. As one anonymous woman wrote, "we need a new group of males in the

---

16 Rose also claimed that enlightenment may also occur at the time of physical death, when ALL of one's energy ceases (if one has lived a prior life dedicated to the spiritual search). It might be said that the tension of this transmuted energy is what finally cracks the "cosmic egg" of the ego-self, leaving one exposed to reality or even propelling one into death.

world, how would the princess ever get saved if the prince had spent all day staring at xxxprincess.net on his computer?"

This quote comes from David Deida and his book *Way of the Superior Man*:

> You will not be able to bypass ejaculation until you have experienced far greater pleasures beyond it...if you have accumulated a lot of tension in your daily life, ejaculation will afford you with a temporary release and relaxation. But as you live your life with more and more true purpose each day, you won't accumulate so much tension. Then you will discover that ejaculation, for the most part, actually weakens you. It feels great for a few moments, but the price you pay for the genital squeeze of ejaculation is mediocrity in your daily life...In a subtle way, excess ejaculations will diminish your courage to take risks, professionally and spiritually. You will settle for doing enough to get by, to be comfortable. But you will find that would rather watch TV than write your novel, meditate, or make that important phone call. You will have enough motivation to live a decent life, but ejaculations drain you of your cutting through energy that is necessary to pierce your own wall of lethargy and slice through the obstacles that arise in your world. Your gift will remain largely ungiven.

We need to move into work on our sex connection gradually, otherwise we may frustrate ourselves over perceived failure and open doorways to entity attack. Remember this work requires us to work on the deepest levels of the structure of our brain. We keep moving forward in small steps. But if you can keep the mind focused, the body will follow, and things begin to even out. It can take quite a long time to complete this task, depending on where you are.

"My barn having burned to the ground, I can now see the moon." (Taoist Saying)

When it comes to sexuality, what will be right for one will not be right for another and is dependent on one's life experiences. An overly sexed individual who has chased it their whole life will probably gain great benefit from celibacy, while someone who has been afraid or ashamed of it most of their life might be better served in walking into this area openly to observe how their mind and body react to the experience. This is a most unique part of the path, but it is one that we cannot overlook. The job is not to eliminate sex from our world, but to include it in the way that is best for our spiritual search and our own vitality. All that is false for us in this area is removed to leave only what is true and helpful for us, to bring sexuality into one's life in a powerful life enhancing way, as opposed to the energy drain it tends to become.

℃℧

Parasite Adversaries

"We have two minds, one from the creator, and the second from the revolution of the celestial spheres." (Iamblichus)

Something that is not really talked about enough in spiritual work is the rule that as we try to take a step forward, something (which could be called a force) is there to try and make that step difficult and, if possible, make us take two steps back. Something does not like the sheep getting too close to the fence. Rather than try to name this specifically (for there are so many parts) it is better to label it *the forces of adversity*—a downward force that wants to keep us earth/matrix bound. Mostly the spiritual community wants to find way to avoid, deny or repress this entire area with beliefs and hopes such as: nothing bad will ever happen if we only have positive thoughts, believing that all is love, or that we can vibrate ourselves to another dimension and never see bad stuff. These are fantastical hopes, rather than an honest study of reality as it is. This subject (of demons, energy vampires, aliens) is a main topic of the writings of the ancients, as among the oral tradition of tribal wisdom. In fact, any area the mass of modern sleepers ignore, or are shamed away from exploring, should be the very area a Truth-seeker looks at in more depth. Studying the forces of adversity is to learn how we are affected by them, how they operate within and through us, so to be aware of what to back away from. We are not doing this to fix or change the world; but to fully know the self that is here now.

The Gnostic writings, (seconded by the books of Carlos Castaneda), claims that members of the human race have a True Mind—which is part of our natural functioning at birth. The problem is that we almost never use it. We have come instead to listen to (and trust) an imposter of this True Mind. This imposter is something the Gnostics called a virus, given to our race by destructive beings named archons. Castaneda in The Active Side of Infinity called this mind a parasite, one which came from beings he called mud shadows or flyers.

This parasite links to our fictional self (belief system, personality and mask) at a very early age. While ego is supposed to mean this fictional self that we use day to day, because of the psychotic nature of the parasitic control of it, generally ego is now referred to the manifestations of the parasite.

Rose also spoke and wrote about this topic, but not in great detail. He claimed that people had to examine this notion that humans really are the top of the food chain, as we are conditioned to believe. Or, if entities who reside in other dimensions are, in fact, eating us. He said these beings are not superior to us, just strategically better off because they operate in a dimension that few humans see. Psychics and young children, and occasionally people on heavy drugs, get occasional glimpses. We cannot see electricity or air, we only know them by their effects. The same would be the case with such entities; we have to test the validity of their existence by watching our own minds. "I see no other explanation for the huge expenditure of energy. It has to go someplace...All the entities want is to keep us reproducing so they can have ever more access to the food source." (Richard Rose)

What are called adversaries are not naughty genies that makes us misplace our shoes and run late for an appointment. This is far from the case. This force is strong, intense, nasty, and often manifests in, or as, human forms. Rose claimed one of the main areas the parasite influences is human sexuality. He claimed that great rush of exhilaration we feel during sex is the sensation of our energy leaving us (mainly on the psychic level). This is evidenced by the great fatigue we feel after. The entities also seem to like the intense energy of trauma—killing, torture, abuse and bloodlust. The nastier a person's behaviour is, the more likely the non-human parasite is in control of the egoic mind. Someone can even be taken over for just a moment, commit a murder or some other act, and then have no idea why they did it. This is not mentioned to open any notion of ducking personal responsibility, but rather to see just how vast this subject is.

"The biggest block in humans is not the invasion of a predatory species, but the hidden attacks in our own minds." (Second Treatise of the Great Seth—NHC)

The first time I came across one was in a retail store in Calgary in 1998. I was waiting for Omri to finish his shift, so we could go for coffee and talk, when I noticed a guy looking in my direction, about 25 or 26, wearing a t-shirt. Nothing would seem out of the ordinary except the cold eyes staring at me. Something about those eyes told me that he was not human. While I knew nothing of archons or demons at the time, I felt that the being was attempting to control me through its stare. I stood there and stared back, while mentally letting "it" know that I knew what it was and it was not going to win. Come one step closer and I would wrap my hands around its throat, strangle and annihilate it. Simple as that. We stood and stared at each other, maybe for two minutes, maybe for twenty. At some point, "it" knew how serious I was, and turned and simply left the store. It took me a while to allow the body to relax, I had become absolutely tight. My friend recognized this scene and what was going on. He came over, looked at me and said, "You can't back down from them, not even once. Once they think you will back down and not stand your ground, they will roll over you the rest of your life."

This force, that either is or manifests as parasitic beings, has been here for thousands of years, and has controlled and shaped much of the recent history of our planet and human experience. All of what we believe to be history and is taught in schools and universities is mostly just a manufactured story, a story so ingrained that many do not even question it any more. Things are now very close to the world foreshadowed by George Orwell in the book *1984,* and Aldous Huxley in *Brave New World.*[17] Thus, one must work with the great force of doubt—doubt everything. If you don't honestly study history, and see the lies, you know little of the present. Any group that wants to control the present, first must control the story of the past. Those who control the present can produce the future. If you really think you want to have impact on the future of yourself or this reality, then the study of history to see if this force is true or not is an important step. Some who investigate these subjects plunge so deep that it leads to depression, anger and supreme paranoia—due to what the findings mean for our day to day world. That is no reason to hide from it, however. Look at an area, understand, and then move onto other things. If we lose clarity during the study, then our work on self-observation will suffer.

---

17   And presented in the movies *Eyes Wide Shut* and *They Live,* which are not metaphoric as people like to think, but much closer to the way things are.

"Every animal has a natural enemy, and so for humans. It is
not disease or death, but terrible creatures that watch over
us until we have a moment of weakness. They lie in wait like
vultures around a corpse. When that happens, we become
broken in spirit. That is when people do terrible, unspeakable
things, or create misery for others." (Harry Wood)

These adversarial beings are interested in humans, for it seems that
unlike the rest of the animal kingdom, humans have a particular
energy that is very nourishing for them to eat. As such they have
installed themselves into our natural lives, and in a sense, they grow
us the same way we grow cattle. What are known in modern language
as demons, are another interchangeable word for the parasite force
among us. I will only provide tiny bits and pointers. More so if these
entities attach to us, they can make us sick or create problems in
our life until we can find them energetically and remove them from
influencing and draining us of energy.

In the famous Greek myth, Prometheus (who represents all of
us) is punished for stealing fire (representing personal awareness)
from the gods to bring it to humanity. He is chained to a rock, and
each day an eagle (emanations of the mind) comes and eats out his
insides (his emotional body or energy). Each night, Prometheus
repairs himself, then wakes up to repeat the cycle of being food again
for the eagle. This is a total representation and comparison of our
human existence in this reality. This cycle, in the myth, continued
until Hercules (representing Horus, the warrior, true wisdom beyond
the dream) comes along to break the chains and give Prometheus his
freedom.

"If people could see their true position and understand the
horrors of it, they would be unable to remain where they
are, even for a second. They would begin to seek a way out
and they would quickly find it, because there is a way out.
But everyone fails to see it because they are hypnotized.

You are in prison. All you can wish for, if you are a sensible person, is escape. But how? It is necessary to tunnel under a wall. One person can do nothing. But let us suppose that there are 10-20 men and women, they can work in turn, and if one covers the other, they can complete the tunnel and escape." (Gurdjieff)

Anyone who starts the process to regain their personal power and freedom is immediately "tagged and targeted" by the system—to do what it can to put them back to sleep, render them powerless, or make them lose faith in continuing. The adverse force will also try and disrupt and sabotage the target (us) by using the people around us who are open to direct manipulation. Sexuality, because of the great energy generated, is an area manipulated especially at a young age, to cause guilt, shame and inner destructive patterns to last a lifetime, thus we have to learn to be extra aware in this area. You will not have to seek these forces of adversity out, as we progress along the path they will find us.

This one takes a while to understand. People you know can be unknowing tools of attack through a weakness in them exploited, to slow you down. So we remain alert, not emotionally reacting to possibly set-up situations. When Mr. Park said we were filled with darkness; he could have also said, we were filled with this mental virus. We see these forces survive in the dark, thus we cannot succeed in fighting them there, as that is their territory. But we can drag them into the light by making their tactics visible, where they lose their power of being unseen. "Whoever cannot stand in darkness, will not be able to see the light." (First Apocalypse of James—NHC) "The lamp of the body is the mind. As long as those things inside you are set in order...your bodies are luminous." (Dialogue of the Saviour—NHC)

"A philosopher must be on guard all the time. You have to watch certain circumstances set up to tempt you, you have

to watch falling through on a universal "set up." So you have
to watch everything. Is it a time for action, or are you being
baited? Do not ignore the forces of Adversity. That could
be as damaging as increasing their substance by giving them
a direct relative form. ...We should ignore the elements of
adversity; yet we should never ignore them. Keep to the
business of observing" (Richard Rose)

We are not as alone against these adversaries as it may originally seem.
As much as there is an adverse force looking to push us down, there
is a similar force looking to help us up. Becoming a warrior, a seeker
of answers, becomes like a call to this helping force. To Rose, the
complete commitment we make in any endeavor in life is what calls
forth these helpers. Commitment was not an act, Rose said, but a
magical act. The results of it will rarely be seen openly, but behind the
scenes in the vast area Rose termed between-ness (chapter 6). Learn
how to stay one step ahead to avoid what may be coming next. This
idea may be what Rose called, running between the raindrops. We
cannot stop the rain, but we can gain a wisdom and a way to maneuver
where we are able to move forward between the falling rain, and not
get wet.

The basic mistake being made in perpetuating all of this comes
from not recognizing that there are two selves. There is a small "s"
self (that gets infected with the parasite), which is everything we
classify ourselves to be. My body, appearance, what I do, where I go,
what I think about, memories, opinions, beliefs. In other words, one
gigantic soup of tiny things that make up a bigger believed whole.
This self is constantly in flux—changing continually. However, there
is also a Big "S" Self that is essentially All-That-Is, which is beyond
form and thought—and is ultimately unchanging. The small self
is a fictional shadow. Ego is nothing but a story. Past events and
memories that are woven together into an album called "the story
of me." Particularly important in this album is any item taken or

translated by mind as an event or item where we felt we were hurt, or in pain, or got no respect.

> "I get no respect at all. Are you kidding me? My wife is afraid of the dark...then she saw me naked, now she's afraid of the light." (Rodney Dangerfield)

Dangerfield's comedy, like many other comedians and musicians, was born from his childhood trauma. Yet most of us haven't discovered the transmutation into music, painting or comedy from our traumas. Instead, we have only found ways to punish ourselves more. The purpose of working on our past and our traumas is not for healing or wellbeing (that is a side effect). Rather, it is to know the current self better. To see how our mind works and why we do what we do. It is not about creating a peaceful mind, but cultivating the groundwork for an observed mind. We don't need more trauma, just to examine fully that which has already been experienced. "Mental and personal delusion is better likened to a cancer of the body system, in which the objective is to locate the cause of the disease and remedy it, returning the organism to wholeness and vitality, not to cut out the offending body parts." (John Kent) To liken the ego to cancer can give us the energy and focus we will need to tackle it. To be like Captain Ahab in Moby Dick who attacked his egoic mind, symbolized by the white whale. "If man will strike, strike through the mask! How can the prisoner reach the outside except by thrusting through the wall? To me, the whale is that wall." (Moby Dick) Ahab chose to give up all in his life except for his battle against the whale. And he did so, in a sense, knowing that as long as ego was running the show of his existence, that he, in fact, had no life to speak of.

> "Thus the core of this area of work is to continuously confront ourselves in every aspect of what we call 'me,' and to dissect it, to find what may be real. It is terribly nihilistic and threatening, and one will encounter tremendous resistance

which can also manifest as procrastination, distraction and depression. That is because what we are examining is not just false, but a parasite." (John Kent)

"So what is the big deal? Anders asks. "Ok, I have this mind. I know that. And ok, perhaps it might be—as you say—something foreign, even a parasite. But that's fine. I can work on that. It's all within. You make it sound like I should be afraid."

"Well, you should and you shouldn't. It's a bit confusing. The problem again is not that I have a separate egoic parasite, and you have a separate egoic parasite. That is one of its main tricks. The issue is: there is only one parasite. What you have, and I have, and the girl at the counter there, and the guy walking funny has—it is the exact same parasite. We have an individual ego, but the same parasitic invader- Slightly adjusted based on environment, life experiences, and personality traits—but the same nonetheless. They know how to communicate with each other, how to hook and get each other to react—for there are just a batch of clone minds all around us. They are constantly sending out waves that try to hook any minds around them. We can be hit by the thoughts of everyone around us. Just a few moments without awareness can let out a single action that causes a wave of destruction around us—either an internal thought carried out, or a reaction to someone else's. Later, for the life of us, we cannot figure out why we did what we did. That is why we need to become a stellar witness of everything going on internally, while at the same time staying alert to what is going on externally. The entire set up of Western civilization and society was created to serve only one thing; the parasitic mind. This really is a bizarre place."

"You mean my house?"

"I mean Earth. This is nut-land. I don't think it was supposed to be nut-land originally, but for sure a main reason for the way it operates now is thanks to the minds of human beings. And since the actions of humans the last several thousand years are doing nothing but creating massive destruction, that in itself is an indication that this mind thing might be a parasite after all. I believe that some of the ancient structures, like the pyramids at Giza, Dahshur, Teotihuacan, sites in Peru, etc. are far older than modern history wants to tell us. Like hundreds of thousands of years old. That is one of the great draws for me going to visit a place like them. It is not just to get a jolt of powerful energy, it is to touch back to a time where humans lived on the earth before mind parasites. I believe there really was a golden age, and few sites around the world still offer a direct link to it. A time before the parasite...what a thought huh?"

Anders is quiet for a few moments. He asks suddenly, "What happens when our parasite gets weaker?"

"You will think you are going crazy. The world, as you have always known it, begins to shift and change and alter. You run to the people you trust the most—family and closest friends—for support. But they, too, have a parasite. And that parasite does not like to see one of its copies lost, so they all fight hard to get "you" back under its control."

"So what is the way through?"

"For me, I needed to take a close look at this thing called my mind. But it is real hard to see the mind with the mind. Impossible almost. So that is why I chose to follow a specific set of actions designed to shake the mind. Along with recapitulation I was also practicing dreaming and not doing. And they were almost crazy things designed to test the mind and reality"

"Did they pass the test?"

"The mind? Reality? No they failed miserably."

One element of this thought examination is dwelling on the possibility that in the future we could reach a point where we could legitimately call ourselves sane. This is not the university psychology model: in which anything the masses do and believe can be deemed "sane". Instead, it is coming to see that the mind we trusted in—for as long as we can remember—is, in fact, insane. And this is only seen by finally looking at the mind from something—or someplace—beyond itself. A deeper part of ourselves becomes activated in this kind of work, which leads to us finally seeing the limited, almost trivial level of perception that we had continuously been operating under. To achieve this feat, we need to see the mind from one level above the mind, in order to really know it. We then begin to adjust and correct the foundation of the insanity that we find—what Castaneda referred to with his term re-organizing the island of the tonal. Once this is accomplished, then as Rose said: "If you like what you see from there, then you are sane." I would classify sane as a mind no longer influenced by the parasite.

> "Our remaining transfixed by the performance is not only due to ignorance and habit. We have also learned to love the fiction we create, while not suspecting that we too are created. We have grown an ego of pride and self-satisfaction in our role, re-affirmed through other's eyes, to whatever extent we are successful in the usual pursuits in life. Yet this conditioned enjoyment is also confronted by the emptiness it really is... You must become an observer, instead of remaining an actor, before an audience of fools." (Richard Rose lectures)

Chapter 6

NOT DOING THE EGO

Costanza's Revenge

"There is nothing noble in being superior to your fellow man; true nobility is being superior to your former self." (Ernest Hemmingway)

The previous information on the parasite and forces of adversity is important. Because without that information, a discussion on what is referred to by ego is impossible. To just believe that the regular human mind is currently in its natural state, makes understanding the bizarre behaviour of humans impossible. When we look closely at people's actions as well as our own, we see insanity. Choices that contradict our best interests, on a planet filled with suffering, war, torture and destruction. A world where half of the people lack enough food to eat. A civilization where a doctor tries to save a person dying of lung cancer, then goes outside to smoke three cigarettes. Yet at times human can show the most logical and helpful actions. So now with this background we can finally delve into the topic of ego. What is it. Where does it come from? What value is there in it? How much of it is false?

We have no clear definition of what is meant in spiritual terms by the word "ego." Most would define it as arrogance or superiority. In Latin, the word refers to myself, as when we use the word "I" today in speech or writing. But what if ego is not something we have, but rather something we are? Or, perhaps, something we think we are. At one level all ego (all we think we are as persons) is false. However, and this is a key point, a human is supposed to have an ego-or better we call it a small individual self that functions within this dream reality. Again the problem is not that we have a small self, but that false self has been taken over, and we have come to believe that self is what we are.

A self that is meant to serve a function, has become the master. In short, we have become slaves of the mind without even realizing it.

℘

"But you keep saying that this egoic mind is actually unreal. An impostor."

I nod.

"If that is the truth, then why should I work so hard to know, battle, and correct a fictional ego?

"Excellent question. The first problem is that we cannot just fly to heaven. Many New Age types try this, and instead of getting wise, they become fruit loops. No matter how much a balloon may want to lift off and fly, if it is still attached by ropes to the earth it is not going anywhere. Pretending we are already flying while still tied to the ground is simply fooling ourselves. So then, why not just cut all the ropes and let the balloon soar? Because if we lose all egos too fast, we can also lose the ability to function within standard reality. That happened to me, and it has been hell to try and get back certain egos needed to function in the dream. Thus, a balanced approach is needed. We want to drop a parasitic ego quickly, we want to drop what we might call our natural ego a bit more slowly. We aim to become a more truthful human here in this world, before working to handle the Absolute Truth beyond this reality. A Christian mystic once wrote about watching the darkness of one's delusions within their mind:

> "As the light grows we see ourselves to be worse than we thought. We are amazed at our former blindness as we see issuing forth a whole swarm of shameful feelings, like filthy reptiles coming from a hidden cave...yet we are not worse than we were, on the contrary we are better. We are better for now we know ourselves and can see all that is normally hidden". (Francois Fenelon, 17th century)

How does this false self work in the dream? The I of the ego cannot see itself directly, just as you cannot look at your own eyes without a mirror. The false self needs a mirror to see itself and validate its ideas. "I am or am not something". Energy is then sent out so that it casts a reflection into the bubble of perception. The easiest way to reflect is to use the egoic structures of other people. The external ego of others has the job of reflecting the signal your ego sent out. If your ego wants you to think you are either smart or stupid, it needs to have other people to TELL YOU, or you must experience situations, that you are smart or stupid. You cannot just tell yourself you are smart because something rightly within always doubts statements of the mind. However, with enough external validation, this inner questioner gets drowned out. There comes at that point a total agreement that we are smart or stupid, happy or sad, ugly or beautiful, talented or a failure. This is how a vast amount of a person's precious energy is spent—to get other people to agree with what they think of themselves. For if someone says we are ugly or beautiful (makes no difference which), then there must be a "me" who is ugly or beautiful and can be seen. "I" must not be transparent, for someone else sees "me." It is like that Dean Martin song, "You Are Nobody Until Somebody Loves

You." Which means: once someone else says 'I love you,' it confirms to the egoic mind that there must be a "me" here that is loved. Whew, another existential crisis averted!

A good example of how this works was when I went for a walk with a woman named Nikki. We met in Stanley Park in Vancouver and talked for about two hours. At the end of the conversation she said, "I hope I didn't bore you today". And there it was. It was a zoom-in close-up of how ego maintains itself. She spent all afternoon attempting to project a persona that was not boring—hoping that at the end of the afternoon I could say, "no you're not boring, you're a lot of fun." Most of her energy was spent preparing to ask that one question. Done so to reflect the answer her ego wanted to reinforce—that "Nikki is fun." This is why adults tire so quickly. Most of one's energy is spent attempting to make others (and the world of experiences) agree with who and what they think they are.

"Dwelling on the self too much produces a terrible fatigue. The fatigue makes one cease to see the marvels all around him. Feeling important makes us heavy, clumsy, and vain. To be a man of knowledge, one must be light and fluid." (Carlos Castaneda)

෴

Not Doing

"Yes, yes. I will do the opposite. I sit here all day and do nothing and regret it...so now I will do the opposite, and I will do something (walks to woman at the counter) Hello. My name is George, I'm unemployed and I live with my parents." (George Costanza, *Seinfeld*, "The Opposite")

"Ok, so can you explain not doing?"

"Not-doing is a concept presented by Carlos Castaneda. It should not be confused with the same phrase that exists in Taoism which stands for a sort of detached action. For Castaneda, the phrase means a series of practices designed to purposely break all our standard patterns (called doings), with opposite actions (not doings). Basically, you could say that not-doing is "doing the opposite.""

"So you lived your life like George Costanza?"

"Exactly. For one episode, he was the king of not doing. If you want to contemplate not doing, the "Opposite" episode of *Seinfeld* certainly helps. Everything in George's life changed because he chose to do things in a different way from his normally self-centered pattern. That old saying, how can we expect anything to be different if we keep doing the same thing over and over, applies. Not doing creates physical change, but if our actions change, thoughts change. And really it is the thought that is the driving force for actions. To really alter what we do, we have to alter what we think. However, we often have to work backwards: break the actions first, and that will begin to disrupt the long-standing thought patterns.

> "It's difficult but not complex. The path to truth seems complex because we have to navigate the complexities and interferences of the mind. As these interferences are removed, the path becomes simpler." (Richard Rose)

We rarely notice that our entire life is one giant routine. We have a habit for everything. We get up at the same time, take the same shower, brush our teeth the same way, use the same mug for coffee. We go to work the same way, take lunch at the same time, and take the same bus home. The first time we arrive in a place, we choose a particular chair that will always be "our seat." We do the same things over and over, staying on the same paths that will eventually wear themselves into ruts. Habits give people a sense of comfort and familiarity, that is why people accept them so easily. However, they are only a false idea of comfort. Life gets boring because we have made it a giant, ongoing set of repetitions. Yet any habit can be dropped immediately if we want to, as in dropping a hot coal from our hand. Most changes that one makes are not really changes, but rather are ways to make our old habits look a little fresher and more spruced up. Real changes are not gradual, but are instantaneous, abrupt, and far reaching. Everything we normally label change is generally another egoic game, and a part of our doing. We are testing our mind's reaction to performing an action in a way that is not our normal habit. Just brushing our teeth with the toothbrush in the opposite hand can be enough to see a small voice of rebellion from the mind. As we expand the limits of what we test, we begin to change.

In ancient tribal cultures, there were special people that the Lakota Sioux referred to as Heyokas—similar to the joker of the medieval world. Heyokas taught through laughter and opposites and were considered sacred teachers by the tribe. One of their tasks was to do everything the opposite way: they would eat dinner in the morning, breakfast at night. They would wash in dirt, say the opposite of what they meant ("I hate you" would mean "I love you"). They lived life as a giant not-doing—in order to show everyone that beliefs and actions can be altered at any time. Their medicine ally is the coyote (trickster), whose job is to trick people into awakened states of understanding—even sometimes tricking themselves. A key of not doing is to learn to laugh at oneself while keeping our compassion. As Castaneda reminded us, "when we have learned how to play the fool, it them becomes easy to fool anyone."

By acting in opposite ways, we put the mind in places it is not used to—to see how it reacts. We begin with little things—what order we put our shoes on, then expand. We eat lunch at different times or have it in a restaurant we never go to. We take a different bus. If we don't ever drink, have one. Never take a karate class? Do so. Afraid of asking a woman out, go find the most beautiful one around and ask her. We are testing our ego's story of "what will happen to me" if I do something I don't normally do. You can go as deeply as you want. Pretend to be like an opposite personality. I cannot tell you how much an "acting" exercises such as this can teach you. The most intense for me was to act as Andy Kaufman's alter ego Tony Clifton for an entire day. It was experience. My mind got very afraid, the mommy and daddy voice was demanding me to stop and go back to standard social behaviour. But then after a few hours, the voice gave up and there was a gap of freedom.

Other not-doings to release patterns include: walking backwards (which is great for it throws your entire system out of whack and dealing with the looks on the people you encounter), talking in gibberish, jumping unexpectedly when walking, spinning at random or falling down, spend a day (or week) not talking. Another good one is to only look at the spaces between objects, not at the things themselves. But when we do these things, and subsequently find out that everything is still alright—ego takes a blow. It is important not to do any not-doing activity for too long, or else that will become our new habit. I mention some walking exercises, which are themselves not-doings in the next chapter.

One of the first stalking exercises I tried was to sit on a bench in a place of heavy traffic, like a mall or by a busy pathway. The idea was to still the mind long enough to get to know things about people without knowing how you know. The test is to then go over and ask them about it. I had Brendon do this one day at a mall. In the course of an hour he managed to know: a woman was there waiting for a friend to watch a movie, a man was shopping for a gift for his wife's birthday, and another needed a pair of dress shoes because the others wore out. When he asked them, he was stunned by their agreement. What he had done was to merge with them for a moment and gain a piece of information that one normally would not know. Of course, one can have this direct mind link with animals, plants, rocks, planets or anything. All things are Mind, thus open to connection. Rose called this rapport.

"So you just held your toothbrush in another hand, and tied your shoes different?" Anders asks.

"To start with yes. You have to start somewhere. Start small. But then I had to begin to build up to more and more difficult tests."

"Like what?"

"Bizarrely the first not doing almost everyone has to practice is something incredibly simple. One has to learn how to breathe. I am not kidding. I never knew until I was introduced to Qi Gong that I didn't any longer know how to do the simplest of human activities—breathe in slow deep controlled breaths. One can use Qi Gong, Yoga, or just learning how to be still and breathe deep to one's belly. As long as someone is taking quick shallow breaths, they are keeping their mind and body in a flight-fight state which means the body can never actually rest. Much of the calm people are seeking in their path can be found just by learning to breathe slowly and deeply."

"What other crazy stuff did you do?" Anders asks.

"One of them was the way I used to walk around my entire house once before entering."

"Why?"

"No reason. And that is the point. I know this sounds stupid—and it is. It is called acting for the sake of acting. Ego only performs actions when it thinks it can get something, so when you do things when mind can see no reason for doing them, it causes it to "check out" for a while. In that checking out, something deeper can arise. When I first began this type of practice, I felt like a soup kettle that had the heat turned up. Everything in my mind began to bubble over, as the activities were like the lid of the pot. Yet, at the same time, I was also the observer—getting a sense for just what was bubbling. That is the power of Not Doing."[18]

---

18 Some examples of this is to take all the books off of the bookshelf and then put them back exactly as they were, or take the longest possible route to work. How about getting bunch of large stones from the river, pile them on your driveway, then as soon as that is done take them back to the river. Any activity that seems to have no purpose to doing it will really test your mind to keep up its normal process.

Eventually I did try out some very challenging not doings. To be invisible, or blend in with nature, to use what are called fibers to pull me up a mountain on a hike. Really wild stuff actually.

"You became invisible?"

"Well not like a superhero in a comic book or something. Just creating a fog around yourself so as to be unnoticed. There are lots of stories of soldiers who are caught in a vulnerable position and were so afraid of being spotted by the enemy, they unlocked this deep stalking power in all of us and were not seen by the enemy even though they were standing in an open field, in broad daylight. There are many who as children due to abuse, learned how to "hide" so their abuser could not see them even when in the same room. You know the person you bump into at a party like you never even saw them. Right. This. If you are doing it well, people will constantly be bumping into you, or will sit on you. Martin Prechtel spoke of something similar in his book, *Secrets of the Talking Jaguar*."

But for me it was the simplest not doings that were some of the hardest for me to learn. Learning how to eat well was something I battled for years. Not as in what food I was eating, but how exactly I was eating it. I leave you with this quote from Marsilio Ficino, the man who translated the *Corpus Hermeticum* in Florence to begin the 1400's Renaissance, "It is important to chew thoroughly before swallowing anything...when food is not digested, the humour does not get irrigated and the rotting food buries the natural heat...the greatest rule for health is that food does no good at all unless you digest it."

☙

The egoic self (what you have come to think you are) is a costume or mask, created to interact in the dream state with other costumes (which are called people). The ego makes itself believe that each costume, or mask, is somehow different and special from the other costumes. This mask—our protective shield—is the only thing preventing us from realizing what is going on here. The chains of Plato's Cave are links formed from the egoic mask, which in itself is the garment of the false mind.

The false mind complains about everything: your girlfriend, your job, the weather, the government. It has many tricks—in fact, it is the world's greatest magician. It can pull the rabbit out of the hat, find your card, saw the woman in half, and never once get you to question anything that it says and does. For its next trick: Tomorrow it will start up the very same show. And like an amnesiac, we watch it all one more time, forgetting that the last performance ended in a crappy way the day before. One of the mind's favourite tricks is a sense of incompleteness. This becomes the drive for more stuff (possessions, titles, opinions, knowledge) in the hopes they will help fill whatever it is that ego presumes is missing. But no matter what we grasp, we still find we are incomplete—so the cycle continues. In another variation of the scenario, it may create an idea of how our self, or how reality, should be. It does this to keep us in constant internal conflict and frustration with reality. Can a fish feel like a loser? What is a good wife, a good parent, a good employee, a good person, or a success? Who made up these rules? This mind is mankind's greatest disease. In fact, it is the only disease. It uses a steam engine of fear to fuel and create what it deeply needs; emotions, which are its food. Since everyone is suffering from the same disease, we believe that all this suffering is normal.

It is not normal, it is sick.

In time, this self gets made up of everything you can classify. Body shape. Appearance. What you do. Where you go. What you talk about. Who your friends are. Beliefs. Opinions. In other words, everything. Each is a thread in the giant weaving of the self. This is symbolized in Egypt by the goddess Neith. The divine weaver, who weaves the dream of something from nothing. Beliefs are not just about God or heaven. They are about everything, big or small, that we think is true. They create boxes around our perception. So instead of seeing the vastness of reality, we only see the walls of our belief box. All beliefs are held in place with an emotional attachment. And that emotion creates a layer of your dreamworld.

> "We come into the world amid the confusion of two individuals who thought they were combining two alternative principles, only to discover that what they were really creating was limitless varieties of newly paralyzed and frustrated units, which they called children." (Richard Rose)

When we view a baby, we know that we are witnessing something very different from the child that they will become. Even at age 1 or 2, there is still little sense of the separation from the world around them. Before this time, the baby is not really in this world, rather in a sort of netherworld. Humans make strange noises, sing songs to it, dangle toys—all to get the infant to focus their attention on this reality. At some point, a shift happens. Something gives up; they forget that other reality and are locked in this one.

I watched a young child with her parents, just at the age of learning to speak. She always spoke of herself in the third person, "Susie wants a drink, Susie broke this toy" …never "I" want or "I" did. This Susie thing is seen as something separate from what they are. But the parents kept hammering her to make her one of the group, "No you're Susie, Susie is who you are, say I want a drink."

That is where it begins, with the acceptance that I am my name, and my body. Finally, one day after months of continuous pounding, she will cave in and say, "I want a drink." Susie and I are now the same, and the prison walls of self are created. To avoid the constant pain of refusal to agree with the beliefs of parents and other teachers, we accept what they tell us about reality and ourselves. Until language is learned, a child is very intuitive. Once it understands the language of the parent, it becomes very easy to seduce that child. That is just the way it is. To get the child to remain here, it has to be seduced into staying in the nuthouse, where it must then start to act like all the other nuts. Usually, conditioning comes in small moments, not large ones. The first real date I went on was with a girl to buy some sunglasses. The pair I chose were the ones in which she told me how good I looked. Without noticing it, I had just been conditioned. For the next 20 years of my life, I ALWAYS chose a pair of new sunglasses that looked very much like that original pair. Trying to keep the feeling from a few seconds long ago continuously alive.

> "Tigers, lions, elephants, bears, snakes, all kinds of enemy, guardians of hell, evil spirits and cannibals. These will all be bound simply by binding the mind, and all will be subdued simply by subduing the mind." (Shantideva)

Once the egoic mind is fixed into place and operating like it does in everybody else, one is called an adult or a normal citizen—as long as we continue to follow the standard rules. Those who don't fix upon this point like everyone else, we call lost or crazy. Modern humans are like any other domesticated animal—dogs, cows, sheep—in that they are a being that was once free in the wild, then trapped and corralled. Cities were designed as feeding pens. Think about your beliefs. Did you choose your religion—or did mommy and daddy? Did you choose anything—or did schools, TV, books, magazines choose them for you? Are any of your beliefs yours?

What the parasite and the ego structure has ended up doing is keeping a person's emotional and mental growth somewhere around the age when the parasite completed its takeover. From that point on, the physical body will continue to gestate, but no longer will that person age any more, either mentally or spiritually. Check this out: Once a little stress crosses any adult's experience, they revert to their true age—usually somewhere between around 8-12 years old. It is an amazing thing to watch when you see it rise and take over a situation. Awakening, in one sense, is not just about breaking the ego self. It is also about allowing the entire human structure to grow at all levels. Anyone you see that is a real adult (whose mental age matches their bodily age), is awake in some way. Many of the powers people search for from workshops and teachers, come simply from being an awake adult. This happens through seeing the dream clearly, and by knowing how it works, and how we fit into it. Forget about trying to obtain groovy powers. Simply slice off your ego layers and walk into your real age. Then be ready for a surprise.

ℰ♫

Dual I's

"An awake person has no idea who they are. The only person who knows who they are is the asleep, they are their mask and roles." (Adyashanti)

Even more confusing is that an egoic self is not one continuous false I, but rather, compartments comprised of specialized I's. Actually I thought I understood this, but only a few weeks ago a post from teacher-friend Amara Strand[19] helped me sort this out. More than simple compartments that are in minor conflict with each other, they are in fact powerful masks that we shift back and forth from, and who actually battle for our energy and awareness. She called them Dual Programs. One personality is in the inside of us, another is on the outside (the personality we try and show the world).

She presented that the primary program is created in childhood. If one was very insecure, maybe bullied as a child, didn't fit in, or weren't well liked by our peers-then an identity program may be created around not being fully accepted by anyone. But something knows this program-personality is false, so in the not so distant future, an exterior personality is created to counter it. This personality may be very outgoing, fun, high achieving, etc. Two sorts of opposites. This program projects a different image of yourself.

---

19   Her site can be found at amarastrand.com.

As such there is not one major false personality, but two, and they are battling each other constantly. One is "inside" constantly reminding us how we are not good enough and can never be liked or respected. The other is always projecting outward a vision of you that is the life of the party and a person everyone should want to spend time with. Once this was explained to me (for in some ways this analogy did mirror myself very well) I realized just how much energy was being used by these two forces. In the case of Nikki earlier, the "I am fun Nikki" used the entire day to get the reinforcement- but I forgot there as an inner Nikki that was also battling to get whatever reinforcement it wanted. "You rarely get any rest from these two seemingly opposite pressures."

Strand reminds that our challenge once we grasp this is to first recognize that neither of these "personas" are the real us. We tend to know the outward one is a mask. I tended to know, even no matter how much I enjoyed playing the role of the comedian- that it was a mask that I picked up around age 8 or 9 to counter the bullying faced from the other kids towards me. Yet that mask helped make me popular, and therefore created a feeling of safety in the mind, so though false it kept being accepted for a long while. The problem is the inner personality (almost always telling us why we are not good enough, a sinner, a loser, weak, unlovable or whatnot) is not seen by us as not real. We believe this inner voice much more, likely because it has been there for as long as we can remember. It was so long before since we were free of the inner voice we forgot what it was like, so we tend to believe it. Whatever might be called a "true self, or truer self" within can never get a second of airtime, for one of these two other programs are always running on every network.

And just like there is a reason a show on TV is called a program (for there is a design to control the minds of the viewers) in a sense these inner personalities get their title of program aptly as well. The first program created within was so extreme and dysfunctional, so to survive we created another outer program to act as a counter — equally extreme, in the opposite direction. Now you experience these two, equally loud and demanding of energy, attention, space. Even personality has created a dual state in the dual world.

To dig through this is part of the work of self observation. All of this is a major project to see how we are constructed within and figure out if any of it is true. It is a long process. We may notice we get ahead of the curve a little bit, so think we have done the job and all is better, but that is just a trick of the mind- hoping we take the carrot and leave the two personalities basically intact.

> "If you choose to confront and heal, then you move ahead, and instead of the monolithic, dark wall in front of you, casting its long shadow, this is now in back of you and has transformed into a source of depth and strength...that literally 'backs you up.' Also, once you've dealt with your first wall, subsequent walls you encounter will be easier to get through. Just knowing that you can do it, and that there is another side of that wall, gives you the ability to move through even the most painful monoliths. And then you keep moving ahead, deprogramming the layers. Along the way, as these two loud programs lose some of their grip over you and recede into the background a bit, what will be left? What now has space to move into the foreground? You start to get to know your authentic self." (Amara Strand)

Why have I put so much from Amara's post here? Because it directly explains some of my experience in the canyon, and thus makes it relevant to me, and hopefully to you as well. When I said that ego was destroyed by the experience in the canyon, that was not accurate. What was destroyed was the outer ego. The mask I wore externally for most of my life. I was basically unable to be a comedian again. I understood that, even though that was odd to no longer have what had been my greatest shield from the world. But I never checked to see if the internal mask was different than the external. Or if that had also been shattered. Oddly it had not. Slightly shaken maybe. The outer mask had been dissolved and my inner personality was re-organized. Thus it all became very confusing.

As she reminds and I want to point out- it all is a process. Even if you see this in yourself, do not think this will change in a few weeks. "It's not glamorous or even spiritual. And it's messy and fraught at times. It doesn't solve all your problems and you won't get any achievement awards from anyone for doing it." (Amara Strand) But you might start to see finally who you are, and who that being currently is, is a cluster of minds, personalities, moods and concepts shifting perhaps thousands of times every day.

What is important is that we watch ourselves playing this game of intra-psychic conflict. Watch the voices, the urges, the emotions, and the values inside. See how they battle for the right to rule over the whole person. Look for who or what makes the final decision on anything, as well as "who or what" is aware that all of this is going on.

"To challenge these mental patterns as invaders, rather than just as naughty parts of ourselves, gives us more energy and focus to examine them, and weakens their spell." (John Kent)

உ

Emotions

"Recognize everything as a lie. Especially the one who recognizes everything as a lie." (Karl Renz)

An emotion is meant to be a helpful tool. A short impulse of energy generated by the body because of perception, to get our attention.

I will repeat that statement: an emotion is meant to be a helpful tool. A short impulse of energy generated by the body because of perception to get our attention.

If an emotion related to hunger arises, we eat, and then forget that we were ever hungry. Desires are a part of our programming, and emotions are the presentation they go through to get to our awareness. The basic desires are for food, for security, and sex. However, the parasite mind learns to take simple emotions and add self-importance so as to personalize it. The parasite cannot eat normal emotions from the body, only the etheric ones (of the mind). If I stub my toe and yell "fuck," and just go back to my walking—no energy is loss. If I stub my toe, yell "fuck," and then think of how I will burn down the house of the person who left the shovel on the ground, then my mind has begun to operate in fantasy mode. The parasite eats that energy. To get as many of these emotional fantasies as it can, the parasite creates "synchronistic triggers," in our environment. Situations arise that remind us of old trauma, guilt, disappointment or of future hopes. All are designed to get us to react mentally. This is a very subtle means of manipulation, and it is rarely noticed.

Of course, if I do not want buttons pushed, then I should endeavor to be rid of all my buttons. In addition, I will aim to neutralize any and all emotional wounds, as well as get rid of my self-punishing subconscious programming. Please make no mistake: this does not mean one that ignores, represses or hides negative emotions. It is mistaken to believe that if we do not acknowledge negativity, but stay happy all the time, then we avoid bad things. What gets repressed, ends up getting stored. What gets stored either turns into an illness, or comes out as an explosion. Thus, we need to examine our emotions and really delve into why we think what we think and do what we do.

What exactly is a mood? We might say "I am in a good mood today," or "he is in a really bad mood, better not talk to him." You could define a mood as an extended emotion. If an emotion—which was meant to get our attention—sticks around continuously it can become a mood. We can have many of these so-called moods and shift swiftly from one right into another. Anything can instantly switch our moods: a song, a look, a book, a bird. When the shift comes, we might not even know we were in a mood previously. Alcoholism is a mood—and once that mood comes, it is impossible for the person to back away from it. Thus, to stop being an alcoholic is not about not having a drink—it is about getting rid of the mood that forces the behavior to arise in the first place.

> "Falling in love with someone, or wanting to kill someone, are both states-of-mind. All states-of-mind are incorrect points-of-reference. That is because they are based on moods which are almost always a distortion compared to seeing clearly. Some moods "especially called negative (lust, fear, hate, depression) are often entity projections into our minds. Thus one has to learn to see themselves so well so as to determine when a mood or state is coming from within, or from an external entity source that is exploiting a vulnerability." (John Kent)

Yet moods are not necessarily negative. Some can be harnessed and made useful. All great poets, artists and musicians know how to create moods. A real painter is not painting, and a genuine singer is not singing. Instead, each are manufacturing a mood for those who approach their creations. Some locations (a football stadium, or a church) will create certain moods for the people who go there. Popular restaurants might be admired less for the food, and more for the atmosphere that the space generates. Advertising is not the presenting a product, but the manufacturing of a mood that we are meant subliminally to associate with that product. We are buying the chance to feel the presented mood from owning the product. That is why ad makers do not need to make "quality" ads, or even ads we remember. They simply must present ads that hit our subconscious to create an impulse, which they hope will get itself associated with their product.

"Fear is the first natural enemy a person of knowledge must overcome." (Carlos Castaneda)

As important as the study of our moods in day to day reality, is the analysis of our dreams, where our emotions may reveal themselves in ways easier seen than day to day life. Discounting what may be called special dreams (ones that contain prophecy or guidance) generally most dreams take daily life and present the resulting material symbolically. Rose wrote that dreams also tend to add one of three moods to the mix; seduction, fear or nostalgia. In a seduction dream, we try to get something or sleep with someone. We then want to take that mood into the normal world and see what we are trying to seduce, and what is trying to seduce us—such as advertising. Modern society is in the business of seduction. This seduction is either for members of the opposite sex, or with the aim of acquiring all the goodies and gadgets that will supposedly make us continually happy. Yet if we study our seduction dreams carefully, we will find that we didn't want what we were chasing. Do we truly want what we chase in life, or just like dreams, we find a very short-lived enjoyment from their fulfillment?

Fear is a core human emotion is fear. Every mask is a mask of fear. Fear disguised as love, as morality, as compassion. This fear is so pervasive that it bleeds into the normal world. A world in which most of the activities that people participate in, especially hobbies, are often not really the ones they actually enjoy the most. They are simply activities that a person has discovered which stops the constant fear from being present for a while. Without constant thought, judgment and worry, the body feels alive, because nothing is stealing its energy. But it is a short-term fix, the fear comes back. Come back strong and continuous enough and it can become a devastating anxiety.

Rose called the third main mood nostalgia, and it is easily the most spiritual of the three. Usually, this word is thought of as a longing for the past (remembering old school friends, or the good old days). However, Rose claims there is much more to this mood if one looks deeper. It is less formed around a longing for the past to be re-created. Rather, it is generated instead through a call back home; to something beyond physical reality (the Self). In a nostalgic dream (or memory), we tend to see things (humans and society) at their best—i.e., how things could be. Nostalgia is the mood that will push back fear and seduction. This mood can shift people into another realm. What is called journeying, (or the Aboriginal dreamtime) might be accessed by creating what is akin to this nostalgia mood, using ceremony. Ancient people understood the power held by certain moods and states, and they purposely created them. However, like all moods, nostalgia has its traps. Some stay focused on the past, and as a result never end up confronting where they are right now. Others try to relive the past, only to find that it can't be repeated as they hoped—while wasting valuable years, money and energy along the way. Again, the mood is not trying to link us to our own past (it feels that way) but to our past before being born, from our real home. Because nostalgia is the mood that creates the most movement from the mind to the heart, it is a mood to study deeply.

As long as moods are there, they will control. Even Cosmic Consciousness (the unity-sense) is a mood, albeit a very pleasant one. However, the work to reach the Absolute State must, by definition, transcend all moods, and all states-of-mind, in order to reach no state-of-mind (which is the only true state-of-mind).

ço

Spirituality

"Religion, has actually convinced people...That there's an invisible man. Living in the sky. Watching everything you do, every minute of every day. The invisible man has a book of ten things he does not want you to do. If you do any of these ten things he has a place full of fire, and smoke, and burning, where he will send you to be tormented to choke and scream and suffer and cry—for ever and ever, until the end of time... But he loves you. He loves you, and he needs money." (George Carlin)

One aspect at the heart of most any society is what can be placed under the blanket term religion—a supernatural explanation for where we are, and why we are here. Religion has a figure (or figures) above us that are there to help us in our lives, only we need to learn the right system of rules of contact (prayer, offerings, ceremonies, actions) that will bring these figures to feel favor towards us and grant us material gifts, make our life easier, or at least give us a much better time of it after death. These beings and deities will help us, but only if we are somehow "worthy" of their influence. On one level, all religions are the same at their core, while on another there are so many variants within them that they can defiantly be classified as separate and different.

For most, the turning away from a Western religion happened when the presented fairy tale was exposed. Some saw that most churches have been concerned mostly with power and money. Others found that religion's main message, that God is a God of love, did not match up with world experiences of supreme suffering (rape, concentration camps, torture, murder, death of a child, etc.). If God loves us, why does he allow so much suffering? Tough question. Most just ignore it, or come up with a simplified answer so they don't have to think about such questions any more. But if God really is omnipotent then he could step in and stop all the suffering which means either he is not omnipotent, or he must love suffering in order to have so much of it and not stop it. From such confusion came the walk into modern spirituality.

As the bigger shift away from the modern religions happened in the 1960's, a new sub-culture was created that became known as the New Age Movement, a combination of Hinduism, Buddhism, Native Teachings, psychic abilities, and positive thinking. On one hand more free than standard Western religion (not looking for some future salvation when dead), it instead promised we can be happy all the time right now. What the New Age people do not seem to understand is that all its premises come from Hinduism, Buddhism, Native Indians, Aboriginals etc., which are religions. Rather than just follow one, the movement has sort of rolled them together like a giant fabricated jigsaw puzzle. A part here, part there. It looks like one has stepped away from religion, but on closer examination, they have walked into a new religion, and a very odd one at that.

As soon as a tradition or way becomes something that gets sold—it must make it attractive to the buyer. There is nothing wrong with the study of various practices from psychic connection to alternative healing to create an organism that is healthier, more intuitive, and more efficient. But the modern spiritual lifestyle requires money. Only the wealthy can buy organic food and fly off to Satsang retreats in Costa Rica. Part of the whole modern spiritual movement is for the "in-people" to showcase themselves that they are doing well. They still have the same idea that there is some sort of eternal point system, and that if they store enough goodies, they will get some big reward, a reward they can show off just like the previous drive for possessions.

Rose felt most spirituality, instead of an honest search for truth, is generally a compensation for unhappiness, suffering and loneliness, rather than to see who is suffering and why. The spiritual crowd is only searching for a "feel good" answer. To ever know, we are going to have to get to know our mind intimately, to see all the psychic pollution that is in there. Even ideas we may have of God, spirituality or society can very well be pollution. Rose asserted that to really begin to understand the mind, we must see that it is a delusion machine, a machine more designed to project than to perceive. "Those who teach disciplines, unless those disciplines are for introspection or for dying, are teachers of systems of orderly leisure, auto-hypnosis, or self-deceit. You don't want peace, you want answers." (Richard Rose) We want to see what we can take and use for our own energy and clarity on our greater search, not as an end in itself.

Rose did not see humans as latent divine beings, needing only to reaffirm our rightful place as joyous rulers of the world. Rather he sees us as pathetic wretches lost in a tragic farce; victimized by our own lack of character into being inexorably trapped in a savage jungle largely of our own making, while wanting to imagine we are in Disneyland...He claimed we are cowards and what we witness about us is "a dynasty of fear, in a playhouse of desire."

> Rose sees humanity as a wretched lot of pathological wind-up toys, who have dreams of building utopia, while not knowing the first thing about their own real nature or the reasons for their continued suffering. The implication of waking up is NOT that the person is not really a robot and should stop being one. The goal is not to not be a robot. The goal is to realize who one's self truly is, and in the end the Self is found not to be the person who really is a robot and cannot be anything else. Making this shift in identity also corrects the ego-caused errors of the robot. (John Kent)

We must stop looking to save the world and think instead about saving ourselves. That means perhaps we should instead look towards those who may have found an answer to the situation in which we find ourselves. These are the ones who decided to do the work to become sane in an insane reality.

℃

The Absolute

"For all things must be one, if they are indeed one. Yes they are one, and they shall never cease being one, in order that the fullness may not be destroyed." (*Corpus Hermeticum* 16:3)

"My me is God, nor do I recognize any other me, except God himself." (St. Catherine of Genoa)

Whenever someone finally has the courage to take their first look inside—expecting to find "something," all they really find—if they are honest—is an empty hole. This hole is not empty, but rather, is the emptiness of Reality. That is scary for the new created ego. Especially when looking outward at what appears to be other real, solid people. It feels it must keep doing things to be like all the others. It makes a mask—pretending to be solid and whole like the rest. The ego is made primarily to try and fill in that hole, which gets covered over and left unexamined any further.

The appearance of separation is a root of the ego. Ego forms from the foundational idea that "I am a separate being, different and unique from all other manifested beings". However, one of the elements found upon an Awakening is that actually there is only One: One Thing, One Mind, One Source. Even a glimpse of this Truth is enough to cause confusion for a long time in a world where duality reigns.

A primary New Age idea is that "we are one," and is used as a rallying cry to always be nice to one another. Yet, how can there possibly be a "we" in One? There is only One. For a "we," there must a "me" over here and something else somewhere that I can define as "we". That means two. All modern religions and the New Age community speak of how all is one, or God is everywhere. Somehow, it seems, they seem unable to allow this to include God in the murderer or God in the homosexual. One means everything, not select things—or more to the point: just things you like. If anything is excluded from The Absolute, then you are not talking about One. To have any experience you also need two: an experiencer and something to experience. That is why you must be careful with an experience of unity, or any mystical states, because by default, they are experience-based. Unity, or a mystical state, like any experience, will come and go; there is a before and after. You may be in unity for a while, but eventually duality comes back, because there is still a "you" experiencing this unity.

The Absolute cannot be experienced.

When encountering the Absolute, the mind will go blank—for it cannot operate without separation. Some compare it to deep sleep, where there are no experiences but existence continues. This is not accurate, of course, but a pointer. It does not mean that the Absolute is blackness, as commonly suggested. Rather, it only means that our ego mind cannot experience it. When a deeper glimpse of the Absolute comes through, it is not the joy or bliss that people expect, as in the experience of Cosmic Consciousness. To actually view no-self—the realization that the personality and mind is a fictional impostor—is shocking. To say the very least. It is the peeling off of every layer of the onion, only to see that there is nothing at the core. Emptiness shows that all we believe we are, we aren't; and that all we believe we own, we don't. Holding on will just make the emptying process more painful.

Ego believes that it is in a constant battle. The general of an army, no less. And like any general, its existence depends upon having a war to fight. Thus, it continuously tries to create conflict. This general is very strategic, and even makes concessions to keep its strength. It gives up area A, only to fortify areas B and C. It looks like you have made advances in one place, but ego simply strengthens its key strongholds elsewhere.

The belief is that ego is overcome by killing it. This is not accurate, though it appears throughout the process as if you are killing it. It is spoken of and referred to in that murderous fashion for you to gain a real contempt for it. But the way you eventually kill ego is to stop fighting the war. We remove all of the soldiers from the battlefield who no longer want to fight an enemy. As a result, the general has no one to command. With separateness gone—i.e., when there is no other—then there is nothing to gain, lose or protect. Ego stops when it sees that it has no job anymore. It can still go on pretending it is a general in a war room, making its commands. However, since there are no longer any troops to follow its wishes, no actions come from its dictates. Every lie (mask, layer) you drop is like another battalion of soldiers taken from the field of battle. Ego's only real fear is not that it will be killed, but that it will be out of a job. So let it keep its job—just take away all the workers. Let it become the general of nobody. The best weapon we have against this force we are calling ego is to observe it. And then to allow something that might be called our center, or our core, to turn away from all that ego suggests. The other great weapon against this parasite is laughter/humour. Recognizing the absurdity in oneself and being able to laugh at the part of oneself that is being ridiculous, weakens mind's hold and allows us to ignore its suggestions.

Please don't mistake this removal of the workers or soldiers as easy, or think that it is not a challenge because the idea of surrender is involved.

This surrender takes everything you have.

"A part of our mind will do everything it could to prevent us from fulfilling our task, finding the totality of the Self. This could include pushing one into loss of meaning, melancholy, and even suicidal depression. The counter measure is to persist in spite of all the disappointments." (Carlos Castaneda)

Hence a big part of the reason I wrote this book. To show that the process of discovering or realizing Who we are, does not in any way look like a nice spiritual journey. Most every modern spiritual book is going to have to be discarded if there will be any progress at all. Because the process is not to make ourselves better, it is to dismantle ourselves and see if anything we thought of as "me" is real.

Answering "Who Am I?" is probably the most difficult task in our lives. This single question threatens to negate all that we know, all that we have, and all that we are. Thus, as a result, one encounters tremendous resistance to inquiry on all levels. This can manifest as the procrastination and distractions inherent in we call normal living. Some may ask, what is the point of all the work if the goal is Totality of the Self? Especially when there is no guarantee that our challenging work will even create this completion or be met with any level of "success". Yet, we can transform our experience and perception even without Awakening. This is evidenced to me primarily through personal correspondence with some of Rose's students from the 1980's and 90's. Within their responses to me is a clarity, selfless-ness, and friendliness that they likely did not have when they made their first treks to Rose's farm in the 1980's. Something transformed, and that something is evident even in an email.

If you do this observing at a deep level, it is likely that awareness will get pushed from your normal mode of perception. You will move from the belief/experience that the body-mind is who you are and, instead, begin to see this body thing as a character in a movie or a play. Awakening is to identify with the actor or the dreamer, and not the role or the dreamed. To say it another way, to believe that the you that is seen in the mirror is you—is defined as being asleep. To start to get the sense the thing you have always believed yourself to be, may in fact be a shadow of much more True Self, is the beginning of awakening. To start to view our thoughts and feelings and actions simply as the experiences of an actor. This is not a call to be in the present moment, or a plea to live as a witness in order to be happy or end suffering. It is to simply be aware of what the character is doing and thinking, from the viewpoint of the actor playing the role of "you." Arjuna and Donnie Darko represent the average asleep person who forgot they are a character. Meanwhile Krishna and

Frank are the ultimate awareness—reminding the characters that reality is simply a movie, and that they have a role to play. [20]

◆◆

"The enemies of hatred, attachment, and so forth—do not have arms and legs, nor do they have courage and skill. So how do they make me their slave?" (Shantideva)

Rose and Castaneda both used the terms of the Hopi/Navajo: that of us being a channel or tube. This tube is connected to the Manifesting Source by a link, or a cord. This almost makes a workable analogy of humans as a television set—a hollow tube attached by a cable cord to the picture source. What we see on the screen is not the source, but a created image sent through the cord. The screen is mistaken as reality. The Hopi claim that our link gets filled with the garbage of ego: ignorance, identification, laziness, lust and greed. All which cause distortions to what is sent through the connecting cord and perceived on the screen. *"This obstruction (of the channel), is what prevents human beings from realizing their true nature, and even muffles intuition that would alert one to the falseness of mundane existence, and guide one home."* (Richard Rose) When the channel is cleared through, a shift in the point-of-reference—from the lesser I (me) to larger I (Self)—then occurs. Self is seeing THROUGH an ego, no longer WITH an ego.

To take the first steps at attempting this shift, we turn the mind on itself. We turn our curiosity from all the shiny objects of reality, to become curious as to who or what is perceiving them, and why. We move the energy that normally goes to our desires, funneling it instead into the desire to find our essence. We turn our deep needs and wants for connection and friendship, into appreciation for our co-workers on the path. "Most things in this world, as long as the

---

20   See *Donnie Darko*

inner parts are hidden, stand upright and live. If they are revealed, they die...so with a plant. If the root is exposed, the plant dries up." (Gospel of Phillip-NHC) Ego, in all its many forms and variations, must be examined under the microscope of your awareness. People will look at everything except their deep-seated beliefs, hopes and dreams. Find them all. Root them out. Someone can meditate for hours, stop eating meat and quit having sex for the rest of their life. But as long as they do not look at their own mind, nothing will really change. Shine a light on the hidden, and it is hidden no longer.

One final reminder is Rose claimed that it is foolish or even dangerous to try and abandon ALL of our egos at once—with the mistaken belief that some sort of instant salvation awaits. Just move away from untruth—the most obvious and harmful egos—first, until gradually we continue to let go, even of the finest layers. The ego of belief in self, survival, and desire for wholeness needs to stay for a while, to help get rid of the other egos such as laziness, weakness, lust, and conceit. The shift towards Absolute Awareness should be gradual, yet the final crossing of the line potentially comes about in a shocking and traumatic way. We have no control of the final moment. Instead, we work hard to physically and mentally be in a place where we can handle what could be a stark scenario, should that particular lightning bolt hit us.

Thus, proper self-observation has given us the vaccination that we required for reaching the Absolute.

Chapter 7

WHAT'S REAL?

Illusion Busting

"The external world is nothing but a concept present in my mind. If my mind ceased to exist, so far as I know, the concept which I call the world would cease to exist." (Evelyn Underhill)

A story comes from the excellent book *The Holographic Universe* by Michael Talbot. He tells of when as a child he saw a man hypnotized in a show at his parent's house. The hypnotist was able to override the mind's conditioning to make the man do the usual: think he was a chicken, or on a boat, etc. That hypnotic suggestions can make us believe a totally different world is existing should raise eyebrows. But it was the last suggestion that I hope makes you question the realness of this reality, which was that the man would be unable to recognize his daughter, that she would in fact be invisible. Upon the hypnotist snapping his fingers, the man awoke and even though his daughter was placed right in front of him, he could not

HOWDIE MICKOSKI

see her. She jumped up and down, with no recognition. Here comes the spooky part. The hypnotist held something behind the daughter's back and asked the man what it was. With a little squinting he could tell it was a watch and read the inscription on it perfectly. He was able to see through his daughter because to him she didn't exist. It was not that his mind just skimmed over her (as we think when we can't find our keys), she was taken out of existence, thus not blocking the watch. So is our mind creating the whole show? What is reality? Is any of it real, or just a computer manufactured hologram?

❧

Dreaming

"I awoke this morning from a dream where I was a butterfly; but now I wonder. Am I a man who dreamed he was a butterfly, or a butterfly dreaming that it is a man?" (Chuang Tzu)

I am sitting in a coffee shop in Canada, talking with an old girlfriend. I haven't seen her in a while, and it is nice to catch up and hear how her life is going. A band plays in the background, which is nice—you don't often have small jazz bands like this playing in coffee houses. We are sharing some fun stories from our time dating together, when I drop some change out of my pocket onto the wooden floor. It makes the most unusual sound. Clank, clank. Almost as if the metal coin is hitting a metallic surface. But the floor is a beautifully stained maple. As I bend down to pick the coin up, I hear the laughter of my old girlfriend, enjoying my clumsiness. Thoughts arise: There is no coffee house like this in Ottawa. This woman lives hundreds of miles away in the U.S. What is she doing here? Why does dropping these coins make such an odd sound?

182

With that I awoke in bed—across the Atlantic Ocean in Europe. I had been dreaming. Normally, I might have begun to explore the symbology of what the coffee house, the change, or the band meant. But this morning I had only one question: Where did my ex, the coffee shop, and the change "come from," and where did they "go?" While I was in that dream, it all seemed so real, every part of it. And more importantly, "I" felt very real. Where did the dream "me" go? I could say it was all my imagination, but then where did the imagination come from that actually did the imagining? What about all the objects in my waking life right now? This pen, this paper? It seems real—just as real as the objects from my dream world seemed earlier. How can I ever know which is which? In a dream, when the monster chases me, I run. When the pretty girl smiles at me, I get excited. When bread is getting baked, I get hungry. Then I wake up and realize that I have been sleeping on a bed, and none of what happened was "real." Or maybe it was all real, existing in another parallel reality that is continuing on—even if I am no longer conscious in it. Maybe the "me" in that reality is going on too?

To really examine dreaming is to examine the foundation of everything.[21]

Dreaming at night is a very interesting occurrence that is usually either under-examined (brushed over or forgotten each morning) or is over-examined (with continuous dream journals and looking for the symbolic meaning of every object in the dream). But something very special is going on. Our body has taken leave of this reality to rest. However, consciousness is continuing to project movie images inside of our head in which we insert ourselves (usually in the same body) to play the main character of the night-time movies.

Dreams tend to have common layouts. Experiencing a normal dream usually involves unresolved information from the day, which is coming up to be "cleared out" of the subconscious. Nightmares

---

21 The various exercises of dreaming are found in the Appendix Testing Dream Reality

are dreams designed to get our attention. Sometimes we wake and instantly feel that the dream we just had was more than a dream, and that it contained a depth and level that cannot be explained. In these dreams are prophetic details concerning the future, or visits to worlds that seem more rich and deep than our own—yet feel equally real. One interesting deviation is when we encounter what is known as being lucid in our dreams. We know we are dreaming, but do not wake up. Perhaps the most powerful lucid dream to have is one where we see our regular body asleep in our bed. We are seeing there is an "us" that can see, but that seeing is not the body we are used to calling us. It is a shock to the normal idea of "I am my body" when we can actually see it from outside itself. Who or what are we then if we cannot be pinpointed to our body?

In my teenage years I had the experience of "seeing" my physical body, while not in my physical body. However, it was not until 2004 that a similar yet completely different experience occurred in the King's Chamber of the Great Pyramid at Giza. Egyptian pyramids were built specifically to facilitate death, the death of the ego, and they assisted in that by breaking the bubble—causing a tear in the usually static thing called reality.

I was seeing from the eyes of Howdie Mickoski, the form crawling into the chamber. Yet I could at the same time also see from the eyes of a formless "something" already in the chamber, seeing Howdie Mickoski enter the chamber. I can close my eyes and do it now. I associate this formless witnessing as "I or myself." Something that I can call a mind of perception was already in the chamber and watching me enter, yet I was also that perception. It was not like I was still in a body (astral, dreaming, whatever). It was also not a feeling of oneness, a connection to everything, or overwhelming love. I have had those experiences, so I know what they are like. What was strange about the experience was that when watching Howdie Mickoski enter the chamber, the thing doing the watching felt just as I normally feel I am, but only without any sort of form or container, there was only a very vague presence as "me" as I normally think of myself, but there was a clear understanding that "I" was watching the entrance. This is very hard to explain. The very thing I always thought of as "me" was not in any way locked into the body thing.

If I as perception have no form body, and can see Howdie Mickoski the body-mind; while at the same time be inside the body Howdie and look into the room from that body where the viewing perception of it is, then what exactly am I? Why have I always been trained to think that "me" is inside a form somehow?

Dreaming is the not-doing of sleep, and is used to find answers, power, and healing if we can keep our awareness. Rules change in dreaming. It is a mirror opposite of our normal world. Generally, things we focus on in our daily lives are what show up within our dreams. But when working with dreaming, in time the things in our dreams will show up in our daily life. And dreams in our daily life are links to what Castaneda called *The Separate Reality*, a much deeper mirror world. The most personal of these dreams coming to us are called omens, messages from the force outside of the cave, trying to reach our attention within. The better our intuition, the better we catch these messages, but they are a form of dreaming and as such when we are awake we need to operate as if we are in an alternate reality to apprehend them totally. Because dreaming (awake or asleep) takes place in a sphere that is not "normal reality," it appears as if nothing has happened. That is because there is often no memory of anything having taken place. What will remain, however, is a feeling which is beyond the rational mind. That is the only way to know upon waking if dreaming has occurred or not—the remaining feeling.

ↇ

"All that we can see is a dream within a dream." (Edgar Allen Poe)

"The world is a passing dream which the sleeper is convinced is real, until unexpectedly the dawn of death frees him from this fantasy." (Rumi)

‽

"So you are not sure reality is real?" Liv asks.

"In the way you are asking it, no. I have perception of this, but it is quite simply has the element of a dream to it. That does not mean I or anyone else should ignore it. To do so is at one's peril. To call it a dream is a metaphor, just a pointer, not how things really are. But for sure I can say it is not as solid as I had always believed."

"Why do I get the feeling I might not like hearing about this?"

"I am not going to tell ghost stories. Though I have had odd encounters there, too. But I can share a few experiences during my practice of testing reality."

"I like my world being somewhat in its place. Are you sure I really want to hear this?"

"You know you do," I smile. "No matter how often humans say they don't, at some level everyone is curious about the workings of the world around them."

"Ya. OK. Let's hear it.'"

‽

Early in the morning during the summer of 2004, thanks to my over-active bladder, I got up early in the night with the need to urinate. I went to the bathroom. Standing, I took a moment to glance around in my half-awake state and looked towards the tank of the toilet. Normally, there are various spray bottles and containers lined up on top. Yet in my half-awake state, I saw a floating IPC bar code, ghostlike, hovering above the toilet yet in front of the wall. It was definitely separate from the wall, not in some way a label that was stuck to it.

186

I wondered, "What the hell is that? An IPC code does not just exist independently and float! It is a part of something, usually some sort of label." At that exact moment, a bottle of cleaner appeared, and the code was no longer floating—becoming instead a part of the bottle's label. It was as if the bottle had just manifested to give the bar code a "rational" existence. I then wondered (as my peeing had long since lost my interest) if in my half-awake state, my mind was not fully "running" yet. Perhaps it was creating, in standard reality, only what was absolutely required; the floor to walk on, light switch and toilet—but did not have enough energy yet to create the everything, just what was needed and some pieces. We rarely check our perception in such moments. Yet something caused me to check that time, and that is when I saw the floating IPC code. That check showed "gaps" in the reality I which was perceiving. In other words, checking seemed to force the mind to instantly "turn on", because a floating code did not register. It assembled the standard reality as I expected, so that the whole question of "where objects come from" could be ignored.

೮⊙

In 1999 a movie came out that changed the terminology that spiritual seekers now use to refer to "reality." That film was *The Matrix*. Along similar lines, I also suggest viewing the following movies: *Pleasantville*, *They Live*, *Donnie Darko*, *The Truman Show*, *Groundhog Day*, *Vanilla Sky*, *Inception*, *Monsters Inc.*, *Waking Life*, *Castaway*, *The Thirteenth Floor*, and a few others. These films offer glimpses behind the screen of life and get us to ask, "What is really going on here?" Many teachers claim that "life is but a dream," but they don't explain why the dream manifests in the first place, or if any of it actually matters. Reality may only be a giant narcissistic illusion. All after-death and other dimensions may also be totally fictional projections. When Rose was asked about helping the world, saving the planet, and helping humanity evolve, he coolly replied, "There is no world, there are no people. Nobody's here, nobody's doing anything. We are but fragmentary characters in a nightmare, dancing to make believe. You have to realize that. The mind has the ability to create, better than accurately witness. With the ability to create comes the ability to delude itself."

Who is observing these possible fictional realities, and why? A step up the ladder of knowledge is to realize once and for all that PERCPTION IS REALITY. So really one cannot test reality directly. Instead, one must test their own perception, and see if altering that will cause any alteration within reality itself. For me, the best way to test them both was by walking.

I have done a lot of walking in my life. Yes, there is the standard "walking to the store and back" kind of walking. But I did spiritual testing as well. I would practice walking quietly in the forest, making no sound—then bring a friend out to see if he could hear where I was. I would walk at night to learn how to walk without using my eyes, but activating other senses instead to avoid holes and tree stumps. Sometimes with a friend, I might try to walk in perfect unison behind them—or perhaps beside them. But the greatest walking I have ever done was by myself and seemed as simple as how one would walk back and forth to the store.

Those walks were more than just simple walking, however. They served the purpose of testing my internal dialogue. It did not take long from the study to see that subconsciously before I noticed external things such as a table, the word "table" had appeared in my mind a microsecond before. It is hard to explain, but somehow the outward table and the word table in my mind were somehow linked. The table did not exist independently beyond what was happening in my mind. Thus came the question, what would happen to the world if the words inside my head were shut off?

"Any meditation that puts you to sleep or makes you feel nice and happy is garbage. We will have plenty of time to sleep and relax in the cemetery." (Richard Rose, 1984 lecture)

Modern meditation is generally trying to force the mind to be quiet. Glimpses of quiet show up enough times to fool the seeker into thinking they are making progress. Unfortunately, making your mind quiet will not get you any closer to what You Are than eating a cheese sandwich. Something in the external world, from stepping on a sharp twig, to a phone call from our disliked sister will plunge the mind out of the happy quiet and back into the world of emotions.

Meditation equals medication. Perhaps I should take a moment to clarify that word, meditation. The problem is that today in our modern spiritual marketplace, this word has become the catch-all phrase to being happy. And usually is presented as sitting quietly with your eyes closed, perhaps repeating a phrase over and over, or just imagining a happy place that you hide in whenever some trouble occurs in one's world. One of the odd challenges years ago was that people (particularly in Asia) studied the enlightened guy. They noticed that the enlightened guy just sat around a lot very quiet and still, so they figured, if I want to be enlightened I should sit around quiet too. And it made them feel a bit better, so they all figured it works. And anything that can make someone feel better can be sold. And it was, hence where we are.

But the enlightened guy did not get enlightened by being quiet, but by intense inner observation and questioning. Each would have their own unique way, but the foundation is the same. That is what meditation is meant to be, a means of driving our perception into ourselves to observe the very thing that perceives. To find anything possibly true in a perception, thought, feeling, or that which feels. Granted most today who say they are doing such an activity really aren't. Simply finding another distraction from it, at least attempting to examine a thought as to its origin and meaning is far better than hoping to avoid the whole process altogether.

Sitting quietly with your eyes closed will never create a still mind. Any activity with your eyes closed is a form of dreaming; a signal that you want consciousness to shift realities. Most mediators close their eyes and fight to stop their thoughts, when in fact if they simply drifted with them, they would open into a whole new dreaming world. If your eyes-closed meditation is not taking you to dreaming, then you aren't practicing dreaming, but some form of auto suggestion (self-hypnosis) or simply engaged in a struggle of fighting yourself. However, there is another form of practice that seems like it is about a quiet mind, but is actually quite different. It is called stopping the internal dialogue.

You are like you are, and the world is the way it is, because you tell yourself you are like that all the time. Internal dialogue's job is to protect our "description of the world." When the dialogue stops, the very nature of static reality stops. Thus, stopping the internal dialogue leads what is called "Stopping the World." This stopping is not just shutting off words, but the entire thought process. Upon doing so, one is light and airy—much like when someone experiences an altered state of reality where they feel as if they are floating. There is a way to stop internal dialogue for certain periods of time. Done properly, it will more likely freak you out than make you happy. That is because the non-solid reality of the world will be directly experienced. The world can break down, as your mind breaks down due to the lack of inner dialogue that sustains them both. Wait until a tree turns into a medieval castle, or your walls or your wife disappears before you start telling anybody you know what "reality as illusion" truly means.

Stopping internal dialogue is not really a practice, but it occurs as an offshoot of an activity that seems designed to do something else. In a sense, we trick the mind so that it will do one thing in depth. Any activity that diverts attention from the normal circular thought into intense concentration can be used, such as: fishing, bird watching, sports or gazing. Stopping internal dialogue is what koans are for. Koans take the mind to a place where it cannot cope, and thus it merely blanks out and goes silent. That is why you cannot try to force silence. In fact, you must do the opposite—flood your mind so much that it checks out in some way. Once that blanking out happens, mind has trouble re-assembling. And like an overloaded electrical circuit, it shorts out for a while. During this blackout, a deeper glimpse of reality is witnessed.

ℰℐ

"My best meditations and observational inspection came when I was walking or working. When I was sitting down, usually I just fell asleep." (Richard Rose)

The first key for my walking was to have no final destination. I was going to walk until I felt like turning around. One key element was to keep a constant rhythm at a slightly different speed than I normally would walk in other circumstances. Usually, for me, that was slower. Castaneda suggested to hold one's hands in a specific way, but that never seemed too important in my tests. It can be done with someone else if no talking takes place. If I wanted to talk, I stopped and conversed, then resumed my silent walking.

The second key part was the stare. My attention had to be kept directly in front of me (but not at my feet). I could turn my head of course, but kept that gaze straight ahead of me. While doing this, the trick was to perceive a full 180 degrees, i.e. notice everything to my sides as in front of me, but not focus on anything in particular. See it all equally. Mind normally wanted to focus on just a few objects in its field of vision, then said a word internally at each object it sees (birch tree, pine tree, mound, dirt path). Try it now. Look around wherever you are. Watch how quickly the mind has labeled everything with a word: apple, table, salt, pen, and then the overall box of living room. It goes so fast that we usually miss it—but it is there. Mind does not see or label every object in a forest, or even in a small room—it just categorizes a few main objects and then sort of fills in the rest of what it expects "should" be there. Really. There have been psychology tests done that found this.

By staring at 180 degrees with intense focus, we are seeing so many objects all at once that the mind cannot keep up its naming of everything in our field of perception. Doing so will leave no energy for internal dialogue. Keep the breath calm and steady. Stay alert for sounds as well. It will likely take you many walks to attain this (perhaps months). I did this day after day, though it appeared nothing was really taking place. Then one day—my mind just shut off. I cannot describe it any other way. The mind was actually blank of all words, all naming attempts, and all thought. Yet perception was ultra-sharp. And that is when things started to get weird. As each new walk shut off the mind, I would experience such events as the ground flowing while the river alongside it was still; a man walking about 100 yards in front of me would disappear (I could see everything beyond him) then re-appear (which blocked the trees which I had just seen clearly). This all matched the hypnosis story earlier in the chapter. It was not a hallucination ultimately, due to the fact I could see perfectly what was beyond him when he was gone. It got to a point at times where objects would change from one thing to another, or became transparent, and others would become droopy like a Salvador Dali painting. The belief the world was solid no longer stood a chance after that period! That was precisely when the words "the world is an illusion" went from a concept in a book to a personal understanding.

The second-best way I had for testing reality was through the practice of gazing. Simplified, it is sitting still and staring at an object, while letting your internal dialogue shut off. I have listed how to properly gaze in the appendix of dream exercises.

e/o

Hologram, Computer or Reality?

"We accept the reality of the world with which we are presented. If his was more than just a vague ambition, if he was absolutely determined to find out the truth of his world, there is no way we could prevent him." (Christoff from The Truman Show)

I am in my bedroom, it is late at night, and I have made it pitch black. The windows are covered, the door sealed over so that no light can enter. Some may think that I am getting ready to perform a night-healing ceremony in what the Lakota medicine men call the "black light." Actually, I have been given a holographic kit from my friend Lynne, and I am attempting to make my first image, that of a toy car, and I need a no-light space for it.

A hologram is created when a beam of concentrated laser light is split into two. One split beam is bounced off an object (such as the toy car) and onto a photographic plate. The second split beam is bounced from another direction also onto the photographic plate, and thus collides with the first. What is captured on the plate is a wave interference pattern that looks similar to a fingerprint, or ripple after a stone is dropped into a pool of water. But once another single beam of laser light is shone on that plate, an image of the original object appears. That object will in fact be three-dimensional, it can be walked around, beside, above and below. It fools the eye. The image will only be perceived as "not there" by placing our hand through it.

I follow the instructions, turn on the laser light at the toy car, so it will then be bounced to the photographic plate behind. I turn off the laser, remove the plate to check the results. The plate looks as it is supposed to look, full of concentric ripples. When I turn another laser on the plate, the waves disappear, and an image of the original object (the car) appears. Well not totally, the car is a bit fuzzy, I must have not set things up exactly correct, but there is my first hologram. Then as I looked at it more closely, I got a bit shocked. What the hell?

ↄ

"Our universe is created and held together by two wave flows, one from heaven, and the other from our soul." (Emmanuel Swedenborg)

Michael Talbot's book *The Holographic Universe* does a good job of detailing how holograms can explain what mystics and shamans have said for thousands of years. An examination of how a hologram is made and stored could be explaining the human body, brain, and manifested universe. These were the radical beliefs of two unique scientific pioneers of the 20th century, Karl Pribram and David Bohm. Our reality is holographic. One of the most mystifying things for centuries is the concept that there is only One—complete and whole at all times—yet around us we experience many. But take any holographic plate, say of a person, and cut the plate in two. When you turn the laser on each half of the broken plate, you will not have a top half and bottom half of the person, but instead get two smaller—a bit fuzzier—original complete images of the entire person. Split the plates again and you will have four smaller complete images. No matter how many times the holographic plate is split, the wholeness of the image is maintained. Each tiny section of a holographic plate contains information to make the whole. That is what is so amazing about them. It looks like we are seeing a part, but the whole is contained in it.[22]

---

22   This feature is only common to holographic plates where the image cannot be seen with the naked eye but needs a laser shone on it. With the more common forms (such as an image on a credit card) to cut the original image will just cut the hologram in two.

This may explain what occurs in the Chinese systems of acupuncture and reflexology, where the acupuncturist can access various organs of the body by pressing points or putting needles on other areas. The acupuncturist can work on the kidney from the foot or the ear. If the body is more like a hologram than solid matter, then every part must contain the whole-just a few specific areas make the overall access easier. A hologram can also explain how it is possible for the body to contain so much. That is what my discovery on the plate of the toy car was. When I shifted my head, so too the image on the plate shifted. The room to the left was there, the room to the right was there. And if I turned carefully, what was "behind" the plate was also there. The entire room, and in fact, me in the room was on that small plate! One square inch of holographic film can store the same information as 50 complete bibles, a massive amount of information for the space.

Hungarian physicist John von Neumann calculated that the brain stores 280,000,000,000,000,000,000 bits of information over an average human lifetime. Scientists have had no idea what mechanism the brain could use to store what would be the same as several super-computers, unless it is contains holographic properties. How can we have supposedly 1,000,000,000 miles of DNA in the body, unless we are more holographic than we have been led to believe. Many images can be stored on a single holographic plate and the angle of the laser will determine what image comes up. Those with multiple personality disorder shift between one personality and another, and when they do, their entire physical form (eye colour, distinguishing marks, illnesses or ailments) can change instantly with the personality change. A hologram becomes one of the best tools to explain what is likely going on, that an internal belief change about who they think they are has caused a shift of the brain's laser of manifestation (what the person looks like) from one image on the plate to another. Is our body really what we think it is?

The placebo effect occurs when an ill patient is given a sugar pill but told it is regular medicine and has a dramatic healing result. That the sugar pill winds up healing may also be presenting a holographic explanation to reality. The brain it seems does not require a real object, just an idea. If under hypnosis you have the patient believe the glass of water is a glass of alcohol, they will soon show physical signs of being drunk. Not just acting, but the actual body sensations occur (diluted pupils, flushed face). Reality of the body is whatever the brain believes. What medicine is given to a patient may be the less important than how the brain "thinks the medicine will work." Perhaps certain herbs are downloaded into our body computer program to have certain effects when taking them, and the brain just follows the pattern. Aspirin takes the headache away as the brain just follows the "willow bark (in aspirin) should remove the headache" program. But that can be overridden. If the brain is re-programmed to believe that aspirin does something else, the something else will result.

This is truly amazing. It means reality is just what the brain thinks it is, and as such, reality is alterable and changeable as often as the brain (or belief) can change. Pribram saw the brain as a hologram and wrote, "Our brains mathematically construct objective reality by interpreting frequencies that are ultimately projections from another dimension, a deeper order of existence that is beyond both space and time: the brain is a hologram enfolded in a holographic universe."

In altered states of consciousness where one is perceiving a different reality, what may be happening is that one is moving to other areas of the hologram. Just as numerous objects can appear on the same holographic plate, coming into view when the angle of the laser is shifted, when consciousness shifts you could say it has moved its laser to a new angle to view something different in potential reality. I suggest reading *Holographic Universe* for lots of bizarre stories of altered and shifted realities and how they can be explained with the holographic model.[23]

Now I no longer need the lasers and plates to make a hologram. A much easier way has been found, a small set given to me by a friend in Oslo. This is two small mirrors, one concave and one convex. The convex mirror has a hole in the center. In the middle of the concave mirror (with no hole), you place any object—such as the small toy frog given with the kit, or a small stone. When the convex mirror is placed over the object in the concave mirror—it produces a double reflection through the opening, and the image will appear to be positioned on top. It seems entirely real, until one swipes their finger through the image. It is so real that I have photographed the image of the frog or a rock. Even the camera agrees it is there. I am explaining this because the device itself looks so much like the human eye that it got me thinking. Is this what our eye is doing? A concave mirror with a center (what we call a pupil) and perhaps another layered mirror under. The image we see is really what is being projected from our brain through the pupil, which is then double projected out as a real object. An amazing thing of the double mirror is that the object in the bottom will appear reversed in its reflected hologram. This too is how science says our eye operates, saying we see upside down. Recall that the word imagination is made up of the word image—thus perhaps referring to the fact that all images are just projections from our imagination.

Quantum physics has taken the world of the hologram into the Universe, based on the theories introduced by David Bohm. One thing they found is that if you keep breaking matter into smaller

---

23 Such as the odd experiences of the Jansenists in 18th century Paris. While getting into a state of incredible spiritual rhapsody, they would experience bliss along with great inner pain, alleviated by having spectators do things to them- like pound them with a sledgehammer, burn them or drop heavy objects on them. No one ever had a scratch. This was witnessed for years by thousands of people. How is this possible that the body can survive sledgehammer blows, unless the body is not what we think it is?

and smaller parts, eventually it no longer possesses traits of objects, it has no locality. Another finding is that particles are actually non-local, they can be in two places (or multiple places) at once. No particle can really be localized to only here but might be thought of as everywhere, just being perceived here right now. They just cannot find anything that they can call a physical object at that level, there is nothing there. More bizarre is that any small object of matter, such as a particle, is always in a wave form (like a radio signal) until WE are LOOKING at it, when it becomes the object we see. This strange interaction between observer and observed literally means that what is behind me in the room right now does not exist as a physical form, only as a wave, until I turn around and the table and chairs are essentially manifested. This is not speculation but quantum science. Is reality objects or something that gets created when I intend to be an observer of it? Is it all just a "frog-like" projection?

For Karl Pribram, this subject made him realize that the, "objective world does not exist, at least in the way we are accustomed to believing. What is out there is a vast ocean of waves and frequencies, and reality looks concrete to us only because our brains are able to take this holographic blur and convert it into sticks and stones and other familiar objects that make up our world." How is the brain (which itself is composed of frequencies of matter) able to take something as insubstantial as a blur of frequencies and make it solid to the touch? According to Pribram this does not mean there are not china cups and grains of beach sand out there. It simply means that a china cup has two different aspects to its reality. When it is filtered through the lens of our brain it manifests as a cup. But if we could get rid of our lenses, we'd experience it as an interference pattern. Which one is real, and which is illusion? "Both are real to me," says Pribram, "or if you want to say, neither of them are real."[24]

The metaphor of a computer also gives a glimpse to exploring the "dreamworld." What is viewed on any computer screen is not the

24   From conversation between author Michael Talbot and Karl Pribram.

underlying "source." Track back and you will find in the mainframe a series of numbers (0's and 1's). How those 0's and 1's are put together—will cause a particular letter, number, game character, or spreadsheet to appear on the computer screen. You the user are noticing only the end product, which of course is just a shadow of the 1's and 0's that are causing it to occur. If I want to type the letter "y" on the screen, I do not need to know the 0-1 code to make that appear, I push the "y" key and the computer does the rest automatically. Our world is also an interconnecting series of two numbers (yin and yang, good and bad, up and down) that interplay in various ways to make a dog or a rock. The dog may have the number 0110101011 while the rock is 1010001011. Everything originates from a central source and spirals out in a grid-web (golden spiral), creating a spiderweb connecting each manifested object with each other and the source. Due to the spiraling nature of reality it is good to make spirals and labyrinths often as it connects to your DNA and beyond.

There appears to be a lot happening here, but really there is only yin and yang interacting with each other. Our computer (brain) interprets these numbers (fibers of light) through the senses and nervous system, which translates the code and creates the inner world we believe we are experiencing externally. If a new program (new set of numbers) could be downloaded into the system, we would interpret reality differently. The ancients saw that reality was a numerical code, and the better they knew the code (mathematics and geometry), the better they could unravel the universe and predict what was coming. You might say the ancient geometers of whom Pythagoras was a descendant, were the first computer programmers, and more so, de-programmers. This was later channeled into sound and music, and through this understanding of the "computer-like" nature of reality that the use of sound became a primary tool for healing the body. The better they knew the code, the better they could predict what was coming; and perhaps alter the code to alter reality. This is still in the theater work, but if done with the idea of helping a tribe or village to avoid a major problem coming then it is of great value—as opposed to an individual trying to use it to egoically win the lottery for themselves.

ↅ

Observing The Dream

"Well, what if there is no tomorrow? There wasn't one today...Hello." (Phil Conners, *Groundhog Day*)

This chapter asks you to test reality. Reality is taken for granted. If I bump into the table, my knee will get a bruise. The belief around it proves my knee and the table are very real. But given the examination of holograms, dreams, and computers—such an experience does not prove that reality is set up as we think it is. The world can very well be just a projection that we have learned how to create. We may be constantly tricking ourselves with visualizations and projection.

Unless we understand how our mind really works—as well as its ability to create delusion—we will not see our distortions which keep us asleep. We only do that by inverting our awareness to deeper and deeper vantage points—in order to see the thing that is currently doing the perceiving. We test the realness of reality, so that we test the realness of ourselves. Just because my knee bruises does not prove that it is real. Is the bruised knee of the video game character a real bruised knee? Or is it just a series of numbers, in a holographic-computer mainframe, that appears on the screen the image of a character with an injured knee?

ↅ

"What's your favourite movie for spiritual stuff?"

"While there are some good ones I mentioned—like Donnie Darko and Pleasantville. However, if I had to pick one for teaching, I would have to say Groundhog Day with Bill Murray."

"The one where he lives his life over and over?"

"Ya. Without even knowing it, the film sets out the path of Awakening pretty well. All the mess, confusion, attempted manipulation of reality, and even the suicidal depression Phil Connors encounters are all real parts of the path—even if most people don't want to believe it. Along with being very funny, and well-acted, it does present a ton of aspects related to spiritual seeking. It's a movie I can use for hours in discussion...Hey Liv, do you really want to freak out a bit?"

"What are you going to do?"

"Just tell you my favourite part of Groundhog Day. The time loops. Living one's day over and over again. Do you believe that you are one of a kind? That there is only one of you, and this day can never be repeated? That sort of thing?"

"Well duh." She looks at me for a while. Ponders some things. "Are you saying I have a double or something?"

"Some traditions talk about that. A look-alike or doppelganger. Castaneda, I think, called it our parallel being. A person on earth who looks and acts like us, but is in many ways the opposite of us. If we are rich, they are poor. If we are single, they are married. Supposedly, there is great power gained if you can find and interact with this being. I came close once. That is another odd story, but not where I was going with you. Have you ever thought that this is not the only Earth there is? I don't mean other planets—as in globes with some form of life on them. I mean other similar Earths just like this place, with similar versions of you, and Anders and this house. In some of them, you are married, in some divorced, in some you've never met. And in some...you are even dead."

"Dead?"

"Ok, here is the story."

It is May 5, 1999 and I am walking by the Kensington Community Center in Vancouver, heading back home from picking up my mail. I needed to be out in the fresh air. The previous night, I was on a bachelor auction date. The auction, run to support breast cancer research, had 200 women in the audience bidding on 25 guys. All the dates had taken place the previous evening at a local restaurant. The woman who "bought" me, turned out to be a drunk. At 39 years old, the only thing she had to discuss the entire evening was how drunk she had been, and what strange houses she'd wound up waking up in. In fact, seeing her behavior finally got me stop my own drinking. But that is a minor part to the whole story.

While walking along the street, I was reviewing the previous evening in my mind, as we all sometimes do. I recalled a question she asked m; "Why did you get involved in all of this spiritual stuff anyway? Seems like a waste of time." Last night, I didn't respond. Today, walking on the sidewalk, I did. My internal response was, "Because if I didn't, I would be dead now." I froze on the sidewalk. The scene of downtown Vancouver began to shift.

I was now looking at the scene of a car accident. A large 18-wheeler truck was crashed in the middle of a two-lane highway. Another car had its side crumpled in. There was a brown-haired woman behind the wheel, and she did not look good. A man, likely the driver of the truck, was very shaken as he was looking at her— probably wondering (as I was), if she was still alive. Then, I noticed there was another car in the ditch, overturned and smoking. I sort of "drifted" over to the car and looked into the driver's window to see how this driver was doing. The driver was obviously dead. And that driver was me.

I knew instantly in that moment, that I was not looking at a metaphor, a message, or a symbol. At 1 PM, May 5, 1999, I died somewhere, in some universe, in some reality. And my body knew it. It was then that the many stories I had read about parallel realities and time loops became possible. There were obviously other "me's," and at least one of them had died right then. Perhaps it was a parallel me that died, perhaps it was my death from the previous loop through that I remembered. At the time the specifics of which scenario were truer was not that important. Later, I managed through journey to find out exactly where that happened. I have always wondered about the brown-haired woman in the car. I do not know if she lived or died in that other reality. And of course, I wonder, if like me, she also had an experience on May 5 in this reality.[25]

࿇

Looping and Parallel Realities

"Phil? Hey Phil! Phil Conners? Phil Conners, I thought that was you. Now hey, don't say you don't remember me, cuz I sure as heckfire remember you." (Ned Ryerson in *Groundhog Day*)

"What's outside of Pleasantville?" "I don't understand." "Outside of Pleasantville. What's at the end of main street?" "Oh Mary Sue, you should know the answer to that. The end of Main Street is just the beginning again." (Mary Sue "Jennifer" and Teacher in *Pleasantville*)

"They go past, go around the block, and come back. They just go around and around." (*The Truman Show*)

Some of the aforementioned movies, *Groundhog Day*, *Pleasantville* and *The Truman Show*, along with the novel *Replay* by Ken Grimwood, present that reality is a looping rerun of the past. In *Groundhog Day*, Phil Connors (Bill Murray) is forced to live the same day over and over. What makes it such a powerful movie, is that it reveals that the

---

25   Time loops, parallel realities and more are discussed in the Appendix.

process of waking to a deeper reality is not as smooth or full of joy as one might think. Connors goes from confused, to very confused, to incredibly detached (when he realizes nothing can happen to him), to narcissistic and manipulative, to suicidal, until finally to a deeper acceptance of living beyond his egoic wants. But it is the loop aspect in the movie I wish to explore here.

The movie *Pleasantville* carries the idea of a recurring loop, as the black and white episodes keep "repeating" over and over. David showed up and at first attempted to keep the story as accurate as he could, to keep the loop running. However, it was his sister Jennifer who first began to interact in a different way than the standard script. When the teenagers questioned why strange things were happening, something moved David to break from the loop, and be honest and answer. For the rest of the people not wanting a glimpse of something new their only response was to try and stop "what was happening."

Looping (recurring) time would mean that the time we experience moves along a scripted path until it reaches the end point, which of course, is the beginning again. "From the past, the present comes; and from the present, future goes." (Stobias) Some suggest this cannot be true, as a recurring loop of time would be quite boring. It seems for each person that there is an underlying set of conditions and circumstances that seem rather unchanging. Those basic characteristics stay—but there can be some variation on theme. A computer simulation has time begin when the game begins. The character does stuff and then they die or the game ends. Push new game and the character starts afresh right back at the beginning of "time" with the same original options available. In any computer game there are many variations of things that could happen, but there are also finite choices. If your game is not programmed for your character to fly or have dinner in Moscow, then those things cannot happen. If it is not in the game it is not an option, but they could go through the blue door millions of times. That is what I call a *Variable Finite Loop*.

Yet, a loop can have many variables, as a mobius strip helps to explain. It is a geometric model where you take a two-sided strip of paper, and rather than join the ends to make a single loop, you twist it once before joining. What gets created is the original two-sided, two-edged strip of paper—becomes one-sided and one-edged, two differing sides get looped into one whole. That multiple strips of paper could be twisted means there could be endless varieties existing within one single giant loop. Taking the mobius further in mathematics with cubes and planes, some believe that this is the geometric explanation for the interplay of space-time in the creation and maintaining of our reality. DNA itself is a form of spiral or loop, and actually looks more like a mobius, which may explain how it holds so much information, for it is turning two sides into one.

Like a DVD on my shelf, the history of the world is there happening again and again each time it is put in the DVD player. World war II is still happening, or as Karl Renz once told me at lunch, "this cup of tea I am having, I am drinking for eternity." This continual nature of time is the reason that the past or the future can be accessible from any moment, for the DVD is there and complete.

How could we know if we were in a loop? Because the whole underlying principle of a time loop is that people keep going through their scripted actions without ever knowing they are scripted. One could say, "We'll I never eat oranges, so I can choose to eat this orange, and that will prove I am not a scripted robot." But of course, that is illogical thinking. For in a time loop you would constantly be choosing to eat that orange, over and over, each time to prove to someone that you are not in a time loop. Even if one realizes they are part of a giant loop, does it make any difference? Can they expect things to be different due to that knowing? In *Groundhog Day*, the only time the rest of the town altered any behavior, was due to different actions from Phil Connors, the only one aware of the loop. Nothing he could do ever "awakened" the other people in the town to have the same realization. When the next day began, each person's "day script" returned to start and their unknowing loop began again.

In a bizarre coincidence, just as I was writing this chapter I received an email from a friend in Holland who had read an article that I wrote where I mentioned time loops briefly. He said that it gave him a sinking feeling as he remembered a part of an Ouspensky book that he read which claimed we live in a world that repeats itself. Just at that moment some odd event happened at the radio station that he was listening to and they wound up playing the same song over and over again for thirty minutes. How much of a confirmation did he need?

Another similar aspect is the concept of parallel universes. This is the idea that manifested consciousness wants "experiences" from the dream, thus needs ALL possible experiences. With only one life, a form would not be close to gaining maximum possible experiences as that individual form. There needs to not just be me, but billions of "me's," in billions of similar-but not the same-earth worlds. Whenever a decision point comes—turn left or right, drink this coffee or not, reality splits. There is one reality where I brushed my teeth this morning, and another reality where I didn't, while in others Napoleon won the battle of Waterloo. However, since conscious perception can only focus on one thing at once, you have come to believe that there is only this here and now. That there are parallel realities is mind-blowing enough, but even more so is the fact that these millions of seemingly separate realities may in fact be intermingling with each other, known as bleeding. There are thousands of accounts out there, the following is one of them.

A man became disappointed to find out that his favourite hardware store was closing. The entire block the store was on was being torn down to make way for a new parking lot. He went to the farewell party where the old customers came in for one last look around the shop, and to pick up the last of the tools the owner did not want to take after closing. The man sort of stayed away from that part of town, no longer enjoying seeing the parking lot where his favourite store used to be. Four or five years later he needed a tool for some work he was doing around the house, when he mentioned to his wife how disappointed he was that his old favourite store was no longer here. "What do you mean?" she asked. The man reminded his "obviously confused wife" about his store being torn down five years ago and him having to shop in other places. "What do you mean. I drove past there yesterday. There is no parking lot." Now somewhat upset at the impasse that was happening, the man to prove a point, drove with his wife to show her the parking lot. Of course, as you can guess, the store and the entire block was there. He went in. The same owner was still there. The man asked the owner, "didn't this all get torn down five years ago to build a parking lot." "What? No, no, nothing like that ever happened. Remember they talked about it one time but then decided against it. You should know that, you were in last week to buy a new cross cut saw." The man, of course, when looking at his home later found no cross cut saw. He was very confused. He was sure he had not hallucinated or dreamed the experience of the store closing. As he began to research, he found hundreds of others with similar strange stories. He began to speculate that somewhere along the way, two realities merged—he moved from a reality where the store was torn down, to a reality where the store never was. Of course, he began to wonder, well what else is now different in his world than was before? Why should we think that this reality is the only reality, and this self is our only self?

My good friend Dave had a similar story of stopping at a restaurant along the highway one night, with the cheapest prices and friendliest service he had ever experienced from an older German couple. He recalled that the entire thing was odd, and how he was the only one in what he called "the best restaurant deal ever." The next time along this highway, he again stopped to eat there. But now the place was closed and looked as if it had been abandoned for decades. So when did he actually stop at that cafe for dinner? The year he drove home, or 20 years in the past?

I know the idea that we may be living in a reality of looping time or one where there are parallel universes is very hard for the normal mind to fathom, but there may be clues this is the case. Even when people use the words fate, destiny, or déjà vu they are describing a tapping into a future moment that must have some sort of solid possibility to be accessed. It could be the transfer of information from a closely parallel reality where a similar but not identical event has occurred (as happened in my view of the car crash). But like the appearance of David in *Pleasantville*, Tech Support guy in *Vanilla Sky*, or Sylvia in the *Truman Show* shows guidance is available and can come unexpectedly, to lift the needle up off the looping record and get a glimpse of reality as it actually is. This takes us also back to Rose who claims we are all robots, and there is not much we can do, except use some of the free energy we have available to go looking for "who or what" programmed us.

❧

"Groundhog Day so intrigued me because the first book I read the day after I came out of the canyon was Ken Grimwood's Replay. The movie was based on that book—except in the novel, the main character is repeating an entire 25-year section of his life and not just a single day. Well written and very philosophic, it has some interesting ideas in it about awakening. Read the novel to look into this stuff."

"So how does knowing any of that help me?"

"Well, you don't know it. You've simply heard some crazy stories from your crazy friend. Even if you believe me somewhat, it is still only a possibility in your world. You can't know something like this unless you know it. Until you have experiences yourself, where standard reality no longer behaves in the accustomed way, it's all just an idea. Of course, one part of this work is just to know the truth of things—if reality is solid. Is it a mirage, or a dream, or whatnot? In my case, once I got that bit of understanding, I could become far more confused at times. During other times, though, I felt far more at ease. Like anything, there is a give and take for a long while with information of this nature. It took years to even start to understand

Castaneda's Tonal-Nagual message.[26] It means that reality is far more creative than we think."

"So like we can control it, make it do what we want?"

"Kind of. The problem is one other side of the equation that generally halts seekers even when they see the world is dream-like. They miss a key element of what that means about themselves. It is the most important part of what life is a dream means.

"And that is?"

"Best I ever heard say it was a guy named Gary Harmon. If you accept that all of this is an illusion, without including yourself, you have made the classic spiritual mistake."

---

26   See appendix.

Chapter 8

THE GAP BETWEEN

Ancient Manifestation

"Can a man choose his future? If, instead of throwing fits in a struggle to obtain, a man just relaxes and lets things happen, he will acquire more things in life. But letting things happen will only work for so long. We must have intricate scheduling and organization." (Richard Rose)

I am out on the deck of Anders' house, looking out at... well, there is not that much to look at. Merely a standard small-town yard, trees and fence. But it is a calm and peaceful setting.

I am sitting at the kitchen table. Anders, Liv and I are finishing up our breakfast and our tea. I am entertaining thoughts about the stone circles we would soon be getting in the car to go visit. For some co-incidental reason Liv asks me if co-incidental has ever happened to me.

"All the time," I respond.

"I mean big stuff."

"All the time," I respond again.

"Can you give me an example?"

I recount the experience of a research trip to Mexico. On the second evening, Roberto—a friend of a friend in Canada—had taken me out to dinner in Mexico City. After dinner, he wanted to show me a "real Mexican bar" in the southern part of the city. It was more or less what I would expect from a bar back in Canada—except everyone spoke Spanish and most of the beers were Coronas. Then I happened to notice a group of about seven girls off to my right. I gazed at a short, cute brunette. She looked at me, then walked right over and said, in accented English, "You live in Toronto, right?"

Stunned for a second, I replied, "Well I used to. I just moved to Calgary last year. Why?"

"I studied for a year in Toronto in 1996, and you look really familiar to me." After a short discussion she revealed that she liked to spend time at Toronto's comedy clubs. "Right, *The Laugh Resort*," she snapped her fingers. "That's where I know you from. You're the comedian...you do impressions."

Suddenly, I was even more stunned. What were the odds of such a meeting? To go to a far-off country, away from any tourists, and meet someone who knew me from watching me at a comedy club years before? It was so strange. We spent the evening talking, and I told her more of why I was in Mexico—revealing that Teotihuacan was my next visit. She left briefly to phone her mother, who was a history teacher at a local high school. When she returned, I was told that her mother and father wanted to take me to Teotihuacan tomorrow, rather than my taking a bus as planned. So back I went to her house. There, her family looked after me for three days. They took me to the main sites around Mexico City before I headed eastward towards Palenque. I did my best at the time to thank Yuri and the Munoz family for all their generosity—but I thank them a second time by sharing this story.

ॐ

"See what I mean Liv? It was really odd. On that same three-week trip to the Mexican Mayan sites, I had probably four more experiences as strange as that one. There is the word "synchronicity" However, when you experience the effects of it, it is far more than just a term coined by Carl Jung."

"Carl Jung developed synchronicity?" asks Anders.

"Well the name anyway. Came about after a session with a patient, his office window, and the appearance of a scarab beetle while working with a patient telling a dream about a piece of scarab jewelry. The experience got him thinking about an interconnected universe far beyond the small way we tend to think of it. He came up with the term and it stuck. Jung of course was more than just a brilliant founder of psychology, he was a true alchemist in his own right, experimenting on himself. Much of what he found about the mind and reality became a part of his psychology books."

Basically, synchronicity is a big word that means co-incidence—occurrences that seem too strange, too "set up" to be random. Generally, most just ignore these happenings, finding a logical explanation for the oddity. Synchronicity points to a deeper connection to the fabric of the dream. The more one begins to realize that life on earth is like a play or movie, there comes a recognition that something beyond is always giving our character messages about what to do and where to go next. "Stage directions" is another way of expressing it. If the dream needs you to be somewhere or meet someone (pertinent to the movie called *life on the planet earth*), not only will it put you in that place, but if you can be still and shut up long enough, will also tell you why. If we need to read a particular book, it falls off the shelf at the library. If we need to talk to someone, they keep showing up all over the place. One women I knew, Candice, never had to call me long distance, she just had to think about me and I called her the next day. The universe is the cosmic director and we are its actors, and it wants the next scene shot without interference. But we all know about the ego of actors, and how they want the scene and script to be different to make themselves more important.

The challenge is to be aware of the omens while they are happening. They are much easier to see after the fact, but that could be too late to do anything about them. It is still an in the dream thing, but what is behind the omen is outside of the cave. To notice the spirit, what Castaneda called the abstract, one must pay attention for we never know when omens or signs will come. It is like a friend telling you they got a small part in a movie, but won't tell you where. To find "them" you have to closely watch the whole movie. If you go to the bathroom, you might miss it. This connecting with the spirit requires our intent to be alert. The more awareness, the more co-incidences we will catch, thus it will seem like there are more happening. This is not true of course, the same amount is always occurring, we are just more aware of them. We must treat the awake world like the dream world to really catch them.

Nothing is random. In the ancient past, synchronicity was "the gods moving our lives around"—it was obvious. The fact that it is no longer obvious, that books and studies must be done on the topic, should show just how far humans have fallen. It is the one area where the idea of "being in the now" has value. After seeing an omen, one must be in no hurry for it to play out. We have to see them, and then have the trust in the spirit to just follow them and see where they lead, like Alice following the white rabbit.

> "Synchronicity is not about acquiring material possessions or fulfilling personal desires. It will always guide you to what you need to do, not what you think you need." (Eddie Traversa)

While one is still asleep in the dream, they look for more and more co-incidences to help them out. Once awake, it's shown that all there is, is co-incidence, and to see the patterns and flow with them. We may not like some things the universe has in store for us, but our number one preference should always be what the universe wants. You don't have to like it or understand it, but it is not happening randomly. It points out something deeper. Accidents or illnesses are the way the universe gets our attention. It fits some larger whole, like a hologram, thus the moment you begin to really see what is happening, you can start to make some good guesses as to what is coming. You also see certain things that would be impossible, otherwise. If you were supposed to run a marathon tomorrow, and it was important for the universe that you do that, you couldn't get sick. It would be impossible because it wouldn't fit in with the universe's wants. Once that gets grasped, your interaction with reality changes totally.

Astrology, tarot cards or the I Ching, are helpful in the dream (to tap you into a part of this wholeness and see a bit of the fabric more clearly), but they become less important when you see more of the totality for yourself. Thus, you have a sort of inner Tarot or I Ching to call on. This does not mean you will live "happy ever after." There is no rule that says an awake person cannot be in pain or difficulty, or they must always get what they want. However, everything that does happen will happen for a very clear reason. It comes to the extent that you BECOME that which you have realized. Thus, you cannot think your way or practice into it, you become it.

Not only is synchronicity amazing, but if you walk into it while it is occurring, it is the place where magic happens. It is in this strangely diverse area where between-ness is found—a more optimal way that humans are supposed to function.

❧

Manifesting

I really don't have much of an understanding of all the vast areas that Rose presents with the term between-ness. But I do see it touches on the miracles and magic that people like shamans can perform. It also refers to our deep intuitive ability, access to other dimensions, and the ability to manifest both objects and situations into reality. This is not about making our egoic desires come true—between-ness is something much greater. The idea of fulfilling our desires is what gets in the way of this unfolding. It is an unfolding which comes when we have walked into a state of surrender to the way things are, as opposed to the way our egoic structures want them to be. Yet being in this state of flow or surrender is not simply a complete acceptance of things in our mundane world. Instead, there is a special quality of guidance, or an alignment, that makes things happen as they are supposed to happen. "You fear that if you let go, you will crash on the sides of the bank, or everything will fall apart, but you will find that everything keeps moving as it should, even better than you expected if you were still trying to control it." (Richard Rose). The real act of manifestation is not to be conjuring objects, but to be continually manifesting ourselves in each and every moment.

The three of us are in the car. Anders is driving, Liv is in the passenger seat. We are still talking about co-incidences and the like. The Liv asks, "So you were really a comedian? Like for real." I nod. "But you're not funny."

"Maybe a lot of my audiences thought the same way." We all laugh. "Actually that is not true, my audiences found me very entertaining. That was a big part of my problem."

"Being funny for a comedian is a problem. Is that why you stopped."

Ohh, nice one. Partially to be a comedian your mind has to work a certain way, you have to see the world and find something wrong, stupid, painful- then find a way to spin it around to reveal it from the side rather than head on. As I focused more on research and inner observation, a lot of that kind of mind had to be put aside. It is a good mind for being a comedian but not digging into the self."

"You should have just followed the Secret."

Liv was referring to the bestseller book from a number of years earlier. "Did it work for you?"

"No. Never got anything I wanted."

"While there are noteworthy elements at the core in a book like The Secret, such works mostly have as their foundation very egoic aims. They are based on self-importance and greed, continually promising you everything that your little heart desires. You're operating in consumer mode, and someone is telling you how to get more. Your greed helped to fuel the greed of the people who wrote that $24 book. That very self-importance is what is getting in the way of Intent, not helping it. Manifestation happens all the time—seemingly without any involvement on our part. The best way is to allow the universe to do its thing with as little input or demands as possible—until we know for sure what truly really want."

"You're saying I don't know what I want?"

"Probably not. You only think that you do. Or maybe you do know, but are not following that pathway. That was the problem of my audiences really enjoying my comedy I was referring to. I really did not like to be a comedian on stage. I did like the crowd and the, I guess you could call it, drug high of a great show. But my only reason for doing it was to get myself a TV show. That was my authentic desire. Being a comedian was not. I figured doing one would lead to the other. It didn't."

"Because you had to just forget the comedy and do the TV stuff?"

"Not so much. Comedy could have been the road, but then I had to be fully authentic in my comedy. Find the type that was right for me, and at the same time would showcase why I was good for TV. That is not how it turned out. I had suffered quite hard after my father had stolen all of my money, and comedy was basically paying for my food every week. So I started crafting material that would make audiences laugh, get me more gigs and more money. But was never what I authentically wanted to perform, or which would have showcased me better to TV."

"You can get what you want?"

"In one sense, yes. You can get what you want in the dream. However, the weird thing is that what you think you want, is not really what YOU want. Thus, this opposing dynamic sets up a gigantic conflict. Instead: Learn what the universe wants, then want that exclusively. And lo and behold, you will find that everything runs much smoother. When you cut yourself, you really need a band aid—not a million dollars or a snowmobile. If you were caught in a blizzard in the Northwest Territories, then maybe there would be a desire and need for a snowmobile. The difference between authentic and inauthentic desires—THAT is what needs to be grasped. With the ego in control, all one can think about is wanting bigger and better: houses, cars, or boobs. For every step we take during our awakening, many inauthentic needs simply won't survive within us. The authentic desires are not about getting more stuff, or strengthening our image—but about becoming simpler and deeper. My want to be a comedian was a non-genuine desire, as opposed to having a TV show where I could really entertain. That was genuine. One was an egoic want for the roar of the crowd, the other a natural want for something much deeper."

While we were children, we all took very seriously all the tiny things that supposedly had huge effects on the world around us. We tried to keep illness away by jumping over cracks in the sidewalk. As we got older, we wanted to sit in a lucky chair, carry a charm, or not wear the red shirt on a date because it was bad luck. It's not really nonsense, for something inside is telling us that we have a way to tap into the universe. We simply don't know how to do it. We experiment with things that might give us an edge. Anything that seems to have worked in the past, our mind convinces us that we try again—just in case it is factor which brings about the luck. However, any supposed edge that we find will only have limited results. That is because we are not totally clear or cognizant when it comes to all the factors.

"So is this something we can control?" Anders wonders.

"In one sense, we intend everything that happens in our reality—but it is tied to what we and others believe. If you don't believe something is possible, even at a subconscious level, then most likely it's not possible. That is why extreme cases of manifesting are so rare. Healers can stop bleeding, but not re-attach a leg. It may have less to do with the healer's power—but rather, the intent of the other person involved. The mountain must believe it can be moved, as the saying goes. A miracle is nothing more than overcoming a locked view of reality, by both self and by those who are around. The more possibility one perceives, the more intent flows. Consequently—the more likelihood inherent that something miraculous happens. For example, the New Testament claimed Christ performed miracles, but not in his hometown. His faith was no match for the "lack of faith" of those who he grew up with. To them, he was still the dumb carpenter's kid who threw the ball against the wall and kept them up all night. Faith's limitations are the boxes people have—compartments which they put around everything. That, to me, is a shaman's main gift. A shaman opens someone's mind—or an entire group—up to the power of possibility. Part of the reason for the ritual they perform is to shift the mind from a state of doubt into one of possibility. Once that occurs, you could say that they step out of the way and allow the between-ness to work its magic."

"So between-ness is magic?"

"It is an aspect of it, one with a truly interactive quality. All of the current books and workshops about manifesting your desires and getting what you want are but a shadow. They present hardly a whiff of what someone who has stepped up the ladder beyond their mind can touch. The workshops are a "how-to book" for the asleep, which allow them to, occasionally, pretend that they are awake. But the asleep do not need to play pretend. What they need is to reach the awake state."

This thing of between-ness is rather difficult to understand. It is even more difficult to write about or share. I was rather lost in it myself until an Australian friend, Eddie Traversa, explained between-ness in excellent detail. He told me that between-ness generally happens within our mind without us even noticing. But if you look for it, what you find is that it is an action, where a thought or wish occurs, and has some reason in that moment. That thought stays only for a second in a gap or space in what we consider normal thought, but then is let go because there is no need for it to happen.

It is very hard to explain in words. But the thought comes and holds a second, and then seems to vanish to the wind. That is, until something occurs—and we then remember: "Yes, I did think about that about two days ago." For me, I have a between-ness when it comes to finding movies for some reason. I just think of a movie that I really want to see, coupled with having an honest desire for seeing it. Then, *voila*. The next day, there it is for sale in some bargain bin. Or is suddenly playing on late-night television. Why movies? I have no idea. But somehow, the secret of between-ness is present there.

A big element to it is the not wanting. The wish can come or go and either result is fine. Any egoic attempts such as positive thinking, visualization, trying to create one's reality are constrained to a limited effectiveness, for they have the ego as part of their foundation of action. Ego wants and needs what it is "wanting". Thus, by default, it is in duality and will call forth its opposite—which will stop the process. You cannot describe up, without also having a description of down. Between-ness begins to work when there are no concepts and no dual natures. It only blooms when "a thought that is not a thought" comes from a non-dual source—and is then quickly forgotten.

"The greatest prayer you can say in your life is thank you."
(Meister Eckhart)

Maybe a short discussion on prayer might help the topic. Prayer is an element of manifestation. If one can open up the hood of prayer, it is possible to get a good look at how it's motor, so to speak, has been built.

"But you can't even change the windshield washer fluid in your car," Anders laughs.

"True. However, I can pray for help, and be thankful when it arrives. Those are two keys: the opening for help, and the thanks and gratitude before it even arrives." Which is very little compared to the medicine people I have met. They are prayer experts and I am just a novice, at best.

Learn to know what the universe wants by learning to listen to what is inside yourself; this core ideal is the basis for what is truly "prayer". Prayer is ultimate selfless manifestation. The reality, however, is that prayer as normally taught is as if the people using it were weak children. Kids who need to ask some greater authority for blessings, (the same as asking dad for the keys to the car). We only get the keys if this higher power likes us. That is what people believe. As a result, they do all sorts of things to try and please the puppeteer, with the hopes he will pull the strings for them in a way that makes them happier. Love and compassion are two powerful elements of human existence—when done selflessly. Yet much of what is presented as "love" is no more than people's way of bargaining with the puppeteer. "Look how nice I have become!" they say. "So now you have to give me all the stuff I want and make sure that I am always happy". It is another reason to really examine how you pray, why you do it, what you think you will get from it, and how you believe it works when it does. Such examination can open up a great understanding for how the dream actually operates.

Basic prayer—as described above—works. But only to a degree.

That is because it is adding an emotional intent to something we focus on. Believe strongly enough that Jesus, Buddha, the great spirit, Krishna, Elvis, or even a stapler will heal—something will generally happen. We can believe it was Jesus or Elvis that saved us. However, that object was just a focus point for our intent; something to aim the power of our emotions upon. There are amazing results that can be found from faith and prayer all over the world. The catch is this: why doesn't it work all the time? There were times when faith was equally strong, and yet there was no result.

The problem has to do with how we understand the universe. Most prayer is specific: I want "x" or make "y" happen instead of "z". This means the prayer itself is limiting. We put a box around possibility, as only "x" is considered acceptable—or "y" must be the event that takes place. Secondly, normal prayer is limiting by default because of the belief that the power being drawn from is outside of ourselves. Being dispensed or granted by some supernatural being. Our petition can become a bartering with what we believe to be some outside force. By default, this sets up a dynamic where the element prayed for requires a supernatural 'other' to dispense or grant it.

I never really paid much attention to the idea of prayer until I began to spend time with my new Native medicine friends. Almost every ceremony they performed had prayer as a main activity, and they told me the first thing I had to learn to be of service was to learn how to pray. It took some time to learn how different Native prayer is. It is not about asking for something, "please heal my sister". Rather, to pray their way—was to say, "thank you". For example, "Thank you for the help you will bring to my sister". It is quite a twist. This is not putting a box around this, only asking for help. In fact, they are not even specifically asking for the sick sister to be healed—simply helped. Perhaps being well is helping, but perhaps it is not. Thus, an entire spectrum of possibility is being tapped into utilizing this type of prayer. Secondly, they are not even really asking, but instead saying thank you—thereby acknowledging that what was asked for is already happening. There is no longer any doubt involved when it comes to the inevitable arrival of what was prayed on. One time, I was out in the forest with my Ojibway teacher Dennis. I was leaving a tobacco offering by a tree for a friend of mine. After I left the offering, he reminded me, "Now that you have left the tobacco -never think of this wish again. This is done and is happening. Forget it." I was being taught the basic principles of between-ness without realizing how deep such a teaching truly was. Everything Eddie Traversa later told me in the course of an hour, Dennis has completely explained in two sentences.

Richard Rose said, "You can move mountains, but the mountains have to agree they should be moved." By doing so he is touching on something with a much bigger implication: in other words, how things happen and just importantly—how they don't happen. We rarely take the time to take a peek into what the objects want before attempting to impose any of our wants onto them. The same is true when it comes to the dream itself. Why should we think that my wishes for a tree, fish, backyard deck, or whatnot should be greater than their own wants? What do they actually wish? Thus, it seems one key part of the manifestation side of between-ness is learning a trick. And that is the trick of getting in touch with whatever external element it is we wish to influence, and then see how it feels about it. If they agree with us, then the manifestation or change will be simple and almost instantaneous. If they are opposed, then we are in a struggle with it. Additionally, we will likely drain ourselves of energy by trying to move a mountain that has no interest in budging.

As long as we think that we (i.e., an individual person, or a group of people—or even the whole planet) are in control of things, then we will be frustrated time and again. That is because there is a master plan when it comes to what is going on here. We want to see all the possibilities available in the dream, and then help to move the dream specifically toward a particular one. You are not forcing an outcome, but helping to manifest a conclusion that is already there. Black magic is forcing the dream to the extremes when it comes to possibilities, solely for that person's own benefit. Thus, black magic can create some very rare prospects. However, it will also by default attract certain kinds of entities to help the black magic itself occur. The entities feed on the energy of those actions and demand a toll (more energy) for what they leveraged. These entities keep demanding rituals so that they continue to keep feeding. In stark contrast, between-ness is about the power of the mind, it is magical, and it remains available to all at all times—if one becomes interested enough merely to look.

It can be started at any place one is on the spiritual path. Only the more Awake one becomes (i.e. the less that egoic wants and fears clog up our basic functioning) the greater the simplicity when it comes to working with these elements. An advanced step on the path is when one realizes that they do not need an outside "authority" to focus their prayer on. The only object required is their own intent, for they see it was really the thing which was doing the manifesting all along. This is not about wishing for things to be different—but rather, merging with the way that things are. The more that this happens, the more one is in a flow—i.e., Morpheus walking effortlessly on the street. Shamans cultivate the interest to manifest only one thing: harmony/balance. They look for what is out of balance with the basic structure of the dream, and then realign it. That is the same prescription whether what is out of balance is the self, a person, a village or the earth. However, creating balance and harmony may not always be what you think it is. Many times, harmony can only come from conflict. Sometimes something must be torn down for another thing to be built. As a result, merely saying that disharmony is bad, and "I" have to fix everything, is not seeing the full picture.

Instead of buying $50 books that promise to make you rich, control other people or alter the weather—instead start by first examining how the dream works. Become a student of the dream world, what it is, and what it means to be in balance. Balance, though, also means being in the mid-point between everything—for in this gap is where the power lies. Understanding the force in the middle of two magnets, for instance, is tantamount to glimpsing the workings of the human mind working a high level of proficiency. This ability to use the middle of any two poles of duality is not just about how to generate experiences in the dream. It is also the way to take a step up the spiritual ladder. For in this mid-point (the gap, as Eddie Traversa called it) is where real power is found.

℅

Energy and Tension

"Brotherhood and peace on Earth are not good (for attainment). Strife and conflict are...Continuing to bang your head against the wall. This prepares you to bang your head against bigger and bigger walls. If you need entertainment or escape, you are asleep." (Richard Rose)

Normally people try to use this idea of between-ness to "make things manifest for me." They don't take things to the next level to see how it could be used in our quest to know the Self. And to understand this is to understand another force about between-ness: tension.

If you place two equal magnets across from each other, at the exact mid-point between the two is a space where a piece of metal can indefinitely be suspended. It is the tension, applied from both sides equally and simultaneously by the magnets, that creates the powerful mid-point. It is this middle ground that Rose was referring to with between-ness. Tension is a main power of the spiritual path. One does not advance by learning how to be happier, but how to have more tension applied, at a level that is not unbearable, so we don't crack—and then using the energy of the middle to move one step up the ladder. Too much tension and we will get ripped apart, too little and there is no energy in the gap. Tension can only come from some sort of polarity. One magnet produces no between-ness. It is good to note that in front of Egyptian temples were always mirrored obelisks, and often paired sphinxes—that one would walk between—as if the act of being between these power objects would do something to our body, mind, and consciousness.

"The consideration of any two opposites creates a third middle force, which may have nothing to do in relation to either...enlightenment is the experience of nothingness and everything simultaneously. The uncompromisable point in the center between opposites leads to a dead stop, this tension creating the third force." (Richard Rose)

ɞ

This use of between-ness in our spiritual path requires using the tension, but not being tense. We must learn to live without the dream, yet at the same time to personally identify with it. We get to the midpoint between tension and no-tension. To do this we learn to live in the gap between everything: knowing and unknowing; longing and emptiness; life and death; hope and despair. This is not as easy as it sounds, as generally we are always egoically pulled to one of the two opposites and thus lose our place in the middle. Some create small aspects of no tension—with alcohol, songs, mantras—things that occupy the mind, and allows a gap of freedom for something else to happen. When we can get the mind to stop moving from one the another extreme, we are left with something like the calm eye of the raging hurricane.

This again may be the entire reason for religious and shamanic rituals, chanting, exercises, dancing and what not—all to occupy the conscious mind, which allows a space for a deeper non-ego place of power to be connected to. The problem is that one cannot focus too much on the songs or mantras, or there will be no gap, only control by the external ritual. Instead of taking one drink to be calm when asking the pretty girl out, we get drawn to take eight and wind up embarrassing ourself. We use our ritual or practice as a doorway, not for peace of mind but instead to create a clear central point.

An article by Bart Marshall, "Ultimate Between-ness," reminds that there is an important aspect of working with our intent. By intent we mean what the egoic mind is thinking and moving towards. And we want to have that part of it as clear as we possibly can, to avoid double negatives. "I don't want to feel bad," automatically introduces feeling bad. Saying "I want to feel well," introduces the focused direction. Hypnotist Derren Brown showed that if he wants someone to forget their phone number, he asks them "try to remember your phone number." By using the word try, he indicates something we are doing but not completing, hence their mind goes blank. This subtle word play is going on continually. How often does a mother say to a child, "don't fall out of the tree," and the child soon falls, for the idea "fall out of the tree" was entered into the child's mind instead of "stay safe while you play." It looks simple, but this use of words—internally and externally, seems to have a great effect on the reality we experience around us.

The wording used to structure the intention is important. The desires of the universe, our egoic wants, and all the subconscious desires and fears—intermingle into a giant soup and create the experience we are having. But as mentioned, to really work we have to focus on something we want, but also not-want it at the same time. We would like an ice cream cone, but are totally fine without it—but should the cone appear, we will show great gratitude for its appearance. This not wanting has to come from a deeper place— not from the mind itself, where the modern manifestation gimmicks out there trap people—because they are focusing only on the want not the being ok if the want never manifests. Thus, the manifesting becomes greedy, and that stops the process.

I should make a short comment on the use of energy in between-ness. Any time you put the mind under mental tension (really think on a problem or focus on something mentally) there is an increase in body energy that can come. However, the results of that tension are not manifested until the tension subsides, or explodes by its own force. Satori itself is claimed to occur as a result of the explosion or going over the top—a very traumatic result of great tension placed on the mind. Art Ticknor described awakening as the moment our internal transistor finally shorts itself out. It can only short out due to energy sent there that overloads it. For most it comes as a trauma—where the transistor is blown in one shot, or can happen gradually over 20-30 years of seeking (as happened in Art's case). While physical energy can be projected from the body and can affect the environment and even heal others, mental energy can also be projected—called transmission. Even the lesser forms of this (esp, telepathy, astral projection) come from the use of this mental energy. This stored energy can be harnessed—as happens in extreme situations, the mother lifting a car off her son, and afterwards the body is not drained at all. Transmission involves routing this energy from physical to mental and projecting it. This part of the topic is quite a challenging one, and should you be interested in learning more about transmission, I suggest you contact one of the Tat Foundation members who spent time around Rose

I will leave you with a final clue about transmission, and that involves healing. Generally, a healer heals by projecting their own stored energy to the patient. It may look like they are giving acupuncture needles, massage, dream therapy or counseling, but a part of the healer's energy is being put into the package (needles, conversation) and is going to the patient which helps give them a boost. When done at a high level, Rose called this zapping, and in a short period of time (a few years) will wear out the healer. At a low level it will keep the curer tired. Rose warned his students about going out to do healing work with troubled people because there can be a great drain of one's energy from the procedure. Rose claimed that healing has to come from the individual by their correcting their inner state, or by dealing with an old trauma or situation that has caused the system to become unbalanced. He is not saying don't help, just not to help those who have no interest in real inner transformation (which is most everyone), or we will weaken ourselves while the patient didn't transform.

A few have learned the greater healing secret of how work with energy similar to Transmission, and do not project their own energy to the patient. This opens a doorway of sorts. As such the healer never gets drained from their work. Nor is this healer needing the patient to get well, they just are there in the mid-point of the tension, and from the eye interact with the hurricane. I leave that with you to ponder on your own. There are a few of these out there, but they are very rare to come across. The natives that I know who do similar things, even when it seems like they are smoking a prayer with a pipe, mixing herbs, or meeting in the sweat lodge—are not so much asking for the spirits to fix someone, but for the spirits to come to show the person what they need to do to fix themselves. The idea is give the person back their power through knowledge of self, which will lead to healing knowledge that will last a lifetime. Part of that comes not from being a healer as a business (which halts possibility) and instead to be a healer just to be a healer. This bringing money into the temple is one of modern spirituality's biggest ignored topics, saying that help and healing should be free but then charging a big amount of money to get the so-called free help. Even the energetic exchange theory that says to get something of value you have to pay for it, does not take much examination to see that it is bullshit. Anything you have of true value you never had to pay for. To be a healer and not lose one's healing power is a challenge few take seriously.[27]

"I don't believe in patching tires, I believe in removing nails from the highway." (Richard Rose)

᠅

Nature

"I have learned more from nature than I have from books." (Bernard of Clairvaux, monk connected to the Knight's Templar)

Now I am resting comfortably, currently up against one of the 11 massive rocks that make up an ancient stone circle. There are three other circles like this here, at this place. In fact, both Anders and Liv have found their own circle to sit calmly in. These terrific stone structures exist all over Scandinavia, but are mostly ignored by the local populations, who have believed the fairy tales they are told in school that these circles are Viking grave sites. Just like the misinterpretation

---

27 A further examination of healing can be found in my Additional Material.

presented about Egyptian pyramids being created for the burial of
a dead king in Egypt, so too has this northern European place of
power been twisted away from its true function. While there are
burials in some areas around the circles, those came long after the
stones were originally in use, like the burials which happened around
great cathedrals. These circles were one of the human race's earliest
temples. They were places to heal, balance, connect with the heavens,
or to get answers. Built with giant rocks—these small boulders were
positioned through sacred geometry to form geometric patterns and
astrological alignments. The stones themselves were also purposely
shaped, to allow each one to create the exact sound and frequency
that the builders wanted. In short, these are some of the earth's great
power places—and amazingly, they are usually left vacant. Swedes
and Norwegians spend large amounts of money to travel to England
to see Stonehenge and Avebury, not realizing that they have similar
structures right in their own backyards.[28]

I treat each stone circle that I find the same way I was taught
to approach and interact with a Native Indian medicine wheel, for
essentially, they are no different. Both are teaching tools of wisdom
placed in circular geometric patterns that can be read and accessed
if one takes the time to learn how to do so. While the stone circle I
am now in could have been considered a distinct place of religious
or spiritual importance by the original builders, it is truthfully beyond

---

28   Actually, Stonehenge is now a dead site. Few know that the site was completely
dismantled 3 times in the 1900's, the last in 1958. All the stones were removed,
trucked away, the site dug up, then the stones (or at least similar looking
stones) were brought back and cemented into place. Yes, that is right they
were cemented into place, and no one in fact can be sure that the location
of the stones is in the exact correct spot. Even a few millimeters off could
mean that the alignments in the sky they related to can no longer be verified.
This certainly explained why in 2010 when I first visited, I was shocked to feel
almost no energy at all at this site. Then a year later I learned about this and
it was understood. If you want to experience a stone circle go to Avebury, it
has the energy of an Ancient Egyptian site. Or of course come find me in
Scandinavia, there are lots of high energy stones here to be visited.

all those things. This is a vortex point where the earth and sky, matter and spirit—even life and death—could be bridged. Given this is a chapter about between-ness, one could say on a simple scale that sites like this stone circle create a gap in most everything. Thus, by joining the gap, we open to the magical essence of the universe. One way to tap into this essence is to learn how to merge with is the force of nature.

Medieval alchemists suggested that learning to appreciate nature is one of the primary tasks in this field. I was taught to never pick a flower or even take a stone without first learning how to ask if that object of nature wants to come with me. I also discovered how to leave an offering of thanks if it does. We would ask a human being if they wanted to come and visit our homes, so why should I not do the same with a rock? This concept of equaling ourselves with all aspects of nature begins a process of lessening the importance we place on the human self. By being in connection with nature, we allow our bodies and our minds to be recharged by the energy that still exists in the natural world. It is a type of energy that has nearly by destroyed in modern cities. We can potentially soak up even more in the places described as power spots. It is not about worshiping nature—the natural world, too, answers to something. Instead, it is about learning to work with nature, and not against it.

The ancient tribal goal was for every member of the community to get to the "enough" point—it was not a climate of more for some and less for others. Tribal life did not result in habits that depleted the planet, but fostered practices that stayed in balance with it. The tribe members lived in groups where each human had a role and responsibility. There was no need for commerce or money; people were in life together, and no one needed to make a profit off someone else. They knew that if they did not have fresh water or air, it would not matter how many riches they acquired. This system maintained a livable planet for hundreds of thousands of years. It wasn't perfect or idyllic, but it was long-term sustainable. As Rose suggested, if people were to start to live in a balanced and inter-dependent way with nature, many of our own (and the world's) problems would be solved.

> "We look out the window at this point and observe the world as a sorrowful slaughterhouse, a place of blood and carnage...Most people are content to remain fertilizer in the organic parade of life, while imagining cosmic importance to their daily drama..." (Richard Rose and John Kent)

Nature on one hand is one of the most beautiful elements of the dream. Without question my cat is a true Zen-master. I need no other teacher, just her, stretched out beside me, wondering why I want to do anything else but stretch out with her. But nature is also something else, the side people don't want to see. People present their views on the meaning of life yet continue to play games of make believe without ever asking honest questions about any of it. Honesty reveals that the only thing that can be proved about the human condition (and all of nature) is that we are here to reproduce prior to death, and then we become fertilizer afterwards, either for the earth or another creature. Rose asked us to think about how many worms must die this second in order to feed all the birds in the world. And what does a worm feel when it dies? Why set up such a system? Perhaps God loves us the same way we love cattle—i.e. that we can be milked and eaten. To assume that the world exists for our education or growth or enjoyment is an ego-centered presumption that still fails to determine WHO is growing, experiencing, or enjoying. We all get sold a fairy tale about how wonderful this place is. However, when we look closely, all we see is a system designed to create carnage.

༄

Power

"Everything we do, everything we are, rests on our personal power. If we have enough, one word uttered might be sufficient to change the course of our lives. But if we don't have enough personal power the most magnificent piece of wisdom can be revealed to us, and that revelation won't make a damn bit of difference." (Carlos Castaneda)

We have been at the stones for about an hour. Anders and Liv are standing, and currently walking around the one with the largest stones. I am sitting comfortably in a small circle about 30 feet away. That is when I notice an older woman, with a long walking stick, come trudging out of the forest towards the large circle. She is walking a bit oddly, and I sit carefully and watch her. She stops to have a conversation with Anders and Liv. Of course at first I figure that since they would be taking in Swedish there was no need for me to go over and slow down the conversation.

But I began to contemplate more carefully. I have been at this set of stones 5 or 6 times, and I have only ever once seen a young couple come by for a short look, than turn around and go back to their car. This woman was different. Very different. And I also began to notice that she was not someone out for a walk in the woods. She was the woods. She was Power.

☙

Power spots are places on the earth, that due to their positioning, cause an intensification of energy. The earth has energy fields that turn it into a giant magnetic grid. These fields generally run in straight lines (ley lines to the English) and where they cross each other the main power points can be found. Plato once drew a map of the earth that showed it as a giant crystal ball comprised of diagonal pieces to show how these earth lines run, it resembled a modern soccer ball—which may be storing this information of exactly how the earth is set up. Our body mirrors this with what Chinese medicine calls meridians. Where these meridians cross are the acupuncture points used to break up blocks, move energy, or heal various seemingly disconnected parts of the body. Power places are the acupuncture points of the earth. Some of the big ones are easy to spot—ancient sites like Machu Piccu or the Giza Pyramids were built on them. When the Christians took over an area, they tore down the ancient sites and built their own church. Most medieval churches in Europe run in straight lines, as they follow the old power layouts. Some power spots are just a simple place in nature that is completely unnoticeable until you stand or sit on it. Power spots are places where we can recharge, stop our mind, find an answer to a problem, or just relax. One of the amazing things these places can do is to push our attention into the other world of Dreaming. You might say they are doorways to jump realities.[29]

℃

Power will make special appearances for us by manifesting through what are sometimes called allies. An ally is "a power that a man can bring into his life to help him, advise him, and give him the strength to perform acts—whether big or small, right or wrong. An ally is an indispensable aid to knowing." (Carlos Castaneda) The problem is

---

29   Natural power spots (without ancient structures) are much easier to adapt with and merge with for they are still at the original level of the earth meridians of energy. Be sure the first few times you go to just relax there so "it" can get used to you, and for the body to attune to the higher energy. Once you have spent enough time where you and the spot become "friends," you carry that spot with you always. You do not have to go back to the place physically to be there, you can go in your dreaming- however as friends, if the spot needs your help for something, it will come and ask for help in your dreaming as well. Power spots are a place of mutual giving. Whenever you come back physically you will have to look after the place in some way, either by cleaning it up, or just seeing what gifts you can bring for the area.

that there are many types of ally. Alcohol or drugs can be an ally, for it can get some to perform acts that they normally don't. So too can the words of a book, a good friend, or a nonphysical being. As such one must understand who or what we have brought into our lives as our allies and see if they come from a space that helps us or hinders us—for many allies (such as drugs) ask a price in return for helping us. We must see if the price we are forced to pay is worth what we are getting back.

When power manifests, sometimes it does so as a thing of nature- a gust of strong wind, a eagle that flies overhead, two deer that appear from nowhere. On the surface it seems like just the wind, or a bird or some deer. Yet once in a while something is different about their appearance. And sometime power appears and manifests as people. They look just like all other people we know, until you look more carefully.

This was not the first time that this has happened to me at a stone circle, or ancient pyramid or whatnot. I have a boat load of stories. But I always get surprised, and of course honoured when power makes another appearance. Though this time it was not for me, it was for Liv and Anders. They spoke and joked for another 5 minutes, when "the woman" kept on walking right to a section of trees next to the forest. I watched her from the side of my vision, to see her but not look directly at her, and saw her in a sense- merge with the forest.

I walked on over to my friends, kind of smiling. "Good chat?" I asked.

"Oh yes. She was so nice and friendly. You should have come to say hi."

"No, that manifestation was for you. She was not a person."

At first Live just kind of looked at me with a sort of, are you being a jerk with us now kind of stare, but then replied "Yes there was something odd about her, but you know she's a bit elderly. But come on. She is a person just like you or me."

"She is definitely not like you or me. That was not a person. Ok where did she come from?" Liv points. "Ok and where did she leave to?"

"Umm, well I wasn't paying attention, but somewhere that direction." pointing again.

"I watched her. She came right out of that area of trees. Not up the path like we did. Then she disappeared, and I say disappeared for that is the best way to describe it, into those bushes and trees, again not up the path. Think about it. She wasn't using the path like us, she sort of just materialized from the forest and merged back with the forest "Did you listen and remember every single thing she said?" I asked.

"Not really," she replied. "Um, I thought there were just people having a conversation, I will try to remember what I heard. Is it important?"

"Very. Well for you two very."

"Well she did say she was out for a walk...that she was the protector of this place...and that she suggested some other stones a few kilometers down the road we might like to see also."

"Protector of this place? Do you really think she is the caretaker or landscaper or something? She is nature. She is this forest She was coming out to check on us, make sure we may not be hurting this place. She obviously liked the two of you enough to come out and make contact with you. You should see it as a blessing. She just appeared and merged back with the woods after sharing a message that you should go see the other stones."

"So we should go find these other stones?"

"Absolutely. When we have the gift of power manifesting for us, and they make a suggestion. We follow it with no questions asked. But when we get there you two can go to the stones first. I will just follow you. At those stones, the gift is for you, and you are my guide."

"So how do you know when they are people, or allies pretending to be people?"

"You sort of get the hang of it with time," I answered. "The first step is to know that power is always around and interacting with us and can do so in various ways, and to know that not every person, rock or tree we see is really a person, rock or a tree. Some things are dangerous and out to get us (negative allies, demons), while others are there to give us a message, a direction, some help (allies, spirits). Most of the time you are with a person, rock or tree. Just by knowing it is possible you can begin to start to tell the difference."

❧

When I look back at my experiences of meeting power and allies, when it appeared as people, on the surface they did not seem that much different from any other human one might meet. That was until I began to ask them questions, to which they never provided any specific answers. Where are they from (around here), where are you going (just over the hill), or they may do odd things that just seem out of place. Once while on a walk with a woman in Copenhagen to help her find ways to expand her dreaming, we noticed a "man" walking in such a manner that can only be described as zig zagging from one sidewalk to the other. It was as if he didn't know what a road or a sidewalk was. Pretending to be a person is the best way I can describe it, and without full awareness in such situations, our mind will just go along with the perception of meeting a strange person—perhaps thinking he was drunk or somehow crazy. Thus, we have to stay alert and carefully examine things our mind wants us to quickly ignore and get back to normal things. Was it just some abnormal behaviour, or was it somehow a show of power for us?

There is another aspect to what is called allies. Not all are there to help us, some are there to hinder us, and these are known as negative allies. The greatest are what are known as the archon-demons, and the parasite they have given us. But there are smaller versions as well. Drugs are another example. Drugs were at times used in the past because they are a simple way to get into dreaming.

The problem with drugs, is that the drug has control, thus the drug has the power while under the influence of it. Any drug has a high demand. By that I mean they work by inflating someone, give you what you do not have in the moment. To the person taking them, the drug seems to provide them all that they are missing and cannot imagine life without it, as such the drug has tricked the person to think they only way they can gain the experience is through the drug and create a latch. Every addict I have talked with knows very well this idea—the drug gives you something, but demands something large as well. Until the demand becomes more than what they seem to be getting it will be heard to break someone off any drug: marijuana, cocaine, pharmaceutical, alcohol, the internet, sex or food. Because one cannot believe they can be good enough without them.

For some, meeting power will be calm and pleasant; other times it will be an experience of pure terror. One friend, Paul, on his way to hear a talk I was giving, had a "man" run up to his car on a busy street and try to punch his windshield. The man was dodging traffic to try and punch his car. This is his particular person's key inner block (resistance) that must be overcome manifested as an outward challenge. We confront this kind of ally when we are ready. This is symbolized in the Matrix movie with Neo (warrior) and Agent Smith (special ally), and when Neo finally defeats Smith he gets filled with an almost unimaginable power.

☙

We made it to other stones and it was now later in the evening. The sun was going down, it was getting a bit cooler. I put my small jacket on to stay warm. They were nice stones, but nothing felt to out of the ordinary. Anders and Liv walked around, sort of feeling that was their special place, but nothing special was occurring. That can happen too. Following power does not necessarily mean magical occurrences. Some of course can be so amazing that one will classify it a religious experience.

Thinking our experience with power was over, we casually strolled back down the path to where the car was parked—not really saying anything (after brushes with power it is always best to try and stay quiet for a few hours and let the experience integrate). It did not take long to see that this power experience was not yet over for us. Beside an outcrop of some very interesting rocks, I stopped. I thought I saw fog roll by from right to left, but it was a night when there should be no fog. I looked again, and again saw the fog, or like a puff of smoke, appear and then move. I pointed this to Anders and Liv and we both stood there for about ten minutes watching the fog/smoke appear and then disappear. At the same time a small light, like a burst, would occur in the middle of the patch of fog.

I noticed that the fog patches always seemed to be over two spots. I walked to the first one and stood on it, and Liv later did the same. We both felt warm as if our back had an energy current. On the second spot my feet felt they were on fire, and electricity shooting up my legs. But just one step over, there was nothing, just regular ground. Then the fog stopped. Our experiences ended, and our bodies were now full of energy. We walked back and saw no more fog or power. We had had our share for one day.

☙

John Kent once recalled that a student asked Rose, "Is it true that everything is already perfect, including the course of our paths—only our understanding or perspective of it is wrong?"

Rose replied: "Now you're starting to get the idea."

A major step, (though not enlightenment itself) is seeing that something other than the individual me is in control. Not some benevolent deity or angry force. But rather, just What Is, operating as it always has. And we are like actors on Shakespeare's stage "playing our roles." The more we see this, the more we start to step out of the way and let between-ness operate. This letting go or surrender is not something "we" can do. We do not surrender as a way of getting something, for that is still an egoic action. Surrender comes from a total acceptance of What Is. In other words, it arrives naturally when we realize we do not really have the control over everything that we believed.

All of our struggling—no matter what path we walk—is really just our own personal way of trying to comfort ourselves as we surrender. And ultimately, that surrender is to know fully that we are a mortal being, and that we will die. We are all dying. That is what life really is, the drawn-out process of dying. That is why Awakening is not about happiness or bliss. Instead, it will come via trauma and chaos, which by default places us before the inevitability of death. Ancient cultures placed seeking the knowledge of death as the utmost priority. That is why everyone must have their own individual path. That is because, as Rose claimed, the type of trauma we each need to finally get a look ourselves, will be unique for each of us. But we do not need to do anything to try and create trauma. We certainly don't need to go looking for suffering. If we are serious about looking for truth, the chaos is going to find us. We simply need to start being aware of this fact. And while always being committed to finding Ultimate Answers—we must view life through the eyes of between-ness.

> "We don't have time for anything. Death is just around the corner. It is a race to know who you are, before who you don't know dies. This has to become your number one priority." (Richard Rose lecture)

∽

Since this is such a challenging topic, and one almost impossible to fully understand, I will add a few more quotes on the subject taken from Rose and compiled by long time student Paul Constant. Maybe something in the quotes will trigger an understanding of what is meant surrounding this very all-encompassing topic.

"You don't want it, so you don't know if it is going to happen. So when it happens, you haven't done it, it simply happened. And if it doesn't happen, so what? It was one of those things that you couldn't change anyway. So you accept it with serenity."

"Yes I believe this. I would like it to happen, but I am not going to try and make it happen, unless it is supposed to happen. Then it will happen, otherwise, I will forget about it."

"Look between the thoughts. In the gap."

"To announce your intentions invites opposition. If a person goes around talking to everyone about his intentions, it is like blowing the horns. To keep silent is the key."

"No effort is wasted, all we can do is our best. You will succeed somehow if you keep doing your best. Every time that something is done in a certain mood, selflessly, it lights a light that keeps things moving in that direction." (Richard Rose)

How do we do it (Awaken)? We do it by carrying water on both shoulders, but not allowing it to touch either shoulder. We stagger soberly between the blades of the gauntlet with recklessness and conviction, but we pick out way through the tulips with fear and trepidation, because the trap of the latter is sweet. We charge the gates of Heaven by urinating our way through Hell, all the while sitting for forty years on the banks of the Ganges, doing nothing. We sit on the banks of the Ganges, not from laziness, but from an anger at angriness, a fury against our inner fury for wasted activity. And we pull back a terrible arrow...but never let it go. And by so holding, with the universe as our target, the universe is filled with terror at our threat. (Richard Rose)

Chapter 9

SUMMING UP

A Toast

"Spirituality means to die to the Truth, not to create what we want....It is understandable to expect that the further along the spiritual path one goes, the more sensible and clearly defined things should become. Towards the end of a search however, one may find oneself becoming less certain about, well, everything. This may cause the seeker to question the worth of the spiritual search itself or simply if one is dismally failing at it. Why do most teachings fail to account for it? The reason is that most paths do not see the need to first accurately define the self who is looking for the Truth, and no final answer can be appreciated so long as the "I" who would be its happy recipient is still identified with any number of false or lesser selves." (John Kent)

I am sitting with Anders for a coffee in a small cafe in Stockholm Old Town. It's touristy, but a nice place on a cool fall day to be surrounded by the ambiance of some 18th century architecture. Along the way, he and I have become friends. We will stay in touch, meet up, and talk about regular topics. Today, however, we are meeting one final time in regard to this book. Tomorrow, I will send the completed manuscript to the publishers. As we both take a moment to stretch in our chairs, he asks a pertinent question.

"So how do you feel about your book?"

And there it comes. I knew he was going to ask that question. In truth, I've been thinking myself about how I would answer that query in the last couple of days. Now that it has been asked, I have no other option but to open my mouth and see what words spill out.

"All in all, I think I am fine with it. I want to thank you for all your effort in this project. There is no way it could have gotten to this place without your questions on the material."

"Oh, I was just doing my job," he said. "And besides, it was fun to delve into topics I never thought of before."

"Fun or not, it had quite an impact on the presentation. Including the decision to add some of our conversations directly to the book to give a kind of personal touch. As for the material, you know that this is over ten years of work for me. I probably wrote at least thirty versions of this manuscript, ripped them up, and began again. Sometimes, I wonder if I could have written twenty or thirty novels during the same span of time. I could have been Dan Brown on steroids. Instead, I kept working on this same book, over and over again. In a sense, I was Phil Conners—and this book my Groundhog Day."

"Does that make me Ned Ryerson?"

"Oh no, Ned was in a class of his own when it came to annoyance. Maybe you were more like the Chris Elliot character. What was his name in the movie? Ah, I hate when this happens—I should know this, should...Larry! Right. You are like Larry the cameraman. Trying to make me look good while not taking too much of a beating from the occasional shot from Phil the jerk."

"Maybe that should be your new name: Howdie the Jerk.'"

"Better than some Indian guru inspired holy-sounding name all these people out there come up with, I guess. There would be no surprises with what the readers are getting."

"Why do you think this book took you so long to complete?'"

"A few reasons, I guess." I pause for a moment to collect my thoughts. "The first is that writing the book was part of my own journey. Taking what I experienced, read, and intuited—then finding a way to write it on paper. Doing that meant I had to own it. That also meant things that were not settled inside would not come out well on the page. Every revision was about finding something more in the text that wasn't owned. Secondly, it is challenging to write honestly. Most of the big spiritual novels are made up fantasies. Things takes longer to write when you know your reader probably won't like it. So that became more of the case when I began to understand that the reader might put items written here into play within their own life. I had to really consider what I was presenting: pointing to difficult subjects, yet not putting anyone in a danger area simply from reading it. I had to write this in such a way which wouldn't suggest blindly following a single word. Making sure everyone realizes this book is only a pointer and offering the suggestion that the reader examine and take heed of all on their own."

"The material came out fairly well, I think."

"This book could be better of course. For quite a while, there was a great deal of spiritual ego in the writing. Be happy that you didn't see some of the early versions. As that view of specialness dropped, more and more was rewritten. It led more to presenting my own experience—as well as some of the books, movies and people that helped to explain some of what I had seen. Something like this could be rewritten again and again for the next twenty years, and still be finding something new to add or said differently. There also comes a time with any project where you feel it has arrived at a decent port, and it is time to let it go and move on. I feel I have reached that place."

I had also wanted to include my chapter from *The Power of Then* on pyramids. So many spiritual seekers have an acknowledgment of Egypt's pyramids and granite stone work, but since they have not studied them or seen the right areas up close, they have no idea just how amazing they are. We CAN NOT cut the granite today, with all our technology. We CAN NOT build the large pyramids, with their perfect inner granite passages today. Let that sink in. What did they know, what could they do, what power did they have? And what of it can cross the boundary of time to reach us today?[30]

Our server comes by and asks if we need anything else. I pause on the thought that maybe some type of pastry might be good, but decide against it. Rather, I decide to get one at another shop around the corner after I say goodbye.

Anders looks at his watch. I am heading off to meet up with my wife at three o'clock at a nearby art gallery. We have a few minutes before I have to get rolling and cross the bridge—with the pastry, of course. He asks a final question of me.

"And what is the message that you most hope a reader will find in here?"

"I guess it would be, as Rabindranath Tagore said, "You can't cross the sea merely by standing and staring at the water." The search for the essence or Truth or Totality requires the combination of commitment and action. No matter how good a book or piece of information may be, it still means little if we do not put our shoes on and begin to walk ourselves.

The second item would be for people to really examine the actions that they are taking. Are those actions designed to get them somewhere, or just designed to make them feel better and safe? Finding Truth may or may not make one feel better. Running to so many gurus and teachers out there, who make big money and importance off the seekers, while doing little for anyone but their

---

30 · The chapter on pyramids will always be up for free on my website www. egyptian-wisdom-revealed.com

own inflated self-importance. I would much rather spend my time with the people who give up their time to care for unwanted animals for no reward rather than most of the modern spiritual teachers.

Hopefully my Jacob's Ladder chapter will make the reader think about all of this. To see that 95% of everything classified as spirituality is truly no higher than the first stage pyramid. That is because spirituality—as it is presented—is all emotional. There always that element infused into prayer, mediation, positive thinking, astrology, Tarot cards, taking with the dead, acupuncture, herbs, reiki, channeling, chakra cleansing—and the like. The emotional element wants us to feel better, be happier. As long as something has an emotional focus for being implemented, it puts that activity in the first pyramid. Again, it's not bad or anything. That is fine—and very useful, too like when you are sick. However, a seeker who really wants to go to the depths—and perhaps beyond the cave—must finally recognize this and take their practice to the next level."

"That would be second pyramid mind elements."

"Right. The second pyramid is mainly Mental. The examination of mind and thought and the dream and whatnot. However, this is done not to feel better or to change it. Rather, one does this to see who is thinking, what thought is, and why thought happens. It is a real shift in spiritual work. Some people do it without a formal practice or having anything to do with something like Zen. Yet that is just because the dream, in some way, became so painful. As a result, they got tired of trying to fix anything or fall into distraction, and instead decided to stare directly at it. That is something I hope the book can get across. What the book has mostly to say is for those examining the self- either already in the second pyramid or heading towards it."

"But not for the third."

"Not really. I could only mention some pointers there. Besides, if someone really is in the third pyramid of work, generally a book is not going to help them much. It would have to be the right book, for sure. At that stage, they are sort of making their own path with each step they take. They truly become a supreme examiner—even if they don't realize it. In fact, something such as poetry or artwork on the subject might be more valuable. A work that can access the subconscious directly."

That leads back to Rose's suggestion with this material that an important part of one's path is to 'pass it on.' No matter where we are, even if we are low on Jacob's Ladder and know it—we still have something to share that can be of help. Even if it is simply sharing a mistake we made. Or an addiction or obsession we overcame—revealing those times to someone struggling with the same thing. To find ways to be of service is a signal to the universe that we will not be greedy with what we get. Such an action reveals that we will share what we know, as we can.

The first major work I wrote was *The Power of Then*—on the wisdom of the ancient world. This book could be seen as a First Pyramid book, going through Nigredo to show how the ancient way could create better functioning. This book is the work of the second pyramid, seeing the mind and reality. Awakening beyond the separate self. My alchemic book of Albedo. Now I can begin what I would guess would be a final book. The work mostly ignored by everyone, like the middle Khafre Pyramid at Giza. Majestic, perhaps the oldest on the site, sitting lonely while everyone stares at its big brother beside or the Sphinx. But this third pyramid stage of Rubedo is coming now, in my life and in my writing.

I think of this current place in my life as I sit quietly just running my index finger around the rim of my coffee cup. Anders seemingly is somewhere in his own contemplation as well. Our coffee is almost finished, and it is time for me to get going. My last thought about this book is that it has been my attempt to pass on a few things from my experience, even if they might be small. The pile of notes that I carried on my back for so long are open to the breeze, to be carried wherever the wind sees fit to scatter them. Maybe there will be another book. Maybe not. But it is time to turn out the lights on this movie.

"Anders, No matter how nice the cave is, sometime, we all have to move on." I hold up my cup with the last bit of coffee in it, "Here's to exit doors."

I swig the last of the coffee, and he does the same. With that, I head to the open door of the cafe, where I hear the sounds of Stockholm again. I turn once more at the exit to wave back to Anders,

"See you soon," I say, before stepping on the street to continue my journey.

APPENDIX

Appendix A

NAG HAMMADI GNOSIS

"The archons are not armed against you specifically, but are armed against each other." (*First Apocalypse of James*)

O ne of the most important documents for the human race is the Nag Hammadi Gnostic Codex, named after the Egyptian town close to the caves where they were discovered in 1945. The discoverer was a Bedouin peasant, who kept them for a few years while trying to sell them. His mother burned a few fearing what she thought were "dangerous effects." Eventually, they wound up in the hands of a Coptic priest who gave them to the Coptic Museum in Cairo in 1947.

Hidden over 1500 years ago to save the books from being burned by persecuting Christians, currently the codex is left with 13 leather books. They are not scrolls as thought of, but one of the first instances of actual bound books. Written in Coptic, they contain 52 texts. Mostly they are Gnostic scriptures, but also three from the *Corpus Hermeticum*, as well as a partial translation of Plato's *Republic*. Most scholars are in agreement that the codexes are not originals, but copies of older documents. They are not the writings of what most scholars believe is a "pre-Christian" group, but perhaps the descendants of the last of the great Egyptian Mystery Schools. This Greek-era group are referred to today as Gnostics, from the Greek word for wisdom. Prior to finding these documents there was little information on these groups, the Christians having destroyed the original Gnostic documents. The Nag Hammadi Codexes are but a small fragment of the original written heritage, and contain teachings to find True Self, as well and rid the force that opposed it. The Gnostics labeled this force the "archons."

The original origin of the documents is a bit of a mystery. Most scholars believe that they came from the monastery of Pachomius, a retreat of Coptic Christian monks near Tabinnisi on the east bank of the Nile. Yet John List from *Metahistory.org* reminds that just across the Nile from the spot of the discovery is the famous Egyptian Temple of Hathor. These codexes may be modified Greek-period "updates" to the famous Books of Thoth, something that has gone unfound for centuries. Perhaps worked around the Corpus Hermetic style, they became stored in the library of the Hathor temple. This fact of their true origin may have been lied about in order to hide that there may be other texts from this temple still hidden in the hills on the west bank of the Nile.

"The Gospel of Thomas" is the most famous Codex scripture because it has great similarity to writings that found their way into the New Testament. Since most get introduced to this scripture first, there is the idea that the entire set of documents is an early form of the Bible. Other than the "Gospel of Thomas," however, most of the codexes are very "un-Christian." For example, the word "savior" appears, but it seems to refer less to a specific person, but to a force. The name Jesus or Christ is never specifically used, but rather the words "IS" or "XRS, normally translated as Jesus or Christos. However, IS can become Iasius which in Greek means healer. Anyone with healing powers was an Iasius. It can even be a handed down derivative of Isis.

There was a Gnostic idea called the Mesotes, an inner guide. A Christ in Gnostic writing is more like this Mesotes rather than an actual historical figure. "I am Christos, the child of humanity, the one who is in you." They saw IS as a revealer of knowledge, whose death was a symbolic representation of the process everyone must undergo, not a historical figure that should be worshiped. At times they compare this word with a male light within—that connects with the female Sophia (wisdom). Christos is the potential, what each person can become. The Gnostics saw humans as trapped seeds of light and Gnosis is what freed this light. "Those who say they will die first and then rise, are in error...one must receive the resurrection while they are alive, or when they die they receive nothing."

We live in a dual world. When one thing appears, so too must its opposite. It should be no surprise that at the same year the Nag Hammadi Codexes were brought to world attention (1947), so too was another find—the Dead Sea Scrolls at Qumran. While on the surface they seem to be similar (the writings of two early Christian groups), nothing is further from the case. The church allows few scholars to even look at the Dead Sea Scrolls and puts out little information about them. Roman Christianity may not have evolved out of Judaism, but from the very fanatical beliefs of a small group called the Zealots, who wrote the Dead Sea Scrolls. At the time, the Gnostics may have seen this group as the great opposition. There is even suggestion that they may have thought they had somehow stolen their writings and twisted them around, as the Apocalypse of Peter is a warning surrounding a new religion taking hold about a man called Jesus, that was a parody or imitation of the Gnostic teachings.

There is the suggestion that the Gnostics saw the newly evolving Christianity as its direct opposite created by the archons. Gnosticism may have been rewriting the old Osiris-Isis-Horus myth into a then modern time equivalent, which the Zealots then used to make the basis of their own ideas. In time, Christianity tried to hide its origins by murdering the Gnostics and destroying all the Egyptian temples and writings.

Appendix B

RECAPITULATION

"The things that are holding you up personally are the negative things that have happened to you." (Richard Rose)

The technique of recapitulation ("recap") is found in all ancient traditions. It is also called purification, throwing off the world, being reborn into the world, the inventory and the little death. It is the remembering, or more precisely, the reliving and recovering of all our past experiences. It is claimed that prior to death our entire life flashes before our eyes to allow us to review it, see how every event was interconnected, and see the challenges we did not embrace and overcome. Because it shows us the truth, many will find it hard to undergo this review. Ancient wise men and women realized that this process "cleaned" us before leaving the world of form, thus to do the review while still alive, we would gain the benefits that we normally wait until death to receive.

We choose the practice of recap to regain the energy we lost from the interactions from our entire life while still alive. In every interaction of our life there has been some exchange of energy. In "would you like fries with that" encounters, the exchange was so minimal that it was barely noticed. With people we have spent a lot of time with, a great deal of each other's energy has been exchanged. In fact, many people are carrying so much of someone else's energy they act like other people (parent, first grade teacher, first lover) without even realizing it. On a larger scale, during very painful events of our life, we gave away our energy and power to try and make the event stop. Recap is about regaining all of our own energy. No one else can use it, as it only gives others a false feeling of strength. We also must give back all the energy of others that we may have for it does nothing for us either, only keeping old events alive that we need to release. Great healing comes from regaining our lost energy and letting go of what is not ours. In a sense this aspect of recap is like a soul retrieval (bringing back a lost part of ourself). In recap, the memory of the event comes first which causes the return of the lost energy; while soul retrieval brings back the energy first, often sparking the memory of the event that caused the "loss."

Recap as a process is also used to deconstruct the story of "me." A true recap involves reliving all hidden memories, patterns and feelings. Thus, for some it can take years, for others less time to fully see the underlying foundational patterns. Though it seems like one can never make it through the review of every moment of their life, there is a catch, for most of our life is one giant repeated habit. The more we find a particular pattern of experiences, we will find them repeated in our past and as such can go through many areas of time rather quickly once the pattern is finally witnessed. For example, early in the review of my life I noticed that at the start of three relationships I was doing the exact same thing, even going to the same places on the dates.

Our mind is constantly interpreting the present based on the past. We don't realize that we have created a mental past that allows our ego to live its habits and use the excuse of "look what happened to me." The tough part of recap occurs as people begin to see that what they thought was their life, is just a mythological past that we keep repeating. Without a recap there is always some event to blame for where we are now. "I can't get into a relationship because of what my mother said, I can't show you affection because my last boyfriend was a jerk, I can't be successful because I failed when I was 14." That is why mind loves the past. No matter how ugly it was, it gives us a great excuse. Our past is like a stone. We drag it with us through our life and are attached to it with hooks. Every hook we release turns that part of the stone into Styrofoam. The load itself never goes away—just gets much lighter. Many people review parts of their life with a psychologist, but that does little. To retell an event the way we think it happened just reinforces the story our mind has created. The psychologist wants to fix your mind, make us normal. But we don't want to be normal, we want to be sane.

Every time we try to change our life for the better "something" stops us, which is our unseen hooks, dialogue, and promises to the past. It is not just the big events that have an impact. From my own recap I found some very small events were a catalyst. Our entire life may have gone off track from one simple event, something so small and insignificant that we can't consciously remember it, but the unconscious has. It may seem like nothing the time our brother threw our favorite toy on the roof, but that event may have caused us to make a secret promise to never trust anyone again.

A recap is done by starting at the present and working backwards to birth. This does two things. First, it helps to unwind our life, like a tape, and free up space on it. We go backwards because it is easier to remember details of what happened yesterday than when we were four. We can't use our normal mind, for it will only show us what it wants us to see, what it wants us to remember. Recap only works when we can get past our normal memory to a much deeper place, our True Mind and True Memory. It is not designed to hide you from your past, quite the opposite, it wants you to see it fully. It wants you to grieve where you should have grieved, laugh where you should have laughed. Lost events will surface that we have no memory of, as we wonder how we could have ever forgotten something so important.

We don't eliminate the event or pretend it never happened, we take back the emotional energy we used to give it life. It then becomes just an event, and in time you may see your whole life as though it were a series of events that happened to "someone else." While self-importance is still in command, recap often brings out a giant dose of self-pity, thus one will also have to stop indulging in the need to be a victim. Remember that to be challenged by an event is far different than to be victimized.

Any drug users, heavy smokers or drinkers will have their recap (as well as their whole life) hampered by the intake of these substances. It is recommended to stop for at least 30 days to let the system clean out before beginning. If someone during this 30 days takes time to look at why they drink, smoke or take drugs—they are engaging in an early form of recap even while waiting for the system to clear.

Recap has many layers, but the actual steps are few. One of the ancient ways was to tell your life story aloud to Grandfather Fire. The process of talking aloud forces you to hear the truth and hear lies from the sound of your voice. A warm up practice is to review the day just experienced before going to sleep. Review the day backwards from the end of the day until the time you woke up (in forward motion of course, no need to see people walking backwards). Review the key events, and then see if anything forgotten arises. It will help you regain your lost energy from the day, thus you will often sleep better. Many of our dreams are simply the way of the mind to rehash the events of the day that were ignored, but by recapping we will have less normal dreams and more that would be classified as "dreaming." This is a good warm-up for a few weeks.

Active recap is the specific exercises, while passive recap comes spontaneously without warning, when hearing a song on the radio or a car backfiring brings up a forgotten memory. We use active recap to wake up spontaneous recap. Active recap is dull, boring and monotonous, but don't give up. It can take a lot of heat to make a pot of water boil, so don't turn off the stove too quickly if it seems like not much is happening.

To perform active recap first one must find their place to practice. We need complete silence and solitude, thus it is best done in the hours when most people are asleep so that we are not affected by other people's sounds or thoughts. It can be done in the wilderness or a secluded cabin to be away from people entirely. Some suggest the need for a box, the symbolic coffin found in ancient pyramids and tombs, used by the living who want to die to their old self. The idea is to stay night after night in the box until one's whole life has passed before their eyes, then symbolically break the box as a symbol they are no longer locked to their old limitations.[31] However, One does not need a box for effective recap, but what seems to help is an enclosed space to squeeze the energy body and better help with the recall. A closet is good, under blankets, in a big cardboard box, even in your car-as long as the space is small and that you are alone.

Once you have found a place, the next stage is to make the list. On this list you write down the name of everyone you have ever met. A daunting task for many right there. Create this list any way that helps you.[32] You can use headings of where you worked, went to school, people you dated, and as you make each list, the names will trigger the names of people associated with them. This list needs to include anyone you had any meaningful interaction with. I looked at it as if there was someone I met whose name I tried to remember when I met them, was deserving for the list. When complete, place the names in chronological order with the most recent person you have met at the top of the list, and mom and dad at the bottom. For each person add an event or two (maybe 10 for key people) to act as a basic guide. Make a short note on that encounter like: dinner, mountains, swimming, fall down stairs, movie etc. to be a memory

---

31   For info on the box and how to build one you can see Victor Sanchez's *Toltec Path of Recapitulation*

32   You can use yearbooks or old phone directories to help find names of all those you have met.

aid, and place those memory aids in chronological order for each person. You won't remember every encounter with a person, and that is ok, but the more you can get the more you will help jog your memory to get to the events you have forgotten.

You will recap your life following this list. You will also want to jot down key events that happened when you were alone—walking through the woods or driving on a country road. In fact, creating the list itself will be a form of recap as many forgotten events and people rush to the surface, and will give you a burst of energy upon completion. Generally, I recommend for your first recap you just do the most important 30 people you had interactions with. That allows you to get to some of the big stuff right away, then later if you want to do the entire list, that is fine, but at least you will get to some of your most important events a bit quicker.[33]

Whatever list you have chosen, begin at the top. I recommend not to start with your current close relationships. Every person you recap will create some form of change, so give your current partnerships some time. Don't be afraid to recap them, but for most people I suggest some leeway. This is why many people are afraid to recap, they know deep down relationships and friendships are not based on trust and kindness, and they want to hide from it. A recap may show you that you should no longer be in a relationship, or may show you how to totally love that other person. The manifested world is all about change. To want to try and keep something exactly

---

33 You can also create a list of people that you had sexual encounters with. They will still be on your main list, but this second list is only the sex experiences, which recapped first. So if you went for three dinners with Sue and sex once, you recap the one sex experience on list two- and when you get to Sue back on list one, you review the three dinners. People will also likely find how boring their sex life has been, or manipulative or how unaware they have been through it all. You can start here because we give away a lot of energy during sexual encounters, so getting this energy back at the beginning of the work will give us the extra boost that will allow us to go through the more "mundane" encounters on the first list.

as it is, is in fact a form of manipulation. If you are afraid of losing a friendship or a lover, what kind of friendship do you really have?

With a complete and ready list, one must now decide how much time they want to invest. My suggestion is to start with one hour a day for a week or two to get used to the work. Once you get comfortable, the usual way to do recap is to begin at 9 or 10 at night, and recap all through the night until morning. It is best not to stop because you are tired and go to "bed" to sleep. It is your mind trying to force you to stop. Some will do such recaps over a weekend or for a week, or until they have completed one phase of their life (such as "university experiences). Sleep really won't be needed because as you are recapping you are regaining energy. I remember several times falling asleep in the closet around 5 AM, then getting up with my alarm at 7 feeling great. You will find your own way that is best for you. It seems that longer sessions for less days (say 8 hours a night for a week) reap more benefits than 1 hour a night for 56 nights. The longer sessions keep the process focused. I also suggest you make a choice of how many events you are going to recap in one night, say you are going to recap 7 nights and you have 140 events to go through, that means 20 a night. After a little practice get to know just how many events you can get through.

Prepare your space to not be disturbed. During your session you could yell or cry or laugh as experiences are relived. Usually you will make no sound at all, but you don't want someone coming to check on you to see if you are all right and break you out of a key recap experience. Find the first person on your list, and the first event for that person. Get a mental picture of what they looked like at that event. Next set the place you were in, the more detail the better. If you were at dinner, what was on the table? What was the waiter wearing, what pictures were on the walls? Don't analyze any of this, just observe it in all its detail. Doing so you are focusing your intent to be back at that event. When you feel that you have a good remembrance of the space and the people there, now try to observe the event exactly as it happened. For many people they may see themselves at this point, as if they were watching a movie. That's fine. You're still in your normal mind here, but you have to get the event rolling somehow. As the event plays, one now needs to use the emotions, for it is the emotions that were generated that will lead us to find out what really happened in the encounter. As you continue to watch the event keep asking, what am I feeling? What is happening around me that I missed? Try and be there fully. If other events come up, just let them pass.

Play the event right through. Most events will just need this one look (the simple movie-like view), but if the event seemed important or intense, then see it a second time, now not as a movie but try to see it through your own eyes. Be "in" the event, relive the experience. To assist yourself you can talk (even in a whisper) everything you actually said or was being thought to help get you more there, you may repeat the name of people at the event over and over, move your body if necessary—anything to get you to stop thinking and go into feeling mode. Now see the event for a third time, again as a movie, but this time you focus on your healing breath and to balance and harmonize the energy from the event—healing the "self" in the movie, and the "Self" watching it. An added help with your recap sessions can be to include breath work. Breathing helps to rebalance our energy. The suggested method is to begins with a deep breath with the chin on the right shoulder, then the head is moved to the left shoulder with the in-breath. On the exhale the head moves to the right finishing that out-breath on the right shoulder. I found this only tired me when done through an entire event, and simply used an in an out breath with intention, then at the end made a couple of such passes to focus the bringing back of lost energy. On the in breath we breathe back our energy that we gave away at the event, and on the out-breath we give back all the energy we have from that event. See what works for you.

This third watch can be the hardest of all, for this is the real healing, where the energy hole gets filled. The ego wants to stay locked in the second stage, (crying or feeling hurt) not letting themselves see it once more to heal. The final stage of the process is to "dream" in a not-doing for you to perform in your day to day world later. You are looking for the pattern that helped to create the event, thus find another part to dismantle. Without this, the band aid you just put on your wound will be easily reopened.

The biggest problem with recap is that there is no real way to teach it, because it involves connecting to your lost feelings, and only we know how best to do that. For that reason only the base starters can be given, then each must modify them as they see fit. At the beginning it will seem we are doing nothing—until the usher appears. It is called the usher because it will usher in a whole new period of recap. You will know when the usher has finally appeared when you are no longer seeing the event or even feeling it, you are fully reliving it. The space you are recapping in may be gone, and you are right back at that event—a freaky thing the first time it happens.

Most of the events and people that you recap will only have to be done once because the investment of emotional energy was very small. Others may be part of many life passes (new rounds of recap over years or decades), yet each life pass you make, there will be less remaining events to "re-see". You know that an event or person is completed when you can remember it or them and have no emotion attached. An example was a woman that I went on a few dates with and had some lingering bitterness towards, but after recapping our time together I felt no emotion, no need to blame her or be upset... the events were now just experiences in the past. I knew that my need to recap her was complete.

❧

After a recap session you may feel light-headed or odd, that is ok it just means that something is changing. Have something to eat and you will likely feel more grounded. Don't worry about trying to rush the process, go at your own pace. It takes years for the average person to make it through just one complete life pass. A reminder that often when we finish recapping someone we may "run into them" somewhere, or someone may bring up their name when out for coffee. It is an energetic check, do you really want the energy evened, or for some reason do you want to return to the old way of lost energy?

Usually the next day, even after a short hour session, one will feel they have more energy. The problem is that people feel they are "back to normal." This is more like an energy band-aid. Those energy wasting habits and patterns have been around for a long time, and there are things you will need to change. Another warning. Recap, if you do it well, may make you think that you are have lost your memory. I'm not exaggerating this point. As the deeper events of your past become known, all your history will become like some maddening game being played on you by some unknown force, as you realize that most of what you thought were the events of your life—were not anything like that at all. This is good, it means your True Mind is waking up and showing you the truth of your life events, and normal mind has no idea how to deal with it. It takes a while for the confusion is lessen, and clear seeing to take its place. Just part of the process.

As a foreshadowing, a few years after completing a first life pass (which will take years in itself) someone might feel they wish to do a second review (to see events and people not totally cleared). The second review will be very different. For me the second was like only tiny parts of the event were focused on, as if the entire event itself is no longer important, only a few seconds of it. There were lots of bursts of unremembered feelings. You are working now directly at the level of the energy. No real need to focus on it now, I just mention it for those who have completed one pass and may wonder what to do next.

Recap practitioners will often continue to review for their whole life what are called omens, synchronicity, when they felt a meeting with the Spirit, or any time where there was a strong presence of death (illness, serious accidents, close calls). What are called "Meetings with the Nagual" (discussed later) should be recapped as often as possible.

Appendix C

DREAMING EXERCISES

"Under the impact of dreaming, the ordinary criteria to differentiate a dream from reality becomes inoperative." (Carlos Castaneda)

The only way to get to deep forms of *Dreaming* is with personal power, thus one needs not only to practice dreaming, but also increase their northern not-doing practice (the southern practice of dreaming is linked to the northern practice of not-doing). They are a pair. All not-doing, from gazing to walking backwards will help our dreaming. The more we stalk and alter our habits, patterns and internal dialogue (rearrange our tonal) our dreaming will improve. Being outside at night is a not doing that helps dreaming.

One exercise to work with is lucid dreaming, which is recognizing that one is in fact dreaming. To open lucid dreaming, you want during the normal day to constantly ask yourself "am I dreaming right now?" You could do this every time you turn on or off a light switch or look at a watch or clock. Constantly ask yourself seemingly nonsensical questions, "Do I own a TV, does my neighbor have grass in front of his house, is my dog blue, is..." then you will catch something, "wait my dog is not blue. I might be dreaming."

Another famous dreaming exercise is to try to look at your hands. Keep trying to bring your hands up so that you can look at them. This seems to be a very hard thing to do in dreaming, and once that happens, it is as if a form of control of the dream comes (objects and events in dreaming can shift quickly—thus seeing the hands becomes a grounding force). The key in a dream is to not let the objects and events shift and change too much, thus to learn how to operate in the dream more like normal reality—of course the trick in normal reality is to learn to let objects shift and change and not be so stable and static.

Another aspect of dreaming practice is what is called the OBE (out of body experience), where our consciousness is in our dreaming body and not our physical body. This dreaming body will have no physicality; thus, doors and walls are not a barrier to it. It is important to see that the double is not some sort of hallucination, but something just as real as the normal body—just used for different things. We can visit other rooms or houses and verify the next day we saw what was there, though there was no logical explanation for our knowing. The big moment of the OBE is when we come across our physical body asleep. It is the most shocking experience one can have, to be here, and yet see ourselves there in the same moment. The confusion is utter, total, and can last for quite some time afterward. But then comes the question, who or what is doing the dreaming? Am I the physical body dreaming this new dream body, or is something else dreaming up both bodies?

> "We can get everything in dreaming. We can open ourself to what is needed there. If we forget to use it, that's ok, it comes back when needed and we remember to open to it." (Karl Renz, personal conversation)

ↁ

I mentioned gazing briefly in chapter 6. It is another excellent practice to go deeper into the make up of reality. You need to devote a few hours specifically for this. Once the dialogue shuts off, as mentioned, that will stop the world—which will allow the supposedly very stable reality to begin shifting. Do this in progression, and don't try to speed up the process. A good procession would be:

- Leaves,
- Small plants,
- Trees,
- Insects,
- Birds,
- Rocks (done later in the work due to the power they hold),
- Rain and Fog (fog is good to see ghosts, rain is good to find power spots),
- Distance and Cloud gazing,
- Fire and Smoke (smoke is good for "seeing" people),

Shadow Gazing. Shadows are of course something resisting light, hence to learn to gaze something's shadow you can learn to understand its darkness and resistance. Thus, learning how to gaze and read the shadows of nature will help you learn how to read the shadows (resistance) of people.

The final gazing practice would be to gaze at Stars and Water. Water can be used by anyone who has become formless (dropped their human form) to gather their second attention and transport themselves anywhere they want to go. It is for that reason that water gazing is not a beginner's practice, but a highly advanced and potentially dangerous one. The better your gazing becomes, the more you will be amazed to find just how deep your dreaming practice becomes as well.

Along with the concept of the double, which in time can allow the amazing practice called bi-location (being in two places at once) is what is known as "finding one's parallel being." This will be another person of the same sex that will be very much bound together. They co-exist in the world at the same time (this is a dual reality so in manifestation everything has to be dual). The two parallel beings are like two sides of the same person. It is a great task to find this parallel being, because there are so many other distracting factors in one's life. But for anyone that could do it, they would find an endless source of youth and energy. Thus, one should ask if the famous "fountain of youth" that everyone in "myth" has been searching the earth for is really, their parallel being?

Something else that can be classified as working in dreaming, are subjects that have in some ways become part of the New Age Movement. And again there is nothing at all wrong with practicing them to have a better function and aware form. Many have their roots in the ancient Native or Taoist practices of the past. I still use many in my day to day life.

What the natives call medicine, is really a power that comes from the earth or spirit realm to humans. AS mentioned it is something that nature will share with us in order to get us to help it out. We were created from nature, and its gifts of healing, help, guidance and protection come from it. All of these things are a form of medicine. Thus, the connection with nature, the spirits, stones, divination and with ceremony becomes a key help in each one of our journeys as an addition to the work on the observation of the self, not the work itself.

Another important area of dreaming is known as working with "clear dreams" (your colour). This sort of active dreaming is found in the Dzogchen Buddhism and the book *Cry of the Eagle* by Theun Mares. In a nutshell, upon creation, the first thing manifested was the white light (One Thing). This one thing, to manifest forms, must split itself into 7 bands, which is mirrored in how sunlight when shone through a prism splits into the 7 colours of the rainbow. The One White Light uses its universal prism, and splits into 7 colours (which are not the same as the seven colours of the rainbow) and from each of these colours, objects manifest themselves. Thus, humans are a layer of manifestation after the splitting into colours, so one human will be from one colour, while another is from a different one of the seven. One is not better than any other, it just means that they have a slightly different origin. Of course, two humans who are from the yellow colour will work better than one red and one yellow. Actually, truth be known, if one could just get into a relationship with someone from their own colour, it would go much smoother. The meaning of all this is not that important until one comes to the ending section on the sorcerer's explanation and the warrior's party. It is mentioned here for its role in what is known as clear light dreaming.

One way to perform the start of this dreaming is just to push on your closed eyelids and apply pressure. Coloured blobs of light will appear. Notice how the patterns change and swirl in and out of each other. What you are seeing of course is your very own perception changing, and instead of being shot outwards to create elements of the outward dream, they are appearing on the screen of your eyelids. You were seeing the movie at the raw elements. Learn to do this without the pressure on the eyes. Find the dots and let them grow. Listen for a sound, like a buzzing of a computer or crickets. You will think the sound is outside, but it is an inside sound projected outwardly. When you notice "your colour" you begin to smooth it out, from blobs to simply having the colour fill the screen that you are looking at, then open your eyes quickly, and the external world and the inward swirls will mingle for a while. The best way I can describe it is seeing the holographic wave patterns of reality. With a smooth colour, allow your "perception" to enter into it. Mares suggests in his book that there are some other things that can be done before entering this colour, one is to work with what appears as a black and white checkerboard, and the examination of a yellow rose. I leave you with his book to study if you wish. Once you have entered your colour, you would say that you have just entered *dreaming,* and the normal world of the rational is gone and what is left is the feeling side of the Nagual.

A slight variation of this is to practice wall gazing, with a white wall. You may notice it begin to break down into standard elements, or see objects projected on the wall. It requires some effort for it will usually take a few hours of gazing at the wall before any "break down" begins to happen. It was from wall gazing that one of my crazy periods began (when all reality itself began to completely break). The main goal of Dzogchen dreaming is to have a clear light dream, where there is no dreamer, no outside, just oneness or the void.

Lastly, I leave you with a couple of warnings surrounding the practice of dreaming. First is that because dreaming takes us to the second attention, a much finer form of the holographic reality, it is the place where all sorts of elements try to get us: aliens, demons and sorcerers. The Gnostic texts show a lot of information of how to deal with archons and demons in dreams, but they spoke little about sorcerer's attacks. I spoke to one teacher of my interactions with a female sorcerer, and how she kept trying to kill me in my dreaming. He first told me that her "teacher" kept appearing in his dreams trying to steal energy from him. He said that all he has to do with these people is to take off his masks (he said take off his armor) and show what he really is. That will scare them so fully (because they are always using a mask to look through and are viewing other masks) that to see no mask frightens them completely. To see ourself without our mask will frighten us too.

Another warning is that because the practice is based in the south, it has its base in power. Because of that many people will get trapped in dreaming while on a search to try and control others or the dream. This is how one gets trapped in the world of sorcery. When one does not get trapped, what comes is not only power but warmth (where real friendship and relationship can be found). In fact, as one gains more warmth they will also gain more feeling, and it is feeling which sets up dreaming. We can get everything in dreaming. We can open ourself to what is needed there. If we forget to use it, that's ok, it comes back when needed and we remember to open to it.

Appendix D

TONAL AND NAGUAL

"What happens to someone whose assemblage point loses rigidity? They think they are losing their mind." (Carlos Castaneda)

Carlos Castaneda created a number of terms that he used in his writing. That does not make them invaluable, but does mean that the terms are his creations- but what they are pointing to is something quite timeless and found in the ancient world. Some of these terms are: assemblage point, tonal, nagual, human form, and parallel lines. I wanted to present these terms, and my understanding of what they point towards in case some readers are now interested to read his books. Again though, I am reminded how poor I feel his first novel is. I recommend that if you want to read Castaneda's work, start with his next three novels: *A Separate Reality*, *Journey to Ixtlan*, and *Tales of Power*. Then read further if you wish.

Carlos Castaneda wrote of something that he called the assemblage point, normally positioned opposite the right shoulder blade.[34] Castaneda said that when one could "see" (perceive beyond normal reality) they would recognize that the world is not made up of objects like we normally think, but instead made up of fields of energy—which he described as infinite threads of light. The Gnostics referred to the world as Emanations of light coming from the Pleroma (Source). We, too, are not solid but a bundle also made up of these threads of light. This "us" is bombarded by millions of these fiber-like emanations, which all pass through this assemblage point, which for unknown reasons chooses some threads to "light up" while keeping the rest of the threads dark. You could say infinite movies are being projected (as beams of light), but only one gets selected to be placed on the movie screen. What we call Earth 2018 is just a small grouping of continuously chosen light fibers. Each person chooses a slightly unique selection, but close enough so that reality seems similar for everyone.

Using the metaphor of a radio, when a radio dial is on AM 1200 we will hear that station and only that station. Move the dial and we get a new station. The old station is still playing, but we can only hear one at a time. If you did not know that the dial could move (because it was locked in place), you would not even guess that there could be other stations. To understand the metaphor of Plato's Cave properly, the chains that bind the prisoner to the seats are not physical, but are more accurately that which keeps this assemblage point static. Move our assemblage point and we access a different frequency. This movement is called dreaming, because of the dream-like quality of any other world, and I guess because how "dreamy" it would be to hear other stations playing.

---

34   I always believed that it was just a metaphor that Castaneda used, but John Last at *Metahistory.org* found reference in GRS Mead's "The Subtle Body in Western Tradition." Here the writings of Damascius paraphrased Isadorus (of the Alexandrian Mystery School) which discusses the augoiedes or auric egg that surrounds the physical body and was one of the deepest secrets of the mysteries, and how the luminous oval is connected or locked onto the physical body at a point on the back, high up on the right shoulder blade.

Part of the way the point is rigidly maintained is through habits and internal dialogue, which for each person is slightly different, but keeps perception within the safe range of station AM 1200 (1190-1210). This agreement of what radio station is playing is called being of "sound mind" (because we hear the same station as everyone else). However, the assemblage point can shift—(being in love, hunger, illness, fear, drugs or lengthy stillness[35]) or the interaction of the Spirit.[36] In a sense this is one of the underlying bases of the movie *Pleasantville*—where the townsfolk can only hear the "pleasant" sounds of 1200, but David and Jennifer come along with knowledge of other radio stations. Move your point far enough and you are in a totally new world (as the people of Pleasantville were at the end of the movie).

A movement of the point is usually forgotten because it does not conform to our normal view of the world. We try to explain the odd event by known beliefs or claiming that we were hallucinating or drunk (the prisoner just sits back down). "Seeing" is the capacity to perceive the world as it appears without the filter of conditioning. When your assemblage point gets loose, reality begins to collapse. You may think you are going crazy, but rather you are seeing that reality is nothing like you have been told it is. One who goes psychotic had this movement happen, but lost their foundation. You want to

---

35   Drugs move the point quickly, which is why they were used in the ancient world, but they also are hard to control, and have consequences for the physical body, thus are not recommended.

36   Anything classified as a ritual is just a way to trap the attention to let the assemblage point move, either for an individual or a group. While ritual works, it is cumbersome. If someone is about to die in five minutes and your ritual takes four hours, no matter how good your ability to shift the assemblage point, you will be of little help. They teach us rituals, so that in time, we will know when we don't need the ritual anymore. But perhaps it was being involved in various religious or spiritual rituals that helped our prisoner to stand up.

encourage the movement, while keeping the foundation of normal perception available.[37]

℘

The ancient writings speak of the need to combine two elements, the Ka and the Ba (for Egyptians), the Eagle and the Jaguar (for the Maya), the sun and the moon (for alchemists). Usually this is thought to be either the male and female halves of oneself, two parts of the mind, or perhaps the mind and the heart. But this combination is much deeper than that. What must be combined are hard to define aspects which Castaneda called the Tonal (the world of manifested objects and all ideas, concepts, and beliefs), and The Nagual (Void, Spirit, No-thing).

It is the Tonal that helps to lock the assemblage point, and thus our perception. It could be said that the Tonal begins with our form's birth, and ends with our death—not entirely accurate, but close enough. The Tonal is not bad or evil, it serves a function in the dreamworld, but that function becomes incredibly warped without the balancing influence of the Nagual. We want to experience a 50-50 connection between the two. The Tonal is compared to an island (the cave), which seems to exist individually and separately from all the other islands in the ocean of the Nagual. We are not trying to escape from the island, but claim it. This island was originally clean, but became messed up over time, our symbolically getting locked into a theater seat. The island has everything our form will need in

---

37　One needs to be ready for shifts is when around artifacts or sites of the ancient world (due to the power placed in the statues and buildings). Thus, one might get very tired. This happened to me in Egypt, and I wondered why all the other travelers I met were also exhausted at the end of the day. The places and the objects were moving people's assemblage points, and in the case of those with any spiritual training, greatly. The recommendation at such sites is to move slowly, pay attention to your overall energy. Take far more breaks to allow the assemblage point "rest time" to better handle all that is taking place and being stored in that movement.

272

this life. The problem is not from the things we were given on the island, but rather the landscaping of them. We began to be told that some things are nice and should be kept and grown, while others are not—so we tried to build up the nice things and hide or shrink the rest. We tried to get rid of things from the island, but nothing on the island can be eliminated, just misplaced. Millions are thinking they are ridding themselves of bad aspects when all they are doing is denying them or pushing them into a more dangerous spot. Instead of trying to eliminate something such as anger, we allow it to come out of hiding and just be there on the island, a tool in a tool box of possibility, used when the outer circumstances demand its use. To repress something just means it will come out eventually as an explosion. This has nothing to do with trying to be a perfect human according to some moralistic religious jargon, but simply to be the complete human you were created originally as...with all the naughty and nice accepted and potentially available.

The parasite mind has come to that island, claimed it for its own use, and developed protections to keep things landscaped for its benefit. The warrior wants to break this hold, but to do so in a way that does not damage his form. He sees illness not as a weakness of his form, but as a reflection of something weak or misplaced on his tonal. Reacquiring proper tonal will save vast amounts of power, for we are no longer wasting energy trying to be something that we are not. When Osiris is shut into the box by Set, he is imprisoned in the Tonal. He needs Horus, who represents the warrior obtaining proper tonal, who can open the box (bubble) and release access to the Nagual. By reorganizing the island properly (regaining our natural clear mind state as when a young child) one will have totally changed, yet at the same time remain the same. We become a younger and wiser version of our current self. Only when our island has been put back in proper order, do we have the foundation to begin to spend time off of it, in the Nagual.

છ૭

"My only advantage over you is that I know how to you get to the Nagual, you don't. But once there I have no more knowledge or advantage than you." (Carlos Castaneda in *Tales of Power*)

The Nagual is the part for which there is no description, no words, names, feelings, knowledge. While not exactly the Absolute, it could be considered the doorway to it—perhaps like what Rose called the Unmanifested Mind. One can talk about the Nagual but never explain it, usually only feel it. Another name for it would be Spirit, or that which lays beyond normal waking reality.

Connecting with this area is the activity called *Seeing*, which is an intuitive grasp that comes when the bubble has been burst, moving perception from The Tonal to the Nagual. It has a visual edge to it, but it is not primarily visual. It is not right to think of it as seeing through objects, or making them transparent, but more that one is able to feel into that object to know more of its essence and history. I would not call it an intuitive feeling either which is something more within the Tonal world.

Castaneda claimed that there were three attentions, what might be called different observation locations on the mountain of Totality, which also makes the three attentions similar to the three sections of Rose's Jacob's Ladder (which is also a three-step process of deeper and deeper observational awareness). Thus, *seeing* is allowing observation from this second attention (the Nagual) while at the same time keeping the regular physical image of the first attention (Tonal, normal reality). However, even when the Nagual appears, few will have any memory of it because the Tonal, through reason, has sucked up all their available energy. There is no energy or power left for someone to examine any oddities and so one just ignores anything such as odd occurrences or lapses in time or memory and goes back to the regular daily routine.

When the Nagual manifests (as an omen, power, unique experiences) we are not supposed to talk or think, only act. Don't view the experience as something special, but instead look at it as something common so your energy will not get drained. Blink. Shut off dialogue and just witness. This happened to me one night. While out at a power spot, an Ibis appeared. This bird is a symbol of Tehuti and is not found within thousands of miles of where I was. It was power, via the Nagual, bringing me a message. If I stayed relaxed and just looked on with wonder and interest, the bird stayed and interacted with me. As soon as I began to think how special this experience was (pushing perception back into Tonal egoic reason), the bird flew away.

The Nagual is personal and individual thing. One will be experiencing it, while others around will not notice anything out of the ordinary, perhaps only trees moving in the wind or a strange light. At times the Nagual itself will rearrange things, set up things in a special way so the person can have the experience without interference. Other times two or more people can be given a similar experience, but even though things may seem almost the same, when one meets the Nagual face to face they are alone. When a physical object is being borrowed by the Nagual, such as for an omen or message, that thing is no longer the normal object—it is the Nagual manifest. A bird is a bird as long as it is reflecting the earthly tonal. If it is reflecting the Nagual, it is no longer a bird and all bird rules are suspended (as something beyond the dream is borrowing the object for a short time). Normally an encounter with the Nagual is frightening for most people because Tonal rules are not in effect. It is why so many people are afraid of shamans when they first meet them. The body recognizes that he/she can open up the Nagual, which can make their parasite jumpy.

We shift or move our Intent to the Nagual and it decides on its own how things should turn out. We can only intend the Nagual and witness its effects, but no one has any idea how it works. In the Tonal we can show something specific to someone else, such as how to drive a car or hit a golf ball. In the Nagual all that can be done is open the door of it for someone, then watch and join along with them. It takes a long time to learn how to be such a doorway for someone else.

Again, there are no objects in the world, simply fibers that come from a force known as the Eagle, which have become caught in a bizarre loop of time. Humans have been conditioned to notice on a small amount of reality and "skim" or ignore the rest. We focus on fewer "items" than we believe. What we select as reality must be constantly renewed, recreated each moment to have freshness. Thus, we must intend "mountain" or "stone" each time we look at one. It is the reason that not-doings are taught which really create "obstruction" in the normal perception of the first attention, thus interrupting the ability for mind to recreate normal reality.

What is often thought of and sold as enlightenment, is really a glimpse into the immensity of that thing/force of Nothingness. Encountering it can leave one without hope, as they see that all they believed to be real are but a shadow of Nothing. Hope is the result of familiarity with the skimmings (normal way of perceiving objects) of our day to day world, and our belief that we can control them. A glimpse shows something else is in control of everything, and that is crushing to the ego. This glimpse is rarely remembered, for trips beyond "the dream" are often only remembered as a moment where there was no memory of activity, or perhaps like being in a fog.

Most would call a glimpse of the great Nothing the enlightenment experience (where there is no experience), but the ancients were clear that when in the second attention, the first attention does not really work, thus the only memory that returns from an encounter is blackness. The Land of Osiris. Until one can train their second attention through Dreaming exercises to handle the Nagual, the only thing experienced will be blackness. But it is not actually black and can in fact be perceived and interacted with. One begins to activate the second attention by forcing it to wake up, and the only way that you can wake it up is to block the first attention's normal hold on us. Are you beginning to see why the standard enlightenment talk is backwards? You wake up the second attention by blocking the first.

The egoic self wants to hold onto the old system of interpretation as long as possible, but it must be blocked. There is no specific thing to do to cross the lines themselves (no doing, no effort), yet at the same time great effort is required to block the normal skimmings of the mind.

Getting to the second attention and staying aware is also called crossing the parallel lines. The first line is where normal Tonal attention (everyday reality) ends and is perceived or felt as a wall of fog-veil.[38] Going through that wall, the first line, is moving towards "the other self" (some may call it the astral body)—and your physical body will generally feel this movement as a shift or a pressure. The second attention (other self) can be found on the other side of the second line. Both lines must be perforated (burst like a bubble) to cross over completely, leading to totally different perception. Between the two lines is an area of awareness that seers call limbo, and where most spiritual shifts of consciousness or Dreaming experiences tend to occur. Limbo is a transitional zone between the two attentions. The closer you are to first line the more the limbo experience will be similar to the tonal, the normal world experienced in a more dream-like fashion. Closer to the second line the experience will become more Nagual like, having similarities to what is called in spiritually the Astral World. Along with journeying, a good way to cross through the parallel lines is by falling backwards. This is what Egyptian false doorways in Sakkara and Giza were designed to do—fall backwards into and cross over instantly into the Nagual.

A reminder is that there is a third line that can be broken as well, taking one to the third attention or third view, where the Totality of the Self can be obtained. However, this information is of little value until someone has become familiar with the second attention, and by that time, they may be able to understand the doorway to the third attention on their own.

---

38   Again, the majority of time slips or rapid movement have been said to have come after the person involved noticed an odd fog or mist.

The Nagual was personified by David and Jennifer in the movie *Pleasantville,* who begin to break all the rules of the town and show there is far more to their bubble. Morpheus and the crew returning to the Matrix-world to interact with a possible person ready to jump their awareness, is another movie aspect of the force of Intent. In the *Truman Show,* Sylvia was the force that made Truman go looking beyond the town of Seahaven (his "heavenly" bubble). Sylvia arrives, and just before being "captured and removed" tells Truman that his world is not real and that he needs to escape. He cannot believe her for it sounds so bizarre, but "something" about her seems unworldly to him, and he never forgets her or what she said. He decides that since he feels he trusts her, he will find a way to start testing reality, quietly, without anyone else knowing. In the process, he notices bizarre or strange things in his surroundings that make him begin to question his world. Truman must have noticed these odd things before, but easily found a logical explanation. After meeting Sylvia, however, all was now open for questioning. In Castaneda terms, Sylvia is the Nagual Woman. In a sense, she acts like a driving force—even though no longer there—but somehow like a beacon. He tries to find a way to her and trusts something in her message.

Maybe the Genesis story of the Garden of Eden is not about paradise, but more of the Gnostic idea of being trapped in matter. Maybe it was not Jehovah who sent Adam and Eve out of "paradise," but Adam and Eve who wanted to leave (finding their paradise was a bubble), and the serpent is really the hero of the story—representing Intent that slipped in to reveal the truth of their situation. Eve is not the force of original sin, but like Sylvia, the passionate focus that got her and Adam to a place beyond what was perhaps a nice bubble, but a bubble nonetheless.

The Truman Show ends as Truman manages to escape the watchful eyes and goes through his final remaining fear (water), which is both the symbol of his confinement as well as the means of escape. His commitment overpowers anything thrown at him. His boat (the Santa Maria) finally punctures the external bubble—shattering the world Truman had always been led to believe in. Before walking up a set of stairs that lead to an exit door, Christoff tries one last time to convince Truman that he is safer in the bubble world, even though it is nothing but a television show. That is when Truman asks in pure Zen fashion, "Then who am I?" The poignant question all must answer if they ever want answers. Truman says good-bye to the only world he has known, and heads for the exit to see reality.

At the end of *Vanilla Sky*, Tom Cruise jumps off the building (a la the Tarot Fool into the Abyss). In *Pleasantville*, Toby McGuire leaves his cheerleader and perfect life behind to return to his crappy nerd world. In both cases they knew that the nice dream was not true reality, and no matter how nice the offer was, they would choose the real and whatever consequences came with it. For David (interestingly the character's name in both movies) even their perfect woman was not enough consolation, for she was still a "fake" woman in a fake world. In Truman's case, Sylvia is the only thing real that he knows, and thus becomes what he heads towards.

ɛ∕ɔ

Losing the Human Form

"Losing the human form was the only means of breaking the shell (the luminous core, of awareness) which is the Eagle's food. The day you don't covet the company of your friends, where you use your shields, that is the day your person has died. Losing the human form is called the clear view, when human pettiness vanishes." (Carlos Castaneda, *Eagle's Gift*)

"I understand exactly what you are going through. When I laugh at you, I really laugh at the memory of myself in your shoes. I too held onto the world of everyday life with my fingertips. Everything told me to let go, but I couldn't. Just like you I trusted my mind implicitly, even though I had no reason to." (Carlos Castaneda)

What Castaneda called Losing the Human Form is a very interesting part of the process of breaking down the egoic structure, and the shields that make it up. What one calls "a human person" is not the body that they carry, but the entire structure of layers of beliefs. To let all that dissolve or fall away is called Losing the Human Form. People act the way they do because they are clinging to the human form, which is a force, a mold. Everything, including plants and animals have a mold—the source, or basic structure of that type of object. When the human mold is witnessed it appears as a radiant light, so strong that it can blind us. Normally if anyone sees this radiant sight, they believe they have seen God, and in one sense they are correct.

This dropping can only happen when we lose our desire to cling. People will cling to anything they like, even the desire to be liked. Losing the Human Form is a rather painful experience, and is described nicely by U.G. Krishnamurti, Richard Rose, and Castaneda. Deeper awareness will burst through and burn everything. Depending how strong one's shields are, will determined how much pain is present in the process. It often leaves only following a massive internal battle that can manifest as an illness, and it is a natural reaction to struggle against it, as if something bad is happening, and in so fighting it we block it. Let go of your fear and let the human form fall away on its own. Losing the human form links to what is described in the Additional Material as the *shamanic initiation illness*.

When Losing the Human Form has finally been completed, the normal human feelings will no longer be there. Then comes an odd aloofness and detachment. Everything is equal and the same, yet the person is totally new. To anyone who knew that person prior to this happening, it will be hard, for they will keep expecting or hoping or trying to make them be the normal person that they were before. Yet following Losing the Human Form, the regular connection to the natural world is simply gone, and nothing comes to replace it. They

don't become a different type of person, but something deeper—
and all the expected rules of behavior and thought get burned out
in the process. The human form is the belief that has caused people
to think they are people in a life game with rules, winners, losers
and advancement. Once the human form is gone—all that is seen to
be far less important than previously. It will also take much of the
judgment and anger about others away, for they were only acting the
way they did because it was their shields that caused the behaviours,
not the deeper reality of someone.

> "He desires nothing, yet instead of playing with his fellow
> men like they were toys, he meets them in the midst of their
> folly. The only difference between them is that a man who
> sees, controls his folly while the average man does not. A
> man who sees no longer has an active interest in his fellow
> men. Seeing has already detached him from absolutely
> everything he knew before." (Carlos Castaneda)

The aftermath of this process takes time. After a true encounter with
the Absolute (Nagual) many will find it hard to return to the Tonal
(world of order, noise, pain). But to stay or return is something that
has nothing to do with one's reason. If one chooses not to return,
they will disappear as if the earth has swallowed them up. Perhaps this
is the explanation for the odd event referred to as *human spontaneous
combustion*, the burning up of a person who lost the human form and
did not want to remain. But anyone who "chooses" to return to the
earth then must WAIT until one's PARTICULAR TASK is finished,
a task each being is given (even if one cannot notice it) and once
we have stepped beyond the normal dream what matters is that we
complete our task. Waiting to fulfill that task is a very special waiting.
If you get impatient or desperate, you will be cut down mercilessly by
the sharpshooters of the universe (the forces of adversity).

 If on the other hand your personal power and effort is such that
you can complete the task—in either SUCCESS or FAILURE—then

each will get their gift of power, the Totality of the Self. I believe that Rose's experience that he had when he was 30 was the reaching of the Nagual—experiencing enlightenment, but not becoming enlightened. He must have had some task (perhaps surrounding his teaching work and preparation) and as that task got completed he became the experience. Even though he knew, he still had to work to finish his totality, which as some point before he began his teaching occurred. Hence it was then what he called "the time being right" for the students to start to come.

When the task is over, and they have reached their totality, they will also become filled with Power. Each will then do with that power what they are drawn to do—some may live as a hermit, another become famous. We might say that Rose's power from completing his task became the TAT Foundation. The warrior will truly understand that they are alone, but they can never be lonely because their love of the Absolute becomes total. For a warrior there can be no greater love than Totality, and nothing else can bring so much freedom to his spirit. It will only make sense when someone has faced his death and aloneness.

Part of the waiting involves examining if you can help other people in the ways we have come to think of as helping. Mostly you don't help people like you think that you would. At first, to find out that the world is nothing but a dream, movie, hologram is depressing. Well, for your ego it is depressing, because it has been spending all its time trying to get more, advance, fix, change. And when we see that none of that can happen, that is where the depression comes. But for what is deeper than the egoic structure all that is felt is a magnificent freedom. One knows it is a dream, but interacts with everything as if they were real, as if what they do matters, offering help or guidance or laughter or whatever in an acting known as controlled folly (see chapter 10). They feel comfortable getting to know the dream and not needing to change it. They simply want to alter a few elements of it. This is mirrored in the myths of the Hopi who talk symbolically of the need to break into a new world, not fix or change the old one.

With this gaining of power comes a new way of working with time. They no longer deal with time the way others do, linear, but instead see time as a tube, similar to looking into a tunnel, and draw from that look the knowledge of how to proceed. In a sense they are no longer looking at time as it passes (normal awareness) but see time before it comes. Donnie Darko suggests this with Mr. Monatoff when he speaks of following God's Channel, thus if one can see what God wants and perform that action they will always be walking in a correct and holy way—no matter how unholy their actions could in fact seem to be within the dreamstate. Doing this also helps them to learn how to be like Morpheus on the street in the *Matrix*, avoiding everyone effortlessly while Neo (stuck in the mind) bumps into everyone and gets his attention drawn to that which is not helpful (the woman in the red dress). Meanwhile Morpheus in his state of flow is able to keep his attention free to find the next mind he might be able to help, the next person who could be brought closer to an encounter with the Nagual.

∾

Meeting the Nagual

I was visiting an old university friend in Calgary and took time to go down to the Hillhurst area and have a coffee and enjoy the nice weather. Memories of previous walks when I was in a good energetic space filled my mind as I headed towards the Higher Ground. Today was a stunning day out and I wanted to sit on a bench outside rather than inside. As I walked in, I noticed a cute blonde sitting, and writing, on the farthest outdoor table. I went in and got my coffee and felt kinda "flirty" and said to myself that if the bench beside her is still free I would sit and just drink beside her. It was, so I sat down. She was writing feverishly, so I got out my notebook and was making some notes myself. Then for some reason I said to her, "want to trade notebooks, you write in mine, I'll write in yours?" She smiled, "I don't know if I have anything to write in there." I said, "ok, if you think of something profound to say, ask for my notebook." She said ok. I looked at her, and had a hard time gauging her age, based on her appearance and clothing. I really noticed her clothing for some reason, a red two strap top and a pair of black tights. It made it hard to tell if she was a first-year university student, or a 29-year-old who had just finished working out. I was just happy sitting there watching the dream characters walk by, when she took a break from writing and asked me, "What are you writing?"

I replied, "I am writing about the dream." She asked if it was a dream I had last night, and I said "no," and pointed with my hands to the street, "this dream." She looked at me in an odd but curious fashion. I asked her what she was writing. She said she likes to look back one year from where she was and write about it, and one year ago she claimed she was in some sort of marathon. I didn't fully catch if she meant she ran in one or organized one. I remember asking her if it was a good experience, and she said it was great.

Around this point I began to recognize that she was responding energetically in this conversation. We did not know each other, and most women would be very reluctant to say anything to a male stranger, but she was very relaxed and talkative. I tried to think exactly what I was doing a year ago. I told her a year ago I was in Europe. She asked what I was doing there. My response was odd I said, "I was doing some talks." She asked on what. I said, "Ancient Knowledge." She asked if I was a scholar, I said no. She asked what I wrote about, I said mostly on the secrets of alchemists and shamans, the hidden stuff beyond what most people think about them.

It was then she hit me with her question. "What is the biggest secret you have found?" It shook me. I had no answer, partially because I wasn't sure. She joked, "Would you have to kill me if you told me?" I said, "No, it's not that kind of secret." At that moment there was a beep from a car horn, and she raised her hand to a guy in a white pickup truck and said to me, "My ride is here, have a great day." She bounded to the truck and I just sat, mostly disappointed that my interesting conversation had ended. I was enjoying it. Oh well, that's how these things go.

I got up and began to walk to the New Age bookstore in the area, then walked back to Higher Ground to have another coffee and relax as my friend was still working for another hour or so. I chose to walk back on the other side of the street than I had walked up. Half way there a white pickup truck pulled over—which I instantly noticed, and a woman got out and rushed past me into a bookstore. There was a sense it was the same girl I had been talking to. I didn't get a good look at her face, just the overall sense of her. Height was the same, and she was wearing the SAME clothes. Too co-incidental. I thought the guy driving (likely boyfriend/husband) might recognize me from the bench and may not be too happy that I turned in my tracks to talk to his girlfriend. So I stopped at a bench beside a gelato store and waited until the light turned green and the truck sped away.

With the truck gone, I stood up and went walking back up the street to find her, when "she" came out of a bookstore. I walked past and stared at her face, only this was not "her." This woman did not have blonde hair, her hair was brown with blonde highlights—but she was the same height, same build, wearing the exact same clothes, exiting the exact same white pickup. A few elements of her face were also slightly different from the woman I conversed with at the coffee shop. This new woman was carrying a huge box. She walked past me without even a hint of eye recognition that she knew me. If we had just talked twenty minutes ago for almost an hour on a bench, her eyes would have told that by glancing towards me. No glance. I was a total stranger. Yet I was also 100% sure, this had to be the woman I just talked to. But how could she not look the same? How could her appearance in certain areas change in twenty minutes?

I staggered past her a few steps, stopped and sort of tried to catch my breath and think about this. For some reason I only spent a moment or two on the oddity, then walked to the restaurant where I was meeting my friend for dinner. I had mostly forgotten all about this until my friend asked me at dinner if anything odd happened during the day. As soon as I retold the story I realized that, shit, it was the same woman. But when I spoke to her at the coffee shop she was in the Nagual, and not a person (at least for my individual perception). The Spirit had altered her appearance slightly to look and act a particular way for me, and when I saw her again she was in her normal person state without the Nagual borrowing her. She was the Nagual when talking to me, a direct Spirit interaction, then to make it clear the dream showed me the real person a few minutes later. It was a meeting right out of a Castaneda novel, meetings that tend to make me question reality. How did I not fully recognize this at the time I was speaking to her? Why did I not pay more attention to every detail of that meeting when it was occurring?

Appendix E

—◦◦◦—

SHAMANS

I am sitting at a table in the back of a small series of apartments in the north part of the Mexican town of Palenque. I am here with Chris Powell, American archaeologist and lead investigator of the team digging in the Cross Group at the Ancient Mayan site of the same name. We have struck up a connection based on that we are both looking for aspects of greater knowledge in the past than the standard books and histories present. He had given me a tour of their latest work, and we have made it to the courtyard behind the apartments where the archaeology team stays at and are sipping on a beer chatting about Palenque's symbolic connections. The third member of our group is a local Mayan man of about 65. He hasn't said all that much, particularly to me. As Chris and I shared various ideas about the nature of time, the old man turned to face me and said very clearly, "There was no time here before the white people."

I heard him, and semi-continued with the conversation, but at the same time something inside was rebelling. What does that mean? No time before the white people. Because there were no clocks? They didn't know the exact time of day? No that is not what he was referring to, for such a comment would not have fit in with the conversation. Was he really saying that there actually was NO TIME? An hour later our chat was finished. The old man patted me on the back, wished me well and walked off. He never gave any further explanation of what he said—like a Zen Master, dropping a koan on me and leaving me to deal with it. This was my first meeting with someone shaman-like.

☙

It still shocks me when I go to a shaman website and see, for example, the main photo of "the group" of practitioners. A bunch of middle-aged white people, wearing ponchos they bought in New Mexico, beads from Sedona, and holding a rattle which they bought in a store with a name like "Buddha's Breath."

It is now fashionable in the western spiritual world to claim to be a shaman. Take some workshops, get a certificate, claim some Native heritage, before then giving drumming classes and building sweat lodges. We have a world full of pseudo-shamans, playing games of power to fool white people for money and prestige. The word "shaman" is a rather mixed up term, anyway. It is a Siberian word for a very specific type of person in their specific tribal culture. The name can be translated as "ghost talker or night walker." White academics standardized this word to indicate any man or woman of traditional culture involved in utilizing healing, medicine, journeying, spirit contacts, divination, prayer, ceremony, or songs for ascertaining a patient's trouble to find a healing cure.

Today *shaman* has become a word to represent a lot of things. But it is a very specific word for me. To me it does not mean someone who is a smart Native Indian, but something which many wise Native men and women became. People of all traditions reached what this word embodies, but that was mostly a long time ago. When I look out there today, just about anyone using the word to describe themselves probably isn't. The few that really are shamans, generally stay unnoticed. And yet, how did the real ones truly become what has been labeled a shaman? Pushed to the brink of death or beyond, they fell into an illness or madness so unbearable that they only way they could stop was to be a shaman.

∽

I am sitting on a park bench in downtown Ottawa waiting for someone I have never met. His name is Roberto, and he is from Brazil. This was early in my study of Native Indian medicine traditions. When I was back in town visiting some friends, I decided to call a few of the people in the local spiritual magazine listing themselves as shamans. I met one yesterday, and she was the typical white-looking New Age type, who became a shaman after a few months in a workshop. We talked for about 30 minutes over coffee when she finally said to me, "I am sorry, I don't think I can talk to you anymore. I have no real understanding of anything you are asking or discussing. But I did meet someone last week that might be more help. He is here from Brazil. This is his number." I appreciated her honesty, and today I wait on the bench.

When he arrives, he is not much of what I was picturing. Roberto is your typical looking dark skinned 50-ish guy, in khakis and a long-sleeved shirt. After getting a coffee he tells me that his daughter is married and living in the country and he is trying to move to Canada as well. He starts to tell me some of what he was taught over the years about trees, how they communicate, and how we can talk with them. He has me perform some basic "tree talking" exercises.

After about three hours together he begins to tell me his story of how he came to learn, one I will only paraphrase briefly, so as to not lose the personal power in it. His grandfather was the healer of his village when Roberto was a boy. When it was Roberto's time to learn as a teenager, he had no interest, so his grandfather walked him into the jungle to a cave. From there he threw the teen in a deep lake. Roberto realized right away that in the lake were all sorts of creatures, one he instantly felt was a crocodile. He screamed for his grandfather's help. Roberto was told to stay in there until his fear was gone. Every time he tried to climb out, he was pushed back in. He finally began to recognize that he was going to die. He then remembered a crocodile he had met as a young boy and threw rocks at it for no reason. He wondered about that. And since he was going to die anyway, he thought he should apologize to this one in this lake. On that he was bumped, and he could sense the creature. It was "talking" to him, about his stone throwing. He "talked" with it until he felt he was forgiven and he felt it swim away. This happened over and over again with various creatures, from snakes to fish to insects. After several hours, he had spoken to most of the animal kingdom, and issued apologies for all of his previous acts and for ignoring them. His grandfather pulled him out. Roberto said he felt better than ever in his life. After that, his teaching began. This sort of intensity of practice, of putting one at the cross of death to create a learning door was not forgotten by me. I took a part of his story with me always.

At the end of our meeting I asked if I could give him some money for our time, he laughed heartily. "You know very well I can't accept your money. Anything real is not something you pay for, it is a sharing. I didn't pay my grandfather, so you don't have to pay me."

"But I should give you something. You were very good for my spirit today."

"You did, you bought me coffee. And you helped me to see that there are a few whites in this country who might be interested in these stories. That is good for my spirit."

☙

The best way to test if someone today really is a shaman is to find out how much they have sacrificed to become what they now are. Have they really tasted their own death? Or have they just played a game of denial, projection, and distraction their entire life—which is now carrying on into this new role being played?

"Unlike the medicine man, the shaman's adoption of his profession in many cases was not voluntary. The future shaman's experience of being called, serves frequently to consist of a compulsive state from which they see no other means of escape except to "shamanize." It is often clear that the one who is to become a shaman consciously does not want to do so at all, but is forced to it by the 'spirits' which drive them deeper and deeper into despair and illness, from which they can find no way out but death, or the assumption of the office of shaman." (Lommel Andrews, *The World of the Early Hunter*)

New Age white people read the books, decided they wanted to be shamans, and an entire modern system was created—taught via organizations and workshops, with a few borrowed practices and ideas from all over the world, then stamped by the name shamanism. What is found in these workshops, while of some value, are not the practices done in traditional native ceremony, nor like the work of the specialist shamans of Siberia. In fact, most of those whites and natives marketing themselves as shamans, are more-or-less slapping the face of the ancient wise men and women who spent and sacrificed their life to learn. A great documentary called *White Shamans, Plastic Medicine Men*, that may still be found on Youtube presents the depths of delusion people will sink into believing they are shamans.

Being a medicine person or tribal wisdom holder was not a career or business. The medicine person was needed. People got sick and it was their job to get them well again, while being sure the right conditions for overall survival were set up to find and grow food, and to avoid serious weather in advance. They could not be involved in spiritual games, and they had to succeed, or the tribe could die off. Just because they did not have hospitals, EKG machines, or Demerol tablets did not mean their methods did not work. They did. If you are looking for a book, I can recommend none more highly than the book *Fools Crow: Wisdom and Power* by Thomas Mails.[39] The shaman was one who had seen first-hand how dangerous and cruel this reality can be, and seemingly chosen, had the task of bringing a small bit of sanity to an insane reality.

To be a real medicine person required training, sacrifice, and constant vigilance. But it was still a calling that one in a sense could be taught via a lineage. The shaman was different. A shaman could not get there due to grandparents, or from wanting to. Which is why the shaman usually came from another path altogether—or if they were a medicine person, they were likely a failed medicine person. The shaman's life before being a shaman is usually riddled with failure, until they found the only thing they are not failing at— being a shaman. For on the surface a shaman and a good healer will seem the same. But there is a different air to what the shaman does—due to the Awakening that occurred. One might say that a shaman is someone who has gone past their religion, their culture, and beliefs. In fact, they died to standard reality. There are shamans of all traditions: Chinese, Cherokee, Christian, Islamic, Buddhist, and simple bus drivers. But each will be coloured by their previous experiences and pathways. Awakening is similar, but the expression of it is unique.

A splash of emptiness touches everything the shaman does, even if to outward appearances they act like other people around them. He or she was more seen as a "healer of souls," one who had gone through so much, that they were respected and feared equally. It is not a profession or sometimes done along with other things in your life. Being chosen by the spirits to become a shaman means your life as a normal person is all but over. It often began as a child, either with a serious illness or when some overwhelming traumatic experience forced them to turn inwards, and from this crack the whole unconscious opens, and the potential new shaman falls into it.

---

39   This is Mail's second book on Fools Crow in 1989, not the first he wrote in the
      1970's

Almost no one who became a shaman just had the process show up at thirty-one, it has been acting on them their whole life. Most must deal with a difficult period known as the Shamanic Initiation Illness where they are on the brink of death for perhaps years.[40]

The shaman, for some internal or external reason, has seemingly been forced to return to the world of people to be of service. To make that Awakening available to those around them, thus generally they will stay within the boundaries of their previous religion or spiritual tradition. That is because they prefer to work with the current belief structure of the people, rather than try to break the structures of everyone, which will just create conflict. They may still perform prayer and ceremony, but they are working on a deeper level. They would be masters of what Richard Rose called "between-ness." Being a shaman means to have come into power. And the greatest power one can find is emptiness. Yet a shaman could not really describe what power is, or how they got it—just one day after years of sacrifice, it was there. The best way to test if someone really is a shaman will be to find out how much have they sacrificed for what they now are? Have they really tasted their own death, or have they just played a game of denial, projection, and distraction their whole life?

The real Shaman is not perfect, nor necessarily traveled through the door to Truth—but they managed to look through that door. To come back to be of service, they had to constantly battle with the deepest, darkest parts of the themselves and the world—but it is this constant battle that allows them to be of service to others who are going through their own dark nights. While the village all lived together, including the medicine people, the shaman lived alone. This

---

40 Read the Additional Material for information on what is referred to as the Shamanic Initiation Illness. Rose went through it. Karl Renz had four years of pounding headaches where he could rarely get out of bed. A Scottish shaman I know, Michael Dunning, was so sick for several years that he could barely walk and spent each day crawling to sit under a particular Yew tree that was teaching him. His is an amazing story of courage and healing.

is an important point. Part of the group yet always excluded from it. They have no organization, are not building programs, or making themselves important or rich. They find it hard to charge anything for their services, believing that what they learned is a gift. If they do go into the modern world to share, it is usually for a very nominal fee (enough for their food and shelter).[41] They are in-between the world of the living and the world of the dead, the world of the physical and the world of the spirit. The best word I can use to describe what they are is a bridge. Part of accepting the call of the shaman, is accepting the call to be of service, usually only seeing people when nothing else has worked for them.

---

41   My additional material on healing describes how charging for healing is a dangerous practice in the modern world, for both healer and patient.

Appendix F

THE MUTUS LIBER

The *Mutus Liber* (Silent Book) was mentioned in Chapter 8, but here I will go into detail on this very unique presentation. Only with a background in Hermetics and Alchemic symbolism can what is here be unraveled. There are many layers, and all I can provide is what I can decipher from them. There is far more to be found than just what I can see. Go through it yourself. What comes to you?

First published in 1677 in New Rochelle, France, this work contains almost no words at all. Instead, within it one finds 15 images. In this way it is similar to the Major Arcana of the Tarot. The first plate of the Silent Book shows a sleeping man with a ladder beside him- while the last place depicts the man risen and the ladder cast aside. I believe the book to be the symbolic rendering of climbing Jacob's Ladder. I will re give that explanation here. Note that the plates are not just reference material meant to be glanced at. They are infused with power, and are meant to be studied and meditated upon, almost as if they were paintings hanging on the walls of a gallery.

Plate 1

The first plate in The Mutus Liber has a few words in Latin that translate as "Mutus Liber, wherein all operations of Hermetic Philosophy are described and reported—as set forth in hieroglyphic figures, sacred to God the merciful, thrice great and greatest, and dedicated to the sons of the Art, the name of the author being Altus." This is the only text that appears until plate 14. We are told it is Hermetic, sacred to the thrice great (Thoth-Hermes) while the author is claimed to be Altus (high, or one who has risen to the top of the pyramid). It is dedicated to all alchemists, philosophers, and seekers—the Sons of the Art.

The First Plate can help explain the first pyramid asleep state. The main focus of the plate is in the middle where a man is bound and sleeping up against a stone. This is obviously Jacob, laying down on his way to Harran, placing his head on what is often called the Grail Stone. Jacob, like us, was asleep, not understanding his suffering, nor the nature of reality. He is bound by ropes and cannot move. These ropes are the wrappings of the mummy and symbolize the egoic mind that binds us to matter and thought. It can also represent Jacob as the chained man in Plato's cave. Interestingly his left leg is raised up to make a triangular shape and represent that duality can only be transcended with a third force, to make a pyramid-triangle. Before him is a ladder, that has two angels blowing trumpets—either as an attempt to wake Jacob, or perhaps as a sound guide to lead him on his dream of heaven. Take notice that the two angels cut the ladder into three sections, certainly no coincidence. Also note that the ladder gets smaller as it rises, suggesting as Rose, that the bottom rungs are much larger.

Above are ten stars (ten starting a new cycle), along with a moon reflecting the light of the sun past the dark clouds that surround it—as if light is there for the sleeper, just right now it cannot be seen directly. Surrounding the middle image is a rose branch that is made to look like the Egyptian ren glyph. The ren surrounded a royal name, but also may represent a cave or bubble. The stems are tied and show two roses, which might represent that this plate is showing that the sleeper, while with king-like potential, is currently stuck in cave-like shadow duality.

Plates 2-7 help explain the lower pyramid of Rose's system and relate to the first alchemic stage of Nigredo. Alchemy is not a religion or spiritual movement (a path that will lead either to heavenly immortality, or some sort of perfected God-like form), but to become one who Knows. Nigredo[42] begins in blackness and darkness with the looking at the Prima Materia (First Matter or deepest aspect of self, ego), which requires a full-scale descent into the mind, Modern alchemic writers say that Nigredo is a death-rebirth process due to the many images of death and destruction that accompany this phase in the medieval texts. The challenge of Nigredo is that there is no resurrection that comes with it. Generally, all there is, is continuing depression at the lies of the world and ourselves. We are dismantling, but not replacing much.

---

42 This stage is said to take place under Saturn (associated with lead -intellect) representing blockages and is shown in illustrations destroying the old king (our mind). Other images of Nigredo include Capet Mortum (decapitated head), the green lion (instinctual force of nature who swallows the sun- ego), ravens (birds of death) a desert of human skeletons/coffins.

Plate 2

The second plate of *The Mutus Liber* is divided into two, with two winged angels in the top half, and a man and a woman on the bottom. The bottom couple is kneeling as if praying towards a castle-like furnace, to fuel the alchemic fire. Nigredo is referred to as "the cooking." The two sections are symbolizing duality. The castle can be thought of as the body of the two individuals (or perhaps they are the male and female halves of the same individual), where the Prima Materia is mixed with fire and then moistened with dew (blood, sweat and tears that appears in plate 4). This compost is then placed in the "philosophic egg' which refers to awareness. This egg (in the castle) must be kept warm, but not hot, thus the need for the fire to be restrained from overheating or the work will be lost. This is a period for the alchemists when breath-energy work such as Qi Gong is important—not to feel healthier, but to generate the vast amount of energy that is required to look at our mind. Nigredo is a head-on, ego-shattering experience, and can bring about a fear of continuing. These reactions came from the Old King (or Queen) in us who wants to stay on the throne and rule. There is no way out, only in. That may be why the couple is praying. They know they are going to need guidance from something more than just their small self.

Behind the couple are a series of drapes, like what one would see in a theater production, helping to indicate the movie like quality to life. But if we look to the midpoint of the card, one of the angel's feet "breaks the plane" that divided the two scenes, a break in the bubble. We see the woman's hand reach up to touch the foot (similar to the Sistine Chapel ceiling where Adam and God touch fingers). The fact that the touch happens on the foot might symbolize that the work is in the very early stages. The angel's foot is like Sylvia in *the Truman Show* or David in *Pleasantville*—the outside force that comes to break the bubble of standard reality. Notice that the angels have a light and dark leg, but it is the light leg—that which dispels darkness, that is what pierces the veil for those below. The couple will have to put in a great amount of energy to break this bubble, and the use of energy becomes a key focus in Nigredo.

> "How much time are we wasting watching tv, or running for a tiny bit of pleasure or distraction? Should we know that we have so little time before death ends our fallacy of living an important life." (Shawn Nevins)

Plate 3

Plate 3 is still broken into an upper and lower section. The middle area is made of three circles, one inside of the other—mirroring Rose's pyramid inside a pyramid. This continuous circular movement can also give the indication of a labyrinth or a spiraling funnel. Neptune (who rules water and dreams) rides on the top. Within the center circle are two fishermen, one fishing, while the other is laying back. Perhaps showing that one part of us wants to do work (fishing is often a metaphor for meditation), while another part wants to be lazy. The middle area has a ram and a bull (symbols of sexual energy that need to come under control at the beginning stage) on a landscape, while below them is a woman with a basket and a man throwing a fishing rod (the rod pierces the circle and goes into the third). The outer circle has a flock of ten birds—perhaps indicating the ten stars from the first card are getting closer to us.

Plate 4

The fourth plate has in the foreground a man and a woman wringing out a sheet of collected morning dew over a tub. Other sheets in the middle of the plate are out and not yet collected. Dew in alchemic symbolism represents the sweat of the work, that leads to additional energy. This new-found energy we want to collect to use for our search, not to waste in our normal useless pursuits. Rose always claimed that the control of the sexual impulse and energy is what will give us the fuel for our intuition. The energy will be collected as we control the ram and bull within. Another aspect to plate 4 is that the bull, ram, and the castle type buildings, match up with the second circle of plate 3, which was covered over by the first circle. It is like we are now seeing behind or directly through the circle of the fishermen. This subtle hint is that much of the process will be hidden, or be easily dismissed, and we must continue to look deeper at all times, turn over every rock as Rose might say. The back part of this plate has the sun moved to the left, while in the middle is a pyramid like structure, almost as if made from rays. But rays of what, for putting the sun in the plate tells us that the rays are not from the sun. They may in some way relate to a seemingly missing part of Nigredo, known as conjunction (joining of opposites), where Sol (male sun) and Luna's (female moon) coupling and eventual death, cause Mercurius (Hermes) to rise from the ashes depicted with wings (phoenix-like) and holding caduceus (the rising kundalini serpents). Not until Hermes is born within will any real transformation or understanding of Self happen.

Conjunction also represents Horus, born from the combination of Osiris (spirit) who was dead, and living Isis (nature), who battles Set, the killer of his father Osiris. However, Horus can never compete the battle, as neither can defeat the other. That is because Set is not evil, but the useful mind that has come under the control of the parasite (the serpent Apop). Horus wins when he stops fighting it, and instead un-hypnotizes it. Eventually when the transformation is complete, it will be Set riding in Ra's boat who spears the serpent Apop, as Set (mind) can no longer be hypnotized, freed thanks to the Hero's journey of Horus (Heru in Egyptian). It might be good for the reader to look over the Greek version of this myth, Hercules, and see what aspects of that myth applies to one's current life challenges.

Plate 5

Plate 6

Plate 7

Plates 5, 6, and 7 of *The Mutus Liber* are similar. Each of the plates are divided in three, and each depiction symbolizes inner work. There tends to be a man and woman in each segment, revealing the work is occurring in duality. It ends with plate 7 where the infant from plate 6 gets devoured (similar to the child in the Osiris myth that Isis puts on the flames to make immortal). Yet we also see the child coddled and held. This child is of course Horus/Hermes and represents the Virgin Birth, which is paradoxically both the start and end of the process of Nigredo. Horus is magically born to a higher realm. This new child might be the top of the first pyramid which Rose calls the Umpire, the goal of the first stage. We see the child puts its hands to the man's lips. This sly Hermetic gesture firstly means that one can only go through the task by inner work, not through the use of words (books), but also that one must stay silent to others while working the process, or be seen as insane or be burned at the stake as a heretic.

The Mutus Liber makes a change by the time we come to plate 8, the symbolic number of Thoth-Hermes. What becomes apparent is that plates 8 and 11 are similar to plate 2. As well plates 9 and 12 are similar to 4, while plates 10 and 13 are similar to 5, 6 and 7. Thus there becomes three sets of three series (the Hermetic number repeating itself), but with slight modifications. Also, interestingly, plate #3 (with the three circles) does not get repeated in the series. To not be confused, I will explain each three-plate sequence together, such as 8, 11 and 2.

Plate 8

Plate 8 (like plate 2) is still divided into two sections, which have the angels on top, and the man, woman and castle below. But the picture has become reversed. The woman is now to the left of the card, the man to the right. While it is harder to tell in upper section, the angels and egg too have been reversed. To me the reversal is calling our attention that something has been turned around, or in this case, shifted a stage upward. Looking to the bottom of the card, the drapes behind have risen—the curtain is rising, the veil of Isis is lifting, and we can now see that there are two pillars that support it. The two pillars are found in Tarot Card two beside Isis, as she sits with the sacred book. Thus, we see that Isis is being alluded to with plate 8. The castle has remained the same, but the two people seem to either have gotten fatter, aged, or both. This is not a drawing error. Everything in these cards has a symbolic purpose. The fatter bodies can indicate that wisdom is being stored in the body. The background has also changed. Originally there was only a blank wall, or perhaps the horizon, now there appears two windows. My guess is that they symbolize the break in the bubble started in plate two by the feet of the angels and have now become complete openings. The upper shows that the angels have changed form, they too have become fatter. Within the egg is Hermes, with his winged hat, caduceus and is standing upon the earth. A sun and a moon can be seen on the land. Neptune (the egoic mind) from plate 2, has been transformed into Hermes. For the angels, the land that they once stood on is gone (now only existing in the egg) and is a sign they have lifted off from earth. High in the clouds, they are now almost being raised by the ten eagles or hawks. Given that there are five on each side, the number of Horus, one could say that it is with the path of Horus that we will raise our Hermetic Egg towards the Sun. The big sun is the Process Observer, the goal of this stage.

Plate 11

In plate 11 the scene shifts as the card is reversed back to the way it appeared in plate 2. This reversal, and reversal back, of the cards might have the idea of showing that one has seen the world as not being real—but then returned to operate in the non-real reality. This is sometimes known as the Zen Mountain experience. Below, the drapes and even the pillars are gone. Reality has been exposed for how it actually is. This might be shown too with a second set of windows added to the wall behind, now more oval shape, appearing to be eyes. Isis has become known. The man and the woman have become much thinner, as they were back in the second plate—mountains are mountains again. On the above, the transformation keeps going. The angels have risen further, as almost all the clouds are gone—the eagles are still there beneath them. It can be easier to see in this plate that the leading birds each have a branch in their mouths. The angels have gotten fatter. Perhaps that while on the physical below things are returning more to normal, on the upper spiritual plane one has gotten fatter (filled with more wisdom). The earth is now completely gone from the egg of Hermes and all that is left is him now standing on the small sun and the small moon—symbolizing that he himself is the third point that the baseline (sun and moon) will be transcended by.

Plate 9

Plate 12

When we move to plates 9 and 12 there are similar subtle changes from plate 4, which was a complete image of a landscape, but now the scene has been divided into two. The original landscape remains above, while below there are scenes with a man, woman, and Hermes. The background has changed. Castles appear when previously there seemed to be only dwellings, while in the middle is a church. One might say that symbolically the material is getting "upgraded." In the sky, the moon has joined the sun (however the moon was there in card 4, but we could only see a small sliver of it). The rays—of whatever they are in the center, now do not seem to be touching the land anymore, but stop above it. The sheets of dew that were laid out have changed to be the tubs that were filled by the man and woman. There are six dew tubs laid out in pyramid form. The Dew of the work—the intuition or stored energy, is now ready to be used. The two animals appear stronger and more vital, as if they have been drinking from the tubs. The scenes below plate 9 are little more difficult to understand. To the left is a man and woman. It appears she has some liquid in a container that is being poured into the jar held by the man. To the right, a rather fat Hermes is giving a bottle which is half-full. It is Hermes giving, for he gives with the right hand, while the woman is receiving with the left—thus the masculine-feminine principles are being displayed, kept harmonious during the exchange. It perhaps symbolizes that the Dew (stored energy) is now getting infused with the wisdom of Hermes.

When we come to plate 12, the best way I can describe the top scene, is that we have zoomed in closer on the landscape. We can now make out the background more clearly, the church can now be seen in full, as well as castle towers. Also interesting is that the rays from the sky now reach the ground, where they did not in plate 9. The pouring continues below, while the woman has gotten fatter, and Hermes has gotten skinnier. This likely symbolized the Hermetic Dew has been transferred to the practitioner which has made them "more powerful."

Plate 10

Plate 13

Plates 10 and 13 are like the group that came in 5, 6, and 7. In plate 10 a man and woman continue to work together with a part of the alchemic process—measuring, pouring, and firing. In the bottom section, the man and a woman stand beside the castle—however they now look youthful, with long hair, and each having a sun on their head (representing the rising kundalini force). They have their hands joined, as if showing the two sides are becoming one—either from the standpoint of male-female, or left brain-right brain. In the distance is a target, and while she holds a bow, no arrow is seen. Plate 13 is similar. It is still in three segments. The biggest change on the top is that the left table appears more like a large wood table. It can be thought of as another "close up" of the scene. The symbol in the bottle changes as well. In plate 10 this was a hexagon made of up seven small bubbles, which has now turned into a sun. In the bottom (with zoomed in appearance), we get a better view of the target. Numbers appear around the two people, which are 100, 1000 and 10,000, then 8 CC. That each is the previous number multiplied by 10 has significance, perhaps indicating a tenfold increase in the work of hitting the target with each stage we master. Eight is the number of Hermes while CC is undeciphered. In Roman numerals the letter C was 100 which could make the last number 80,000—or 8 200, 208, or various other possible variations.

This process of Coagulation-Citrinius can be found in Plate #14. This is a unique plate in the set. The top has three similar looking castles to what we have seen all along. Notice that there are three complete structures—representing the three phases of the process. You may also notice that all along, each castle has had three smaller castles on top. There are no people in the upper sections with the castles, but the two windows and the drapes appear again. The second level of the plate has three people (two women and one man) engaged in a similar process. The woman seems to be of normal size, but the man appears almost as if a dwarf or midget. All are pouring liquid. Beside each is a Roman number, read across, 6, 2, 10. It is hard to know why those numbers are chosen. However, to add them up reaches the total of 18, which in the Tarot is the card of Moon (the only card in the Tarot without people). In numerology when the 1 and 8 are added together, this makes 9. In the Tarot, 9 is the number of the Hermit, the older man with the staff and lamp, completing the progress and moving to share his knowledge.

Plate 14

The third section of plate 14 has two eggs in a box on top of a large fire. This can represent the fire and work not only of Coagulation, but of the stage to come Rubedo. The box on the left is marked with a moon, the right with a sun. Each show ten rays (completion) coming from its face. Between the boxes is a balance and a spoon (suggesting it will be spooning out something that was being carefully measured), while below is what can be called a mortar and pestle (to grind and mash). This could also represent the Grail Cup. On each side of the box is a small ball or bubble, in which are three small round objects (perhaps grapes). Grapes were sometimes used by the Cathars in Southern France to symbolize the Grail. A vase is in the middle that has the glyphs of sun and moon fused together, to say the lunar and solar principles cooked separately above, are now linked as one. Below this are the words "Pray, Read, Read, Read again. Labour and Discover." A reminder like Rose that all one has is their commitment to finish the process. The man has one finger raised in the air (a sign of Knowledge seen in card five of the Tarot) while the woman makes the bull-ram horn Amun sign which surprised me. Both are placing their left fingers to their lips to represent a similar message in plate 7. That the same gesture appears in both plate 7 and 14 indicate that each is the bridge point in the process, the first pyramid going through plates 1-7, the second 8-14. Each thus lasts 7 plates, a complete chakra cycle—as some alchemic systems are set up around seven stages instead of the usual three. *The Mutus Liber* has thus combined both symbolic representations of alchemy into one.

Plate 15

The final plate of the *Mutus Liber* (15), indicates the end of the work. Jacob has risen, and the ladder is discarded. While Jacob was asleep in the first plate, while here he is on the ground dead. The death of the self has occurred. The objects around suggest the dead figure might be Hercules, the Greek hero version of Horus (Heru). The seeker, the challenger, has ended. A sun and a moon shine above the dead body. A figure rises above a final rung, but this is not the Jacob that lays on the ground, this is a new Jacob. Notice the ladder is laying on the ground and what the man and woman hold for the climbing figure is something like a solitary hurdle—an apt metaphor. Again, the final step of Jacob's Ladder, is also strangely, not a part of the ladder one has come to know through the process. The two angels crown him—symbolic of the opening of the third eye-pineal gland, or to say that one is now king of all knowing, having realized the Absolute State. The original ren sign, is now open at the top and the sun (absolute knowing) shines through. The bottom is no longer two rose flowers, but has turned into two bird heads—likely representing the Phoenix-Bennu, the Egyptian bird that will rise out of its own ashes. The symbology that to reach the top of Jacob's Ladder, one is going to have to die, and then resurrect. A scroll of words comes from the mouths of the man and the woman, who hold hands. The word scroll, via the two people, creates the oroborus—the serpent that eats its own tail, indicating continuous cyclic time, as well as representing unity. The words on the scroll say, "Provided with eyes, thou departest." This would be the all-seeing Eye of Horus in Egypt. What is being departed would be the dream of separateness.

In the distance the ladder is laying sideways on the ground, while the risen Jacob is moving up from it. What is interesting is that Rose said that to make the shift from the second pyramid to the third pyramid, one had to make a 90 degree turn. "When you lose your logical mind...if you make a right turn–you find Nirvana," moving away from time-space, as well as a reliance on normal senses and thought. It is an about-face: the observer turning around to stare with direct-mind into the ultimate source of one's own I-ness. This is the ray of awareness that leads back into the Self. Retroversing the projected ray is following the light of the projector in the movie house back to the source (another dimension) and seeing that reality as we know it is relative/subjective. To go outside the mind is to go inside the Self. One can pull out the plug to end what is on the tv screen, or one can decide to travel through the plug to find out who or where the pictures were coming from. Another reminder about needing to fit through the eye of a needle. This ray we follow is revealed to us as INTUITION.

I wish to add one more reference, that being the famous Pyramid Texts at Sakkara. Carved in the walls of selected Old Kingdom pyramids, they are the oldest religious documents in existence. During sections 37-57 a ladder is referenced. In section 50 Unas (King or Awakened being) claims, "I have embraced this my father who has become tired (asleep), so that he may be quite healthy again (Awake)." The sleep has been overcome. This embrace must not be seen as something happening between two things, it is not a merging into one. It is the embrace of One by One. Osiris can be healthy again as he has realized what he is (Absolute). Jeremy Naydler remarked that following the embrace in the Rameseum *Dramatic Papyrus*, food and cloth are brought in. One of the cloths is purple and is identified with the Awake king. Priests called "Embracers of Akh" enter, wearing jackal-baboon masks and "create" a giant ladder to reach the sky, which the king climbs. The priests swing clubs to keep Set back, an action that seems to magically produce the rungs of the ladder at the same time. This is one of the most interesting parts of the ritual. Symbolically the priests waving the clubs (keeping Set the mind back) makes the ladder, which is somehow being manifested by the ritual (or process). This again relates to the idea that we cannot know where we are going on the path, only where we are now, where we swing our clubs—doing so, the next part of the path will reveal itself.

Additional Material

This work is sections that I wrote that still have value, but were not included in either the main work or the appendix of this book. It will be around 120 pages and can obtained through my website www. egyptian-wisdom-revealed.com.

The topics included in this Additional Material are:

- Post May 28 (Diary notes of the few weeks after my Canyon Experience)
- Secrets of Gender (Ancient understanding of masculine-feminine)
- Personal Dreams and Journeys (explanatory)
- Control of Reality (A deeper look at the parasite and forces of adversity)
- George Carlin (how is comedy can be used to awaken)
- Stalker's Rule (Castaneda's rules for life interactions)
- Love (what is this force)
- The Shamanic Illness (The marker that creates a true shaman)
- Understanding Healing (Is there a secret to healing, and how many have it)
- Rule of the Eagle (A Castaneda concept that might have lots to say)

Bibliography

Suggested Reading of resource materials used in this work.

- Adyashanti: *End of Your World*
- Carse, David: *Perfect Brilliant Stillness*
- Castaneda, Carlos: *Active Side of Infinity*
- Castaneda, Carlos: *Tales of Power*
- Gilchrist, Cherry: *Alchemy*
- Hauk, Dennis: *Emerald Tablet*
- Harding, Douglas: *Little Book of Life and Death*
- Kent, John: *Finding Reality by Finding the Self* (Ph.D Thesis)
- McKenna, Jed: *Spiritual Enlightenment, The Damndest Thing*
- McKenna, Jed: *Spiritually Incorrect Enlightenment*
- Melville, Herman: *Moby Dick*
- Mickoski, Howdie: *The Power of Then*
- Norvill, Roy: *Hermes Unveiled*
- Renz, Karl: *The Myth of Enlightenment*
- Rose, Richard: *Psychology of the Observer*
- Rose, Richard: *The Albigen Papers*
- Rose, Richard: Various Lectures 1976-1993
- Tat Foundation: *Beyond Mind, Beyond Death*
- Thoreau, H.D.: *Walden*
- Traversa, Eddie: *Truth Realization* website
- West, John Anthony: *Serpent in the Sky*

Suggested Movies

- *Donnie Darko*
- *Groundhog Day*
- *Pleasantville*
- *They Live*
- *Vanilla Sky*
- *13th Floor*
- *Man From Earth*
- *Fearless*
- *The Truman Show*
- *The Matrix*
- Any Stanley Kubrick film but specifically *The Shining* and *Eyes Wide Shut*

About The Author

Howard Mickoski is the author of *The Power of Then—Revealing Egypt's Lost Wisdom*. He has also written *Twelve Months of Mystical Wisdom* and *Hockeyology: Digging Up Hockey's Past*.

In 1997 he began to the study of the world of the Ancient Egyptians and Mayans for wisdom that could be useful today. He shares what he has learned from the many teachers of various traditions that have crossed his path through the last 20 years. Originally from Canada, he now lives in Europe.

His website is
www.egyptian-wisdom-revealed.com